EMPIRE'S END

EMPIRE'S END

Transnational Connections in the
Hispanic World

Edited by Akiko Tsuchiya & William Acree

Vanderbilt University Press
Nashville

© 2016 by Vanderbilt University Press
Nashville, Tennessee 37235
All rights reserved
First printing 2016

This book is printed on acid-free paper.

Library of Congress Cataloging-in-Publication Data on file
LC control number 2014047487
LC classification number JV4017.E47 2015
Dewey class number 303.48'21756—dc23

ISBN 978-0-8265-2076-0 (hardcover)
ISBN 978-0-8265-2077-7 (paperback)
ISBN 978-0-8265-2078-4 (ebook)

DEDICATED TO THE MEMORY OF
Christopher Schmidt-Nowara
(1966–2015)

In the last stages of producing this book, the contributors and editors lost a dear friend and colleague, Christopher Schmidt-Nowara. Vanderbilt University Press has graciously allowed us to add this *in memoriam* note to acknowledge a person whose contributions to the various fields represented in these pages and to the various scholars writing here cannot be easily measured and certainly far outpaced his age. Chris was both a stalwart and a central pivot in the developing fields of transatlantic intellectual, political, social, and cultural history and was keenly attuned to the place of literature in modern life. This volume speaks to his key interests and the kind of scholarship that was his hallmark. Not just ideas but their application, how history moves in currents defined not just by the ideas that motivated people but also how these ideas played out in practice were always Chris' key concerns. We are profoundly saddened that he is not here to see this work completed.

Perhaps more importantly, Chris was a model of collegiality and a lovely person. All those who knew him knew he was an equal opportunity mensch, always generous, always available for advice, conversation, and laughter. His passing is a shock and a tremendous loss. While his absence from the many fields of historical study will be long lamented, the impact from his scholarship and life will always remain.

Contents

Acknowledgments

The studies included in this volume originated in a symposium, "Empire's End: Transnational Connections in the Hispanic World, 1808–1898," which was held at Washington University in St. Louis in February 2012. The essays that form the chapters of this book represent the product of the intellectual debate and dialogue that grew out of the symposium, and we thank all of the participants, as well as our colleagues at Washington University, for partaking in this exchange.

We appreciate the institutional support that made the symposium possible. In particular, we thank Elzbieta Sklodowska and Harriet Stone, former chairs of the Department of Romance Languages and Literatures, and Gary Wihl, former dean of the College of Arts and Sciences at Washington University for sponsoring the symposium with the Program for Cultural Cooperation between Spain's Ministry of Culture and United States' Universities. We also acknowledge the support of our wonderful departmental staff, Rita Kuehler, Kathy Loepker, and Anne Eggemeyer, as well as our graduate students, present and past, Irene Domingo and Megan Havard, who provided invaluable help in organizing the symposium. Finally, we thank Roberta Johnson and Jo Labanyi for their assistance during the grant application process.

We are grateful to Eli Bortz and the entire team at Vanderbilt University Press for supporting this project and shepherding it through the publication process, and to the two anonymous readers, whose comments were invaluable in improving the final manuscript.

Introduction

Akiko Tsuchiya
Washington University in St. Louis

When Napoleon's forces invaded the Iberian Peninsula in 1808, the world's most powerful empire was already beginning to fracture.[1] During Charles IV's reign, the ministerial tradition in force during his father's monarchy weakened following the second appointment of Manuel Godoy as Spain's prime minister (1801). This appointment led to an endless series of political crises resulting from the repercussions of the French revolution, as well as from challenges to the absolute monarchy from both within the Iberian Peninsula (Catalonia and the Basque Country) and the colonies abroad in Spanish America. The crisis of the ancien régime, provoked by a mob of soldiers and peasants who forced Charles IV to remove Godoy from office in March 1808, led two days later to Charles IV's own abdication in favor of his son Ferdinand VII. The latter, in turn, was forced by Napoleon to relinquish the throne in favor of the French emperor's brother Joseph.[2] With the Napoleonic invasion, the end of the Spanish empire was all the more imminent; in fact, the independence wars marked a critical step toward decentralizing power and loosening the stronghold of absolutist monarchy. While Ferdinand VII remained in captivity in France, provincial juntas sprouted to rule in his absence, and a constitution was forged in Cádiz that was to form a framework for the future of the republican nation.

The idea of Spain as a democratic nation crystallized with the ratification of the Constitution of Cádiz in 1812, which marked the beginnings of a modern liberal society. This document established the sovereignty of the nation and fundamental rights for citizens, such as the freedom of expression, "universal" (masculine) suffrage, and the right to property. The new idea, formulated by this constitution, "of the Spanish nation as a unified and self-determining entity," however, did not come into being without a prolonged process of conflict and compromise (Kirkpatrick 230). In fact, the Constitution of 1812 gave rise to a political debate about exactly *which* subjects, according to liberal discourse, could be considered citizens of this nation. In spite of the democratic ideals the Cádiz delegates believed themselves to be implementing, Spanish nationality did not always translate into citizenship with the right to exercise full political rights, as political expediency dictated that differentiations be built into the definition of citizenship on the basis of gender, class/estate, and race. Some groups of individuals could be recognized as Spaniards, but not as citizens of the state (Herzog 159).[3]

Susan Kirkpatrick has shown how the Cádiz delegates struggled with the contradictions between "inclusive and exclusive definitions of citizenship" (237). Women were automatically excluded from citizenship through the Constitution's Article 5, which defined Spaniards as "all *men* born free within the kingdoms of Spain, and the descendants of these" (qtd. in Kirkpatrick 230, my emphasis). Class distinctions were implicit in Article 25 of the constitution, which stipulated a number of conditions under which citizenship could be suspended: "in cases of debt, domestic servitude, lack of employment, and from 1830s onward, illiteracy" (Herzog 158). And while the constitution granted universal suffrage to white and indigenous men, it barred those of African descent from citizenship, thereby diminishing the representation of the colonies in relation to the metropolis and guaranteeing the supremacy of the latter (Schmidt-Nowara, *Slavery* 110–11). Thus, distinctions between the metropolis and the Spanish colonies most frequently surfaced as questions of race, and the exclusion of sectors of the colonial population from definitions of the nation created divisions that would influence significantly the course of history on both sides of the Atlantic.

While Spanish liberals in Cádiz were working out their definitions of nation and citizenship, they did so against the backdrop not only of Napoleonic invasions but also of the dissolution of their largest colonies. Two years before, in 1810, Mexico, Argentina, and Chile formed juntas to govern in the name of the king (held prisoner in France), launching a period of over ten years of devastating wars in the Americas. By 1825 Spain had lost all of its American empire except for Cuba and Puerto Rico. The independence movement would eventually culminate in the Spanish-American War, with the loss of Cuba and Puerto Rico, Spain's last colonies in the Americas—and with the simultaneous loss of the Philippine Islands in the Pacific. Though undoubtedly a significant episode in the crumbling of empire, the Spanish-American War did not bring about its end completely, as Spain retained possessions in Africa—in Morocco until the 1950s and Equatorial Guinea until the 1960s. As a compensatory gesture for its imperial losses in Spanish America, the Spanish government embarked on repeated attempts to recolonize northern Africa, culminating in events such as the Spanish-Moroccan War of 1859 and 1860, the Melillan campaigns of the 1890s through the 1910s, the Rif War of the 1920s, and, most recently, the 2002 invasion of the islet of Perejil off the Moroccan coast by former prime minister José María Aznar, through which the conservative Popular Party reasserted the nation's legacy of imperial control and violence.

The "End of Empire" of the volume's title refers to the commonly held belief that the official end of the Spanish empire was marked by the Spanish-American War of 1898, in which it lost the last of its American colonies. Yet, in light of Spain's continued efforts to cling to the vestiges of imperial power by colonizing elsewhere, we need to problematize any attempts to demarcate temporally the endpoint of empire. Even within the borders of Spanish America, the "end of empire" is, in fact, a process that occurred over the course of the long nineteenth century and that continues to have both real and symbolic ramifications beyond this period. Prior to the official declaration of independence by a number of Spain's largest colonies in Spanish America, the 1780 uprising in Peru launched against royal authority by the Indian noble Túpac Amaru II and his followers exposed fractures in the pacification of indigenous groups. This shows the problem of limiting the temporal framework of the empire's end strictly to the nineteenth century, from the first declarations of independence to the Spanish-American War, as events that both anticipated and followed these historical watersheds demonstrate empire's far-reaching impact. In Spain, repeated allusions to the "Disaster" of 1898 in academic, cultural, and political circles up to the present reflect the long-lasting legacy of imperialist discourse and ideology. Thus, even as we evoke the commonplace of "end" of empire, one of the objectives of the volume is to question this notion of the end as coinciding with a fixed date or a historical event.

Nor can empire's limits be demarcated in clear spatial terms, as demonstrated by Hooper's reconstruction of the "entangled histories" (52) of Spain's peripheral communities with those of other nations' port cities. Empire and its legacy in the nineteenth century, as much as today, encompass a transnational Hispanic world that extends beyond the borders of Spain and Spanish America. In fact, the Hispanic world included—and continues to include—the United States and parts of Great Britain, with Liverpool and London representing two of the most critical spaces of transnational exchange. As William Luis argues, there is no doubt that the end of one empire—the Spanish—made way for the emergence of others, most notably those of the United States and, more recently, China, to embrace expansion in the Hispanic world.

Latin Americanist scholars, who have focused on the moment of independence as a political, economic, and cultural watershed defining modernity and who have renewed their attention to independence as Latin American nations begin to celebrate bicentennials, have shied away from tracing the dissolution of the empire over the entire nineteenth century.[4] On the peninsular side, as one of our contributors, Alda Blanco, has stressed, there has been a dearth of efforts to theorize modern Spanish identity as that of an imperial nation-state ("Spain" 4). She thus identifies the need to analyze the inscriptions of empire in the cultural production of Spain as a nation that continued to remain the metropolis of an empire, even after the loss of a majority of its colonies ("Spain" 5–6).[5] Sebastiaan Faber, in fact, argues that in the cultural realm—which is, of course, an ideological one—Spain's failure to interrogate critically the implications of its imperial status has been such that Latin America has been elided almost entirely from Spanish cultural history, notwithstanding the impact of Spain's former colonies on its own culture. One could add that the Philippines, as well as Spain's (former) colonies in North Africa, have met a similar fate in Spanish academic scholarship. Mejías-López goes even further in maintaining the difficulty of addressing empire in the postcolonial Hispanic context "without simultaneously resurrecting empire in the process."[6] The question he poses is an important one, which the contributors to this volume tackle in different ways: how to critically approach the notion of end of empire as, in itself, a problematic concept, even as empire has eventually been forced "to come to terms with its own end" (204–5).

Finally, as William Luis's contribution shows so convincingly, the fact that the end of the Spanish empire in the Americas coincides with the rise of the United States as an imperial power complicates the transatlantic and transnational shifts in power relationships, as Spain desperately clung to the symbolic remnants of its empire, many times unconsciously, while the newly emergent Spanish American nations sought to legitimate their very existence by disconnecting themselves from the imperial center. The inevitable transformations in social hierarchies—between the metropolis and the colonies, naturally, but particularly with regard to race relations—that resulted from the dissolution of empire affected the transnational Hispanic world, leading to important debates about the new national communities in Spanish America. A fundamental premise of our anthology, to paraphrase Sebastiaan Faber, is that the political independence of Spain's former colonies did not mark a break in transatlantic or transnational relations. Rather, the ongoing negotiations between the metropolis and postcolonial societies, on both the material and discursive levels, continued to play an instrumental role in the development of both regions. Consequently, the anthology will focus on the circuits of intellectual and cultural exchange—and the concomitant power relations that such exchanges implied—between Spain and its former colonies throughout the "end" of the Spanish empire.

The chapters that comprise *Empire's End* break new ground in nineteenth-century Hispanic literary and cultural studies in a number of significant ways. First, by considering the "end of empire" as a process that occurred over the course of the long nineteenth century and beyond (in the case of Spain's African colonies), these studies depart from the tendency to focus almost exclusively on two key historical moments: the political independence of the Spanish-American colonies in the first decades of the nineteenth century and the wars of independence in Cuba, Puerto Rico, and the Philippines at the end of the century. While the volume as a whole centers on the nineteenth century, many of the contributors also consider Spain's imperial legacy beyond this period, all the way up to the present moment. In addition to addressing the political, economic, and social implications of the end of empire, this volume emphasizes the *cultural* impact of this process, with "culture" encompassing a wide range of symbolic and discursive representations that often formed the basis of transnational connections and exchange: among them, literary fiction, literary histories, periodical publications, scientific and anthropological texts, national symbols, museums (as well as other architectural monuments, such as *indiano* mansions), and tourist routes.

Furthermore, the anthology addresses the ramifications of Spain's imperial project in relation to its (former) colonies, not only in Spanish America but also in North Africa and the Philippines, generating new insights into the circuits of cultural exchange that link these four geographical areas rarely considered in conjunction with each other. In fact, only recently have important book-length studies, such as Susan Martin-Márquez's *Disorientations: Spanish Colonialism in Africa and the Performance of Identity* (2008), Michael Ugarte's *Africans in Europe: The Culture of Exile and Emigration from Equatorial Guinea to Spain* (2010), and Alda Blanco's *Cultura y conciencia imperial en la España del siglo XIX* (2012), begun to address the impact of Spanish colonialism in a context other than that of Spanish America. An attention to those "other" colonies of the Spanish empire undoubtedly complicates our understanding of Spain's imperial project as one that is not merely transatlantic and, as Joyce Tolliver has suggested, tests "the limits of Spain's conception of its empire" in the nineteenth century and beyond (108).

Finally, we hope that the interdisciplinary scope of the volume will make its contents appealing not only to Hispanists but also to a broader readership of scholars engaged in nineteenth-century literary, cultural, and historical studies in a transatlantic and transnational context. We bring together both Peninsularists and Latin Americanists, historians as well as literary and cultural critics, to debate productively the problem of empire and its cultural impact in the Spanish-speaking world. *Empire's End* grew out of a symposium held at Washington University in St. Louis in February 2012; the event showcased the work of scholars in literature, cultural studies, and history, centering on crucial issues such as mappings of the Hispanic Atlantic, race, human rights, and the legacies of empire. Given that these thematic groupings provided structural coherence to the symposium as a whole, we have titled the four principal sections of this volume accordingly, with the understanding that these categories are fluid and mutually related.

Titled "Atlantic Cartographies," Part I centers on the ways in which the empire and its relation to the (trans)atlantic space were conceived and visualized, both literally and metaphorically, in the cultural imaginary of the nineteenth century and beyond. Sebastiaan Faber's piece, "Hispanism, Transatlantic Studies, and the Problem of Cultural History," appropriately frames the debate on "empire's end" by scrutinizing Hispanism as both an ideology and a material reality shaped by and within the institutional framework of academia. In particular, he reflects on the role of the field of transatlantic studies as a possible challenge to the hegemony of an outdated Hispanism and, thus, as a way to achieve a more complete understanding of the cultural history of Spain and its former colonies. Charting the physical and symbolic spaces of inclusion and exclusion in representations of "pan-Hispanic" identity on both sides of the Atlantic, Faber's work raises broader theoretical questions concerning the production and evolution of fields of knowledge within different national and institutional contexts and, ultimately, the purpose of national cultural histories since their rise in the nineteenth century.

Kirsty Hooper, for her part, rethinks established spatial frameworks through which scholars have approached the Hispanic world by investigating the role that the British port city of Liverpool played in the long nineteenth century as a crucial hub for the formation of postimperial global networks across the Hispanic Atlantic. Hooper reconstructs the "entangled histories" of port cities located on the peripheries of the nation-states that host them: more specifically, the networks of social, cultural, and commercial connections that linked Liverpool with Spain's "peripheral" communities—Basque Country, Galicia, Valencia, and the Canaries—as well as with Portugal, Cape Verde, the Philippines, and South America. Her materially grounded analysis of four interlocking dimensions of global history—routes, bodies, ideas, and objects—serves as a model not only for recovering obscured nineteenth-century networks of circulation but also for stimulating a reflection on the "geopolitical logic underpinning our practice as Hispanists" (35).

Part II, "Racial Theory: From Imperial Formation to Nostalgic Celebration," addresses the centrality of race in defining both imperial and postimperial social relations, especially as they relate to nationality and citizenship.[7] Historian Joshua Goode, known for his scholarship on racial identity in late nineteenth- and early twentieth-century Spain, focuses his attention on the scientific debates of the period around the loss of empire, bringing to light the ways in which different historical contexts shaped the anthropological view of race to serve political ends.[8] In particular, he shows how Spain's anthropological communities used the idea of racial fusion and hybridity that predominated shortly before and after 1898 to explain the losses of empire, as well as to justify Spain's colonization of North Africa, through which the imperial power sought to compensate for the loss of its colonies in Spanish America. Goode concludes that the idea of racial fusion was a "portmanteau" (64)—or a "traveling text," to use Said's term—that was adapted to the different contexts to which it was applied, allowing for a transatlantic exchange between Spanish and Latin American scientists. Along similar lines, Alda Blanco examines the deployments of Spanish racial discourse at the turn of the century and, in particular, of the idea of *mestizaje* at the core of Spanish racial theories through which Spain imagined America. The racial discourses produced in Spain (at the Congreso Geográfico-Hispano-Portugués-Americano in Madrid in 1892) and in Spanish America (by Argentina's Domingo F. Sarmiento and Mexico's Justo Sierra, who envisioned the future of the nation very differently) serve for Blanco as examples of the divergent meanings that colonizing and colonized nations ascribed to racial hybridization at the end of empire.

Joyce Tolliver, for her part, turns attention to the largely neglected case of the Spanish Philippines in Hispanist scholarship, illustrating the inextricability of the concepts of race and nationhood in the Philippines in the late modern empire. The emergence of pseudoscientific racial theories in the last decades of the nineteenth century in Spain forms the backdrop for the production of notions of Philippine nation and identity at the end of empire. She explores the role that the fantasy of "purity of blood" played in the racial discourse both of the colonizers who sought the national unification of the Philippines under the flag of Spain and of the Philippine-born nationalists (the Ilustrados) who sought to stake a claim to their right, as Filipinos, to a place in the Spanish nation. Tolliver recognizes the irony of the Ilustrados' reliance on the same racial fiction that was foundational for the imperial rule that they themselves had struggled to abolish.

Part III, "Slavery, Empire, and the Problem of Freedom," represents an extension of the previous section, focusing on the legacy of race in shaping national communities during the end of empire and beyond. In the early nineteenth century when abolitionist thought began to take force in Spain, the Cortes of Cádiz formally launched a debate on the legality of the transatlantic slave trade. However, in the end, this legislative body both left the traffic untouched and, as Christopher Schmidt-Nowara notes, also "formalized slavery and racial discrimination in the colonies" (*Slavery* 110). As the abolitionist movement gained momentum throughout the century, transatlantic slavery and the slave trade came to an end (with Cuba being the last Spanish colony to abolish slavery in 1886), yet the abolition of slavery did not occur without leaving a legacy of racial (as well as class) tensions and fears, resulting from the "hierarchical and segregated order" maintained in the colonies and recodified in the Constitution of Cádiz under the guise of liberalism (Schmidt-Nowara, *Slavery* 111).[9]

In his contribution to the volume, Schmidt-Nowara explores the ideological adjustments Spaniards made in response to the contraction of empire and the expansion of slavery, noting the contradictions in their attempts to negotiate their aspiration to liberty and equality, on the one hand, and the demand for colonial submission and slavery, on the other. Focusing on the accounts of prisoners of war, both Spaniards and American royalists, in Europe and the Americas in the early nineteenth century, Schmidt-Nowara explores both the commonalities and differences in the visions of freedom, slavery, and civility that emerged among victims of captivity. While some, like Joseph Blanco White, used the experience of captivity (of his brother Fernando) to imagine universal emancipation from slavery, others, like the Spanish royalist soldiers who were captives in America, maintained a counterrevolutionary, antiemancipatory stance. These comparisons, in Schmidt-Nowara's view, shed light on distinct visions of what it meant for Spaniards to be free or unfree during empire's end. William Luis's work centers on Spain's impact on its last colonies in the Caribbean, revealing how the social, economic, cultural, and, particularly, racial conditions responsible for the collapse of one empire led to the birth of another, that of the United States. Luis focuses on the political and cultural contacts between the Caribbean islands and the two imperial powers—Spain and, subsequently, the United States—that contributed to the formation of each island's sense of national identity and culture. The paradox is precisely that the new empire's presence in countries outside of its national borders created patterns of migration from the Caribbean "periphery" to the neocolonial center and produced a postcolonial condition in which colonizers and colonized occupied the same time and place, influencing the culture of the imperial center.

The fourth and final section of the anthology emphasizes the cultural legacies of empire as they find reflection in literary fiction, literary histories, and popular culture. The subject of Michael Ugarte's study is the obstinate persistence of Spain's imperial designs as it turns its attention from Spanish America to Africa. He focuses on Spain's colonial presence in North Africa through an examination of the specifically Spanish brand of orientalism in the realist author Benito Pérez Galdós's representations of the Spanish-Moroccan War of 1859 in two of his historical novels published at the turn of the century: *Aita Tettauen* (1905) and *Carlos VI en La Rápita* (1905). According to Ugarte, the ambiguity and paradox of Galdós's literary discourse in these two works reveal how Spain is at once a producer of orientalist discourse and an object of it. The ambivalence of Spain's relationship to orientalism, manifested in debates throughout the long nineteenth century on "the precise nature of Spain's 'African legacy'" (Martin-Márquez 12), is an often-neglected aspect of the discussion on the cultural legacies of the Spanish empire. For Ugarte, Galdós's self-conscious interrogation of orientalist discourse in these war novels anticipates later-day postmodern and postcolonial readings of empire.

Lisa Surwillo, for her part, analyzes the triumphant narratives constructed around the figure of the nineteenth-century *indiano* (Spanish colonists from the north who emigrated to the Americas with the goal of "hacer las Américas" and returned home, having accumulated wealth in the New World) that continue to be recast, well into the twentieth century, as (re)affirmations of the nation's imperial legacy. These reinscriptions of the *indiano* occur in diverse manifestations of contemporary culture, including television programs and *indiano* mansions and monuments constructed to attract tourism. She takes as an example *La Señora*, a popular

Spanish television series that aired between 2008 and 2010, which reflects unresolved issues in contemporary Spanish society around empire, especially as they relate to the connection between wealth and slavery. In light of these cultural manifestations through which neo-imperial fantasies continued to be reenacted in everyday life in contemporary Spain, Surwillo questions the finality of the end of Atlantic empire even after the loss of Spain's last colonies in Spanish America.

Finally, Alejandro Mejías-López's provocative chapter closes the volume with the claim that nineteenth-century notions of empire continue to define the ways in which scholars view the development of Hispanic literatures, from the disciplinary lines drawn between peninsular and Latin American studies to the ways in which authors, aesthetic trends, and literary history are generally understood by Hispanists. In his view, not only has the empire never ended, but it has "returned with a vengeance" (211). While critical of the ways in which he believes many scholars of transatlantic studies have perpetuated the "imperial dynamics by which Latin America can only be the object and Europe only the subject," he also concedes the possibilities of a transatlantic perspective to challenge "inherited patterns of Hispanism" through a recognition of Latin America's agency as a "renewing and modernizing presence" in shaping Spanish literary culture (214–15).[10] Mejías-López's work and the opening piece by Faber serve as bookends framing this volume of essays: both address problems of literary historiography within the field of nineteenth-century Hispanic studies, encouraging scholars of peninsular and Latin American studies to historicize our disciplinary assumptions and to explore the possibilities offered by transatlantic and transnational approaches to literature.

The contributions in this volume are a testament to the continued legacy of the Spanish empire on both sides of the Atlantic, in the Philippines, and in North Africa. *Indiano* mansions and the tourist routes built around them (Surwillo) are not the only remnants of empire in Spain. From Spain's commemoration of the quincentennial of the "discovery" of the New World, to political disputes over an insignificant islet in the Strait of Gibraltar, to the Junta de Andalucía's proclamation of Cádiz in 2012—the bicentenary of the constitution—as the City of Liberty, these examples confirm that the nation's identity as an empire, presumably repressed from collective consciousness (Blanco, "Spain" 1–2), continues to be resurrected in the late twentieth and early twenty-first centuries. In Spanish America, governments have established commissions to celebrate the bicentennials of independence, with lavish fiestas and major infrastructure projects from Mexico City to Santiago, Chile; the international community was even treated to a rare glimpse of Simón Bolívar's skeletal remains in a dramatic Venezuela state TV production in July 2010, followed by Hugo Chávez's unveiling of a three-dimensional reconstruction of the liberator's image. In addition, a host of films have appeared to celebrate the bicentenary of the Latin American liberation. Even as this volume goes to press, *The Liberator* (2014), on the life of Simón Bolívar, has hit the screen; financed by Spanish and Venezuelan producers, it is one of the most expensive Latin American cinematic productions to date. All of these events and initiatives are about making sense of the postcolonial condition—and what many Hispanists have taken for granted as the "empire's end"—some two hundred years after the process of independence began in the Hispanic world. The contributions in this volume are meant to take on the challenge, to borrow Mejías-López's words, of engaging in new theorizations on empire "that can help us reimagine the circulation of culture and power" (215) in the transatlantic Hispanic world in the postcolonial era.

Notes

1. I would like to thank my colleague and coeditor Billy Acree for his careful reading and suggestions on this introduction and, in particular, for his instrumental role in organizing the symposium from which the idea of this anthology arose.
2. For a more detailed account of the political crises that provoked the Independence Wars in Spain and accelerated the independence movement in Spanish America, see chapter 3 of Carr, "The Crisis of the Ancien Régime 1808–1814" (79–119).
3. For a more extensive discussion of the historical context in which the Cádiz delegates determined "Spanishness" and Spanish citizenship, see Herzog (152–62). It goes without saying that the discourse of nationality reduced Spain to a monolithic unity, even within the metropolis, in spite of the fact there were subjects (from Catalonia and Basque Country, for example) who did not identify with the nation-state. For more on the historical impact of the Cádiz Constitution in the Iberian Peninsula and in Spanish American colonies, see *Bulletin for Spanish and Portuguese Historical Studies* 37.2 (2012).
4. For a sample of recent scholarship on independence in Latin America, see Chasteen; Briggs; Adelman; Davies, Brewster, and Owen; McFarlane and Posada-Carbó; Rodríguez O.; and Guerra.

5. See also Loureiro's discussion on the "ghosts of empire," a reference to
   Spanish discourses on its former colonies, which, in his view, began
   in the mid-nineteenth century, reached their peak in the first decades
   of the twentieth century, and continue to occupy the Spanish cultural
   imagination to the present day (1).

6. As Sebastian Balfour maintains in his study, *The End of the Spanish Empire*,
   "the loss of the mainland was not seen by Spain's élites as the end of the
   Empire. On the contrary, it was viewed as only a temporary setback."
   Even in the face of the loss of its richest colony, Cuba, Spain sustained the
   illusion that it was "still an imperial power of some rank" (1–2).

7. Negotiations of race in Spain, particularly during the period of imperial
   decline, were complex and oftentimes contradictory, representing an
   interplay of both biologistic and cultural notions of ethnic or national
   identity (Martin-Márquez 12–63). Throughout the history of the Iberian
   Peninsula, "race" has always been an unstable discursive construct that
   referred alternatively and in some cases interchangeably to what in modern-
   day discourse would be called religion, ethnicity, or nationality.

8. See Goode's *Impurity of Blood: Defining Race in Spain, 1870–1930* for
   a history of racial thinking in Spain and its role in forging notions of
   national identity.

9. For a more detailed discussion of the tensions produced by these
   hierarchies, see Schmidt-Nowara's *Slavery, Freedom, and Abolition in Latin
   America and the Atlantic World* (110–15).

10. See, for example, Mejías-López's *The Inverted Conquest*.

Works Cited

Adelman, Jeremy. *Sovereignty and Revolution in the Iberian Atlantic*. Princeton:
   Princeton UP, 2006.

Balfour, Sebastian. *The End of the Spanish Empire, 1898–1923*. New York:
   Oxford UP, 1997.

Blanco, Alda. *Cultura y conciencia imperial en la España del siglo XIX*. Valencia:
   Publicaciones de la U de València, 2012.

———. "Spain at the Crossroads: Imperial Nostalgia or Modern Colonialism?"
   A Contracorriente: A Journal of Social History and Literature in Latin America
   5.1 (2007): 1–11. Web. 5 Feb. 2015.

Briggs, Ronald. *Tropes of Enlightenment in the Age of Bolívar: Simón Rodríguez
   and the American Essay at Revolution*. Nashville: Vanderbilt UP, 2010.

Carr, Raymond. *Spain, 1808–1975*. 2nd ed. Oxford: Oxford UP, 1982.

Chasteen, John Charles. *Americanos: Latin America's Struggle for Independence*.
   New York: Oxford UP, 2008.

Davies, Catherine, Claire Brewster, and Hilary Owen. *South American Independence: Gender, Politics, Text.* Liverpool: Liverpool UP, 2007.

Goode, Joshua. *Impurity of Blood: Defining Race in Spain, 1870–1930.* Baton Rouge: Louisiana State UP, 2009.

Guerra, François-Xavier. *Modernidad e independencias: Ensayos sobre las revoluciones hispánicas.* Madrid: MAPFRE, 1992.

———, ed. *Las revoluciones hispánicas: Independencias americanas y liberalismo español.* Madrid: Editorial Complutense, 1995.

Herzog, Tamar. *Defining Nations: Immigrants and Citizens in Early Modern Spain and Spanish America.* New Haven: Yale UP, 2003.

Kirkpatrick, Susan. "Constituting the Subject: Race, Gender, and Nation in the Early Nineteenth Century." *Culture and the State in Spain: 1550–1850.* Ed. Tom Lewis and Francisco J. Sánchez. New York: Garland, 1999. 225–51.

Loureiro, Ángel. "Spanish Nationalism and the Ghost of Empire." *Journal of Spanish Cultural Studies* 4.1 (2003): 65–76.

Martin-Márquez, Susan. *Disorientations: Spanish Colonialism in Africa and the Performance of Identity.* New Haven: Yale UP, 2008.

McFarlane, Anthony, and Eduardo Posada-Carbó, eds. *Independence and Revolution in Spanish America: Perspectives and Problems.* London: Institute of Latin American Studies, 1999.

Mejías-López, Alejandro. *The Inverted Conquest: The Myth of Modernity and the Transatlantic Onset of Modernism.* Nashville: Vanderbilt UP, 2009.

Rodríguez O., Jaime E. *The Independence of Spanish America.* Cambridge: Cambridge UP, 1998.

Schmidt-Nowara, Christopher. *Slavery, Freedom, and Abolition in Latin America and the Atlantic World.* Albuquerque: U of New Mexico P, 2011.

Ugarte, Michael. *Africans in Europe: The Culture of Exile and Emigration from Equatorial Guinea to Spain.* Urbana: U of Illinois P, 2010.

PART I

Atlantic Cartographies

1

Hispanism, Transatlantic Studies, and the Problem of Cultural History

Sebastiaan Faber
Oberlin College

Is it possible to narrate the cultural history of nineteenth-century Spain as if Latin America did not exist? Absolutely. Cecilio Alonso's recent history of Spanish literature from 1800 to 1900, which constitutes the fifth volume of the monumental *Historia de la literatura española* coordinated by José-Carlos Mainer and published with much fanfare by Crítica between 2008 and 2012, manages to dedicate eight hundred pages to the nineteenth century without once mentioning the work of José Martí, Manuel Gutiérrez Nájera, or Rubén Darío.[1] To be sure, this may be more shocking to some than to others. What can sound unbelievable to someone working in transatlantic or Latin American studies in the United States may well seem entirely appropriate to a Peninsularist working in Spain. In fact, these different levels of potential shock are what I am interested in exploring. They point, I would contend, to fundamentally diverging notions of the relationship between disciplinary boundaries and the nature and scope of cultural history.

It is safe to assume that to most of the contributors to the present volume, the absence of Latin Americans from nineteenth-century Spanish cultural history is well-nigh inconceivable. After all, the transatlantic nature of this very collection—its focus on the circuits of intellectual and cultural exchange between Spain and its former colonies—implicitly posits the central importance of these circuits for understanding the cultural history of Latin America and Spain between 1800 and 1900. If the contributors gathered here can agree on anything, it is that Latin American political independence did *not* mark a break in transatlantic relations; rather, these relations continued to play an instrumental role in the development of both regions. Studying nineteenth-century Spain as if Latin America did not exist may well be possible, but to most of us it would make very little sense indeed. Why, then, do leading scholars of Spanish literary historiography continue to do exactly that?

The wider concerns that drive this chapter are not limited to literary history. Still, I want to approach the problematic from that angle, asking three basic questions: What explains the chronic exclusion of the Latin American dimension from mainstream peninsular Hispanism? What are the alternatives? And what needs to happen for those alternatives to take institutional hold? In this context I particularly want to revisit the uneven rise, lukewarm acceptance, and problematic features of transatlantic Hispanic studies as a proper academic field. As we know, its proponents have welcomed transatlantic studies as a much-needed bridge between, and necessary renovation of, the estranged two branches of Hispanic studies: Peninsularism and Latin Americanism. Critics, on the other hand, have dismissed transatlantic studies as, at best, an ephemeral fad with an inadequately articulated critical methodology (Trigo) or, at worst, a reinvented Hispanist wolf in sheep's clothing (Resina). What role, if any, can transatlantic studies play in solving the persistent sense of crisis in Hispanic studies?[2]

Although I am ultimately interested in questions of ideology—that is, the ways in which meaning, in this case the configuration of scholarly fields, reflects and is put at the service of structures of domination[3]—I want to begin this discussion by thinking more practically about the problem of "fit" between disciplinary framework and object of study or, to put it differently, the relationship between the *materiality* of cultural history and the *institutionality* of academic work. Ideology and institutions are of course closely intertwined.[4] It is no coincidence, for example, that Hispanism, as a term, refers to both an academic field and an ideology. The field—as an institutional reality—has long been the *embodiment* and *vehicle* of the (Pan-)Hispanist ideology that constructs the cultural history of the Spanish-speaking world through a Castilian- and Spain-centered lens (Faber, "Hora"; Resina). Within the academic field of Spanish and Latin American cultural history, in fact, Hispanist ideologies have manifested themselves in different ways: as a blanket assimilation of Latin America into the Spanish fold—a negation of difference based on an alleged "spiritual unity" of former colonizer and colonized (Pérez Montfort 10; see also Pike; Van Aken; Valle and Gabriel-Stheeman)—

or, as we just saw, as an outright exclusion of Latin America from Spanish cultural history.

Many critics working on the wider Spanish-speaking world within institutions located outside of Spain have come to see the Hispanist paradigm as an obstacle to any full and true understanding of the cultural history of Spain and its former colonies. And yet, although over the past couple of decades critiques of Hispanism as a field of knowledge have been extensive, ruthless, and seemingly lethal (Resina; Moraña),[5] its institutional presence remains remarkably strong. More importantly, critics of Hispanism have, as of yet, been less than successful in rethinking, let alone reforming, scholarly practices dealing with the Spanish-speaking world at all institutional levels, including not just research but also more recalcitrant structures such as departments and curriculum. This relative lack of success even affects the most promising alternative at hand, transatlantic studies.

That the process of reform has been slow and uneven is due to several challenges, of which I would highlight three. First, inasmuch as *all* institutional structures embody an ideology and all disciplinary structures work through mechanisms of delimitation—of inclusion and exclusion—we are inevitably replacing one set of limitations with another. Second, new institutional proposals have to be powerful enough to overcome inertia and vested interests, whose weight is never to be underestimated. They, therefore, require a persuasive legitimating narrative. And, as Abril Trigo has pointed out, in the case of transatlantic studies this narrative has been less than coherent or convincing (38). Third, given the wildly different situation of Hispanic studies in different institutional settings (Spain, the United States, other European countries, and so forth), the need for reform is felt much more acutely in some institutional spaces than in others (Faber, "Economies"). This imbalance has done little to improve the existing fragmentation of Hispanic studies across national-institutional boundaries. Some critics have recently sounded a cautionary note, warning that we should not exaggerate the extent of this fragmentation.[6] Still, the rift is evident, not only in that leading authorities of Spanish literary history in Spain remain firmly entrenched in the Hispanist framework—with some important exceptions[7]—but also in that they apparently feel they can safely ignore the bulk of the work done elsewhere. Alonso's history of nineteenth-century Spanish literature, mentioned above, dedicates the bulk of its eight hundred pages to romanticism and realism. While the prologue by the series editor promises to take into account the "critical pluralism" of the field and its various "states of the question" (xi),[8] the volume almost completely bypasses the last thirty years' worth of research around those topics done in Anglophone peninsular Hispanic studies. In fact, the twenty-page bibliography contains not a single reference to the work of Diane Urey, Noël Valis, Jo Labanyi, Michael Iarocci, Catherine Jagoe, Hazel Gold, Lou Charnon-Deutsch, or Geoffrey Ribbans, just to name a handful of colleagues with groundbreaking nineteenth-century scholarship. The *ninguneo* from across the ocean is so blatant it is almost funny.

It should be clear by now that this chapter is driven partly by sheer professional irritation: a deep-seated frustration with a particular kind of peninsular Spanish philology. But it is inspired in equal measure by two other sentiments: inspiration derived from the terrific work being done in transatlantic studies and apprehension about the future of the "field"—and, for that matter, doubt about the future *possibility* of any "field" in terms of both scholarship and teaching. In what follows, I hope to channel this contradictory mix of sentiments into a productive attempt to think more generally about the shape and legitimacy of academic fields of specialization as institutions in and of themselves. What factors determine the emergence and evolution of academic fields of knowledge? How do these factors differ in different national and institutional contexts? How do we interpret and evaluate the evolution of academic fields? It is tempting, for instance, to think about institutional and disciplinary changes in terms of scholarly advances or, conversely, to denounce regressive and reactionary tendencies in systems that remain stagnant. But is it still warranted to speak of progress at all?

Fields and Cultural Capital

If Latin America is all but absent in Alonso's volume, Mainer's own subsequent tome, which covers the years from 1900 to 1939, does not do much better. Mainer's eight hundred pages, which centrally cover *modernismo* and the avant-garde, once again relegate Latin America to the margins of cultural history. The first chapter, on *modernismo*, does not mention Latin America once, although Rubén Darío is incorporated as a kind of honorary Spanish writer and cultural operator. By contrast, references to Europe abound. Mainer's approach is, in fact, a good example of what Mejías-López describes as the tendency among Spanish writers and critics to "narrate the Spanish American transformation of Spanish letters as a pan-Hispanic opening to other 'European' literatures" (104). "There is something troublesome," Mejías-López adds, "in pleading for inclusion in 'Europe's' select club, especially in doing so by turning the peninsular back on Spanish America's modernismo." As Mejías-López points out, and as Mainer's *Historia* confirms, this approach "is rapidly gaining ground" (Mejías-López 114).

Tellingly, neither Mainer nor Alonso feels the need to justify the fact that they do not take into account Latin American cultural production in the development of cultural history in Spain. "Why in the world," one imagines the unspoken reasoning, "would anyone writing a history of *Spanish* literature want to include *Latin Americans*? We'll leave that to our Latin Americanist colleagues next door—or, better yet, to the Latin Americans themselves. *Zapatero, a tus zapatos*—the cobbler should stick to his last." It is a purely bureaucratic argument, of course, based on a particular division of academic labor. Yet it nevertheless masks itself as a substantive argument.[9] It does so precisely to the extent that Mainer's history claims to present a totalizing, integral evolutionary narrative of literary production in Spain—a narrative to which Latin American culture is assumed to be almost entirely alien and, in any case, nonessential.

Importantly, the institutional arrangements that allow for this exclusion embody in themselves a set of ideologies. First, they clearly embody an ideology of cultural nationalism: a worldview that conceives of nations as self-sufficient "organic beings" with an essential national character that functions as a "creative life-principle" and that is reflected in, as well as shaped by, the work of great national writers and artists (Hutchinson 122). (Incidentally, this cultural-nationalist tendency is also evident in the marginalization of scholarship by non-Spaniards just mentioned, which a benevolent soul might describe as a kind of scholarly protectionism, an intellectual tariff imposed on work done abroad.) Second, these institutional arrangements embody an ideology of empire. As Mejías-López argues, the institution of Hispanism, as a scholarly discipline, is chronically oblivious to the possibility of the former colonies *influencing* the former metropolis. Conversely, that we take notice of the exclusion in the first place could indicate a waning of these ideologies, a suggestion that they have become, in Raymond Williams's terms, residual— at least in our corner of the field (Williams 40–42). Among other things, of course, our bafflement at a literary history of modern Spain that manages to ignore Latin America almost entirely is, in the end, rooted in the increasing realization that strictly national literary histories have lost their legitimacy and explanatory power (Hutcheon 5). But our shock at our Spanish colleagues' blind spots is only productive if we address the fundamental questions that it raises about the relationship between the nature and scope of our object of study and the nature and scope of the disciplinary structures available to approach that object.

How do we tackle these fundamental questions? For starters, it may be helpful to think of both our object (that is, literary or cultural history) and the institutional space from which we approach it (that is, academia) as "fields of cultural production" in Bourdieu's sense. This would oblige us to analyze both as social-institutional-historical realities with a clear *material* presence and impact; as entities whose dynamics are shaped by rules, interplays of power, prestige, interests, and cultural capital; entities built on, embodying, and reproducing ideologies that are also in constant transformation as they react, and are forced to adapt, to challenges of different kinds. Invoking Bourdieu's notion of the field has the added advantage of leveling the hierarchy between an ideology-free "us" working in the present and an ideology-bound "them" located in the past. In other words, Bourdieu helps us complicate the essential overlap between ourselves as intellectual actors embedded in a particular structure and the intellectual actors and institutional structures we aim to investigate. To see ourselves as operating in a field of cultural production forces us from the outset to adopt a healthy dose of self-reflexivity. It compels us, in Bourdieu's words, to step outside of the *illusio* that governs our daily practice: the self-deception that is indispensable for "players" to stay involved in the "game" (Bourdieu, *Rules* 230).

In the case at hand, Bourdieu can specifically help us understand not only the nature of the historical relationship between Spanish and Latin American cultural producers, but also the shape of academic structures and the behavior of academic specialists as an *effect* of the ways that capital and competition function in the humanities in Spain—an effect that, in practice, *mirrors* this historical relationship. As Mejías-López and others have shown, for instance, the postcolonial relations between Spanish and Latin American cultural producers have been marked from the outset by a struggle for hegemony or cultural capital that Spaniards continued to claim for themselves long after they had lost it in practice (Mejías-López 104). A cursory glance at the institutional history of Hispanism makes clear that a very similar dynamic has marked the relations between academic experts in Spanish and Latin American cultural history (Faber, "Economies").

Hispanism and pan-Hispanism, then, can be studied as ideologies and as institutional realities (academic, economic), but also as cultural-historical realities consisting precisely in the "circuits of intellectual exchange" that include the type of transatlantic public sphere we could refer to as a kind of material pan-Hispanism. This materiality is made up by bodies, boats, and books, by ink, imports, and itineraries. Although he is left out of Alonso's volume, Martí did, after all, live and publish in 1870s Spain. Unamuno frequently wrote for Latin American papers and for an explicitly Latin American readership (Mejías-López 59; Ouimette; Rama 145). And Mariano José de Larra was wildly popular in the Southern Cone (Mejías-López 59). Both Spaniards and Latin Americans, moreover, avidly read French novels in translation—translations that were incidentally often produced by North American or Central European publishers (Mejías-López 55–56). The key point is the fundamental insufficiency of any totalizing cultural history whose very conceptual framework impedes it from taking phenomena like these into account.

Hispanist Philology, Alive and Well

If Mainer's massive *Historia* shows us anything, it is that Hispanism as an ideology and institutional practice—the construction of the cultural history of the Spanish-speaking world through a Castilian- and Spain-centered lens—is far from dead. The volumes of the monumental series have been received to great acclaim as an innovative and daring intervention in Spanish intellectual life.[10] In a short preface that appears in each volume, Mainer himself emphasizes the project's fresh approach. What justifies yet another new national literary history, he points out, is the tremendous progress made in the field. Mainer speaks of "methodological innovations," of the "excellent moment for intellectual production emerging from the university" (even in the face of "confused reforms, ignorant teaching bureaucracies and, above all, our ancestral fear of the future"), and of a large number of new approaches that have expanded what we understand as literature and how we think of the processes that govern its production, inner workings, reception, and circulation (ix–x). Mainer also celebrates the fact that works like this *Historia* now have a wider readership in Spain than just academics and university students and that critics have abandoned their dry scholarly style in favor of a return to "the noble art of the essay" (ix).

Read from my vantage point, this optimistic, self-congratulatory reading of the state of the discipline has one key problem. It rings false. The truth is that, over the past couple of decades, the disciplinary fortress of peninsular Hispanism has been the target of coordinated attacks from multiple directions. Most prominent among these assaults have been those coming from two directions: the proponents of Iberian studies, who denounce the privileging of Castilian over other Spanish languages within the territorial space of the Spanish state, and the promoters of transatlantic studies, who aim to move beyond the artificial separation between Spanish and Latin American culture while questioning the presumed hegemony of the former over the latter. In addition, the legitimacy of Hispanist philology has been weakened by the rise of cultural and interdisciplinary studies and by the more general questioning of the cultural-nationalist foundations of national literary histories.[11]

Mainer, however, prefers to misread the assaults on the foundations of his discipline as mere innovations and new approaches, a "healthy critical pluralism" that testifies to the continued strength of the Hispanist citadel (x). Indeed, Mainer's presentation overflows with satisfaction and self-confidence. He makes clear to the reader that, much like a nude in a painting by Rubens, the sheer corpulence of this *Historia*—nine volumes, almost eight thousand pages—has to be read as a sign of health. A health that, Mainer maintains, the discipline shares with its object of study: Spanish literature.

We see the same neutralizing move, a similar attempt at minimizing conflict, in the way Mainer deals with the controversial adjective "Spanish." "The notion of what is Spanish has undergone enormous mutations" over the past centuries, he writes in the second paragraph of his prologue: "our language—the language in which the literary works we are referring to here were written—can just as legitimately be called 'Castilian,' a name that alludes to its origin and has something of a comfortable domestic denomination (although it should never have a diminishing intent), as 'Spanish,' a term that has stuck over time and which is the name under which it is internationally recognized" ("nuestra lengua—la lengua en que están escritas las obras literarias a que nos referimos aquí—soporta con idéntica legitimidad el nombre de castellano, que alude a su origen y que tiene algo de confortable denominación doméstica (que nunca debiera contener ánimo de menoscabo), y el de español, que se ha ido afianzando y que es el gentilicio que la reconoce internacionalmente") (vii). Telling here is the off-handed way in which Mainer, in one smooth move, accomplishes three things simultaneously. First, he identifies the adjective "español" with the Castilian language. Second, he *appropriates* that language as "ours," without specifying the scope of the *nosotros* invoked. And third, he lets his readers know that, naturally, this massive project covering a thousand years of cultural history in the Iberian Peninsula will exclude literary works written in Basque, Catalan, or Galician.

Despite Mainer's decision to ignore the embattled state of the academic humanities in Spain and elsewhere and of peninsular studies in particular, as well as the serious challenges leveled at the legitimacy and intellectual authority of the discipline, it is not hard to read the monumental effort of this series as an act of disciplinary defense, even retrenchment—something like the Hispanist equivalent of a Maginot Line. At the same time, the fact that *Historias* like these can still be written also suggests that the challenges have not been strong enough, at least not within the institutional space of the Spanish academy.

What is the purpose, really, of national cultural histories? Here, once more, Bourdieu can help us. As we know, since their rise in the nineteenth century, national cultural histories have fulfilled important functions as key elements of modern nationalism (Hutcheon 4–6, 9; Epps and Fernández Cifuentes 11–12). They have constituted monuments of sorts, given the tremendous investment of effort and resources that they require, as well as their aspiration to be milestones, narratives, and rock-carved canons meant to last. To put this differently, national cultural histories are themselves institutions that, as such, exercise considerable power. They are in the business of consecration (Bourdieu, *Homo* 102). They include or exclude works, writers, or movements and incorporate them into a narrative structure that traces the history of cultural production as the privileged expression of national identity. Finally, national cultural histories, as "an enterprise in the prescription of knowledge and the canonization of the legitimate heritage," also serve to legitimate fields of knowledge and to cement the claims to hegemony of their authors (Bourdieu, *Homo* 101–2). "Every critical affirmation," Bourdieu writes,

> contains, on the one hand, a recognition of the value of the work which occasions it . . . and on the other hand an affirmation of its own legitimacy. All critics declare not only their judgment of the work, but also their claim to the right to talk about it and judge it. In short, they take part in a struggle for the monopoly of a legitimate discourse about the work of art, and consequently in the production of the value of the work of art. (Bourdieu, *Field* 35)

What, then, is the vision of Spanish cultural history that this *Historia* aims to legitimize? By dint of its very setup, the nine-volume series defends the idea that Spanish literature can fruitfully be studied and understood separate from two of its closest neighbors: the literary production *in Spain* in languages other than Spanish, and the literary production *in Spanish* produced outside of Spain or by writers not born in Spain.[12] Again, the absence of any justification or explanation for this monumental decision indicates that we should assume the reasoning is self-evident. In reality, of

course, it is anything but. As Mario Santana writes in response to a different text by Mainer, in which Mainer questions the legitimacy of "regional"
Iberian literary histories (Catalan, Basque, Galician, Valencian, and so
on),[13] Hispanism is constitutionally incapable of recognizing the inevitable
regionalism of Spain's own "national literature" (115), within the peninsular as much as the transatlantic space. Quoting Andrés Sánchez Robayna,
Santana writes: "if the language is the only criterion that allows us to speak
of an 'own literature,' then Spanish literature itself would, strictly speaking, be nothing more than a regional literature" (116). In other words, "If
literature in Castilian, or Spanish, has become identified with 'Spanish literature' it is because we conveniently forget that this restrictive definition
results from a project of national invention" (116).

Indeed, if Catalans, Basques, and Galicians are right to protest their
exclusion from Mainer's *Historia*, Latin Americans would be just as right
to contest his and his collaborators' brazen appropriation of the Spanish
language through a first-person possessive pronoun—a *lengua* that is not
only identified as *nuestra*, but whose literary production also appears to
stop at the Atlantic coast. The self-satisfaction evident throughout Mainer's prologue is clearly rooted in an uncomplicated sense of ownership and
identity. This is *our* literary tradition, written in *our* language, of which
we can be proud *as Castilian-speaking Spaniards*. Mainer claims authority,
then, not only as a prestigious philologist but also as a native Castilian
speaker and as a citizen of the Spanish state.

That all this can remain unsaid, and that all these boundaries and ex-
clusions can remain unsubstantiated and unquestioned in the work and
its various paratexts, suggests that Mainer's *Historia*, for all its effort and
investment, is living proof of the glaring inadequacy—one might say the
intellectual bankruptcy—of Hispanism as a humanistic paradigm. To be
sure, all academic disciplines single out a particular parcel of reality to the
exclusion of the rest, making some things visible and comprehensible at
the expense of rendering others invisible and inexplicable. But the Hispanist paradigm has long lost its explanatory potential; as a scholarly practice,
what it renders invisible now outmatches what it serves to make visible or
comprehensible.

The Uncertain Promise of Transatlantic Studies

In sharp contrast with Mainer's brand of undertheorized, cultural-nationalist
Hispanism, the field of transatlantic studies seeks out "comparisons, influences, intersections and crossings in the wake of the nationalist frag-

mentation of knowledge" (Gerassi-Navarro and Merediz 617). But is it a viable alternative to replace the bankrupt Hispanist tradition? While the work being done under the transoceanic umbrella is quite diverse, the rise of Hispanic transatlantic studies over the past fifteen years has not yet resulted in real consolidation and lasting institutional reform. This is, in part, because Hispanic transatlantic studies is held together more by a thematic focus than by a particular methodology or theoretical approach and, in part, because it has not been able to convincingly counter some of the critiques it has garnered. The most trenchant criticism has ironically been leveled by some of the staunchest enemies of Hispanism.

Among critics and practitioners of transatlantic studies, three views of the new field vie for dominance. The first is a celebratory view of transatlantic studies as a kind of neo-Hispanism, emancipated not only from its colonialist burden and its concomitant baggage of superiority and resentment, but also from needless theoretical complexity. Its most prominent exponent is Julio Ortega. For Ortega, transatlantic studies sprang, in the mid-1990s, from a recognition of "the exhaustion of dominant critical models, the limits of the theoretical narratives that occupied the academic market, and the authoritarian derivations of some normative groups," and was characterized by a "return of the Subject as an agent of memory" and a "return to the text" (Presentación 105). In Ortega's view, transatlantic studies allowed scholars to emancipate themselves not only from "disciplinary genealogy" and "regrettable division between a 'Peninsular' and a 'Latin American' field" but also from the "liberal *parti pris* that condemns the subject to the role of victim (colonial, sexual, imperial, ideological, etc.)" ("Post-teoría" 113–14). Ortega's neo-Hispanism is evident in his embrace of Spanish as "the *lingua franca* of the new cultural internationalism" ("Voces").

A second view is also optimistic, although more critical and theoretically self-aware, and particularly attuned to the persistent danger of lingering pan-Hispanist nostalgias. Here I would place the work of Joseba Gabilondo, Alejandro Mejías-López, Nina Gerassi-Navarro, and Eyda Merediz. For Gabilondo and Mejías-López, the transatlantic framework serves in different ways to rethink cultural and political history from the ground up. Gabilondo argued in 2001 that the "Hispanic Atlantic" forces us to rethink key concepts such as "modernity, race, postmodernism, globalization, sexuality, postcolonialism, subalternity, gender, and class" (93), whereas Mejías-López turns the notion of Spanish center and Latin American periphery on its head by showing that, starting in the nineteenth century, the vectors of influence ran eastward, not westward. Gerassi-Navarro and Merediz, for their part, celebrate the tremendous potential for cultural and political history of the transatlantic paradigm, not just because it moves beyond traditional disciplinary divisions but because it gives proper weight to the category of *space* after long privileging that of *time*. Yet they, too, acknowledge that transatlanticists risk ending up trapped "between Spanish global expansionism, the dominance of the U.S. academy, and indifference in Latin America" (614).

The third view, which ranges from skeptical to outright dismissive, is most prominently represented by Joan Ramon Resina and Abril Trigo. Resina sees transatlantic studies as an opportunistic attempt to shore up the hegemony of the Spanish language as the basis for any Iberian or pan-Hispanic identity. For Trigo, transatlantic studies is little more than "a renovated Pan-Hispanism" (2), a desperate attempt on the part of American peninsular Hispanism to reposition itself in the face of a precipitous drop of its value in the US academic market.[14] Trigo's doubts, expressed from the institutional comfort of a flourishing Latin Americanism, do not concern specific research projects done under the transatlantic umbrella. Rather, Trigo questions the need for a new disciplinary umbrella in the first place. The strongest argument in the face of these critiques is the actual work being done. Mejías-López and other colleagues in this volume show that a transatlantic perspective *can* prove extraordinarily productive for nineteenth-century studies as much as for twentieth-century studies.

Still, the real question at hand is to what extent transatlanticism can serve to achieve the *institutional* reforms without which Hispanism will maintain its outdated hegemony, a hegemony that even in the US context remains firmly embodied in survey courses, textbooks, reference works, reading lists, language requirements, and the structure, names, and careful political arrangements of departments of Spanish and Hispanic studies—often still based on a clear division of labor between the peninsular and Latin American sections.[15] The rise of transatlantic studies, moreover, does not just destabilize the division of labor and power within Spanish departments but also opens the floodgates in a different fashion: by way of pan-Atlantic studies, it breaks open the boundaries between the academic units that deal with the Spanish-speaking world and those that study Anglophone, Francophone, and Lusophone fields.[16] With this expansion of geographical scope, the whole notion of field becomes tenuous, as do the notions of discipline and department. To the extent that we have come to experience fields, disciplines, and departments as limiting more than enabling, this collapse of the levees is to be celebrated. But before we break out the champagne, it behooves us to think through what this dissolution might mean for the daily reality of our curricular and administrative lives—which, as Bourdieu would point out, will continue to unfold in an institutional context marked by competition for resources and cultural capital. In addition, we would do well to consider whether any real reform has to be accomplished in conjunction with scholars in Spain and Latin America. We should ask ourselves, in other words, what our responsibility is for institutional reform on both sides of the Atlantic.

Notes

1. José Martí is not mentioned once in the whole volume. Gutiérrez Nájera makes one appearance, as the addressee of a letter by Antonio de Valbuena chastising him for his bad Spanish (Alonso 27). Rubén Darío appears half a dozen times, but only in passing and without any discussion of his literary work, let alone his key role in the evolution of Spanish literature and the decisive shift in literary hegemony from Spain to Latin America, as described by Alejandro Mejías-López (4).
2. The notion of crisis is persistent indeed; it is difficult to find any moment in the history of the academic field of Hispanism in the non-Spanish world when the feeling of crisis was not present. For a more detailed overview of the chronic sense of embattledness in the institutional history of Hispanism, see Faber, "Economies."
3. The concept of ideology can serve to help explain "the ways in which meaning can be used for maintaining or contesting power" (Faber, "Trope" 134).
4. The theory of ideology as formulated by Marx, Lukács, Eagleton, Žižek, and others has long seen ideology as embodied not just in the ideas of groups and individuals, but in practices and institutions as well (Faber, "Trope" 140–41).
5. "It is necessary," Resina writes for instance, "to allow for the possibility that Hispanism no longer has a future as an academic discipline. . . . Spanish philology, to the extent that it claims to be Spanish, that is to say, to the extent that it claims to clump together the cultures that, for better or worse, coexist with the Spanish state, cannot continue to be solely or mainly a 'philology'" (Resina 202–3). Throughout this essay, I am using the term "Hispanism" and the adjective "Hispanist" to refer not to every branch of scholarship that occupies itself with Spanish or Iberian cultures, but more narrowly to that part of the discipline that, growing out of the philological tradition, studies the literary and cultural production within

the borders of the Spanish state as a largely self-contained corpus primarily
defined by the Castilian language. Hispanism thus defined has been the
primary target of the critiques of Resina, Moraña, Santana, and others.

6. Epps and Fernández warn against too readily invoking a "national divide by
   which more 'questioning' and 'self-critical' Hispanists in the United States
   and Great Britain are pitted against more conformist and conventional
   Hispanists in Spain" (18).

7. Among the scholars in Spain today who are emphatically working against
   the Hispanist paradigm, in transatlantic directions, is Pura Fernández at
   the Consejo Superior de Investigaciones Científicas. See, for instance, her
   introduction to the special transatlantic issue of the *Revista de Estudios
   Hispánicos* she coordinated in 2012 (Fernández).

8. All translations from Spanish are mine.

9. The same is true for other humanistic disciplines. Gerassi-Navarro and
   Merediz write that "Spanish historiography has traditionally been the
   bulwark of an intellectual vantage point that tends to divide the field of
   knowledge into Americanism on the one hand and Peninsularization or
   Spanification on the other" (610–11). The lack of interest is mutual; if
   large sections of peninsular Hispanism feel they can safely ignore Latin
   America, Latin Americanists do not very frequently see the need for
   transatlantic approaches either.

10. Carlos Geli called the project "innovative and daring." Reviews have
    praised its broad perspective; its disciplinary, cultural, and political
    pluralism; and its attention to "works in languages other than Castilian"
    (Prieto de Paula).

11. Gerassi-Navarro and Merediz point out that the "Atlanticization" of
    Hispanic and Latin American studies is inextricably linked with the rise of
    interdisciplinary and cultural studies (613).

12. As Mario Santana writes in reference to earlier projects of Spanish literary
    history: "The literary nation is thus mapped restrictively according to
    the intersection of two disparate geographies: one political, according to
    which Spanish literature is that produced by Spanish citizens (hence the
    inclusion of authors from colonial America); the other linguistic, according
    to which the unity of a literature presupposes the use of a single language.
    The problem is that these two geographies do not match, and their pairing
    results, once more, in the silencing of the works of either a significant
    portion of Spaniards (those who do not express themselves in Spanish)
    or the majority of Spanish speakers (who are citizens of *other* countries)"
    (114).

13. "In Mainer's view," writes Santana, "the lack of metacritical reflection on
    their foundations would convert the majority of the regional histories into

mere instruments at the service of political interests that are far removed from literary valuation" (115).

14. Gerassi-Navarro and Merediz point out that this skepticism is widespread in the US academy: "Many Latin Americanists and Hispanists in US academia, unlike those in Canada or Great Britain, have a conflictive relationship with Transatlantic Studies, which is seen not only as an administrative strategy to cut down on specialized personnel and resources, or to fuse programs, but as yet another catalyst feeding the colonial tension between Peninsular and Latin American Studies" (617n17). Trigo's critique is particularly acute. "Transatlantic Studies," he writes, "do not constitute a new critical paradigm—since they rely on paradigms already widely accepted—or yet another discipline—since they do not have a particular object of inquiry, nor propose any specific methodology, nor pinpoint a set of specific theoretical problems, all of which they partake with different disciplines (e.g. history, anthropology, literary criticism), established fields (e.g. cultural studies, postcolonial studies), and the current theories in the academic market. But even more importantly, Transatlantic Studies are the result of a dual shift: a geographical displacement provoked by the geopolitical de-bunking of area studies, and an epistemological rift produced by the bankruptcy of the socialist block and the unstable consolidation of a flexible and combined regime of capitalist accumulation" (38).

15. The shorthand phrase "Departments of Spanish and Hispanic Studies" masks a deeper problem of naming. The broadening of the field in all directions—in terms of geography, theory, methodology, and object of study—along with a heightened awareness of the ideological charge or cultural claims inherent in department and program names, has made it a challenge to find a proper way to identify, for institutional purposes, what is taught and analyzed. If the traditional notion of "Spanish" is seen as too centered on language study (and exclusively Castilian language at that), "Hispanic Studies" appears to exclude the Lusophone world and has an unwelcome resonance in a US context, where the adjective "Hispanic" carries a very definite political charge. "Iberian Studies" as proposed by Resina is an adequate name for the field that studies the cultural production of the Iberian Peninsula as a multilingual, multinational dynamic whole, but even Iberian studies has a complicated relationship with Portuguese cultural production.

16. "The hybridization of European, American, and African cultural productions in the pan-Atlantic challenges us to think outside national canons, and allows for the inclusion of hispanophone, francophone, and lusophone texts alongside anglophone ones" (Almeida 8).

Works Cited

Almeida, Joselyn M. *Reimagining the Transatlantic, 1780–1890.* Burlington, VT: Ashgate, 2011.

Alonso, Cecilio. *Historia de la literatura española. Vol. 5: Hacia una literatura nacional, 1800–1900.* Coord. José-Carlos Mainer. Barcelona: Crítica, 2010.

Bourdieu, Pierre. *The Field of Cultural Production: Essays on Art and Literature.* Ed. Randal Johnson. New York: Columbia UP, 1993.

———. *Homo Academicus.* Stanford, CA: Stanford UP, 1988.

———. *The Rules of Art: Genesis and Structure of the Literary Field.* Stanford, CA: Stanford UP, 1992.

Epps, Bradley S., and Luis Fernández Cifuentes. "Spain beyond Spain: Modernity, Literary History, and National Identity." Epps and Fernández Cifuentes 11–45.

———, eds. *Spain beyond Spain: Modernity, Literary History, and National Identity.* Lewisburg, PA: Bucknell UP, 2005.

Faber, Sebastiaan. "Economies of Prestige: The Place of Iberian Studies in the American University." *Hispanic Research Journal* 9.1 (2008): 7–32.

———. "'La hora ha llegado': Hispanism, Pan-Americanism, and the Hope of Spanish/American Glory (1938–1948)." Moraña 62–104.

———. "The Trope as Trap: Ideology Revisited." *Culture, Theory and Critique* 45.2 (2004): 133–59.

Fernández, Pura. "Redes trasatlánticas: el espacio editorial en castellano en el campo cultural contemporáneo." *Revista de Estudios Hispánicos* 46.2 (2012): 177–200.

Gabilondo, Joseba. Introduction to *The Hispanic Atlantic*, special issue of *Arizona Journal of Hispanic Cultural Studies* 5 (2001): 91–113.

Geli, Carlos. "Memoria histórica para la literatura." *El País* 23 Mar. 2011. Web. 24 Jan. 2013.

Gerassi-Navarro, Nina, and Eyda Merediz. "Introducción: confluencias de los transatlántico y lo latinoamericano." *Revista Iberoamericana* 75.228 (2009): 605–36.

Hutcheon, Linda. "Rethinking the National Model." *Rethinking Literary History: A Dialogue on Theory.* Ed. Hutcheon and Mario J. Valdés. Oxford: Oxford UP, 2002. 3–49.

Hutchinson, John. "Cultural Nationalism and Moral Regeneration." *Nationalism.* Ed. Hutchinson and Anthony D. Smith. Oxford: Oxford University Press, 1994. 122–31.

Mainer, José-Carlos. *Historia de la literatura española. Vol. 6: Modernidad y nacionalismo, 1900–1939.* Coord. Mainer. Barcelona: Crítica, 2011.

Mejías-López, Alejandro. *The Inverted Conquest: The Myth of Modernity and the Transatlantic Onset of Modernism.* Nashville: Vanderbilt UP, 2009.

Moraña, Mabel, ed. *Ideologies of Hispanism*. Nashville: Vanderbilt UP, 2005.

Ortega, Julio. "Post-teoría y estudios transatlánticos." *Iberoamericana* 3.9 (2003): 109–17.

———. Presentación. *Iberoamericana* 3.9 (2003): 105–8.

———. "Voces de una saga migratoria." *Babelia* 13 Oct. 2001. Web. 24 Jan. 2013.

Ouimette, Víctor. "Prólogo: Unamuno en *La Nación*." *De patriotismo espiritual: Artículos en "La nación" de Buenos Aires, 1901–1914*. By Miguel de Unamuno. Ed. Ouimette. Salamanca: Ediciones U de Salamanca, 1997.

Pérez Montfort, Ricardo. "El hispanismo: fundamento del pensamiento conservador en España y México." *Breve antología de documentos hispanistas*. Ed. Pérez Montfort. Mexico City: SEP, Centro de Investigaciones y Estudios Superiores en Antropología Social, 1990. 7–18.

Pike, Fredrick B. *Hispanismo, 1898–1936: Spanish Conservatives and Liberals and Their Relations with Spanish America*. Notre Dame: U of Notre Dame P, 1971.

Prieto de Paula, Angel L. "Los renuevos del viejo Humanismo." *El País* 26 Mar. 2011. Web. 24 Jan. 2013.

Rama, Carlos M. *Historia de las relaciones culturales entre España y la América Latina, siglo XIX*. Mexico City: Fondo de Cultura Económica, 1982.

Resina, Joan Ramon. *Del hispanismo a los estudios ibéricos: Una propuesta federativa para el ámbito cultural*. Madrid: Biblioteca Nueva, 2009.

Sánchez Robayna, Andrés. "Literatura e historia: el caso de Canarias." *Literaturas regionales en España: Historia y crítica*. Ed. José María Enguita and José-Carlos Mainer. Zaragoza: Institución Fernando el Católico, 1994. 117–28.

Santana, Mario. "Mapping National Literatures: Some Observations on Contemporary Hispanism." Epps and Fernández Cifuentes 109–24.

Trigo, Abril. "Global Realignments and the Geopolitics of Transatlantic Studies: An Inquiry." Paper presented at Title VI 50th Anniversary Conference, Washington, DC, 19–21 Mar. 2009. Web. 24 Jan. 2013.

Valle, José del, and Luis Gabriel-Stheeman. *The Battle over Spanish between 1800 and 2000: Language Ideologies and Hispanic Intellectuals*. London: Routledge, 2002.

Van Aken, Mark Jay. *Pan-Hispanism: Its Origin and Development to 1866*. Berkeley: U of California P, 1959.

Williams, Raymond. *Culture and Materialism: Selected Essays*. London: Verso, 2006.

2
_____

Liverpool and the Luso-Hispanic World
Negotiating Global Histories at Empire's End

Kirsty Hooper
University of Warwick

In 2004, the British port city of Liverpool, hitherto largely dismissed within the UK as a textbook example of postindustrial decline, was recognized as a World Heritage Site by UNESCO, which described several clusters of eighteenth- and nineteenth-century buildings in the city center as constituting a "supreme example of a commercial port at a time of Britain's greatest global influence" (UNESCO, "Liverpool"). In 2008, when the city took up its place as European Capital of Culture, its past presence on the global stage was a central pillar of a marketing strategy in which the city's historical identity as Britain's second port, a crucial hub in the vast eighteenth- and nineteenth-century maritime networks that supported the expansion of the British Empire, would once again bring Liverpool to the world, and the world to Liverpool.[1] Visit the city's extensive network of museums today and you will see an eclectic selection of material symbols of this history, brought together under various rubrics that speak to the twenty-first-century revival of Liverpool's global ambition—from the new Museum of Liverpool and its Global City gallery, opened in July 2011, to the International Slavery Museum and World Museum Liverpool. Liverpool's global claims, of course, relate to a distinctly partial version of the globe, one that revolves around the former British Empire and its cultural, commercial, political, and linguistic dominions. However, as I will suggest in this chapter, the city has also been a crucial pivot in another set of global histories: during the long nineteenth century, Liverpool operated as an extraimperial and therefore largely unseen hub in the transnational and postimperial networks of the Luso-Hispanic world.

I propose that, unlikely as it may seem, recovering the obscured nineteenth-century networks connecting this northern British port city with its peers in the Luso-Hispanic world is a productive means by which to stimulate reflection on the geopolitical logic underpinning our practice as Hispanists. In particular, this inherently relational approach may provide a valuable perspective from which to reassess the spatial frameworks we use to make sense of the Hispanic world, with the aim, as I once wrote, of finding a "relational model [that] returns power to the margins and interstices of cultures, languages, nations, and histories" (Hooper, *Writing* 33). To investigate nineteenth-century Liverpool's close ties with Vigo, Bilbao, Las Palmas, Funchal, or Manila is to place the spotlight on connections between spaces that are too often dismissed as local, regional, or peripheral to the familiar macrohistorical frameworks of nation, state, and empire. And the recuperation of connections between spaces that normally reside within *different* macrohistorical frameworks requires a very deliberate effort to read against the grain. As Antoinette Burton reminds us, a project that aims to investigate histories of the global cannot be limited to a simplistic division between "the local" and "the global." Rather, she says, it "requires a self-conscious engagement with questions of method and scale. . . . [It] requires attention to translocal processes and identities as well as putatively global ones" (326).[2] This, I would add, is even truer when we study the histories of spaces and networks that reside in the interstices between distinctly articulated versions of "the global."

Burton's call for "self-conscious engagement" with the tools at our disposal is especially important when we consider how to deal with these translocal or interstitial spaces in the context of two "global" spaces such as the Anglophone and Hispanic empires, whose histories have so often been articulated in terms of distance or opposition.[3] Scholars working in vastly differing disciplines have come to similar conclusions about the need to rearticulate the different modes of reading available to us as practitioners working across global, transnational, and relational frameworks. In an important 2007 essay, the historian Eliga H. Gould argues that "there is a need for Atlantic historians to think . . . hard about what it means to write entangled history of the sort exemplified by the English-speaking and Spanish Atlantic worlds" (785).[4] The subtitle of Gould's essay, "The English-Speaking Atlantic as a Spanish Periphery," underlines his powerful case for rethinking established geopolitical assumptions regarding the relations between these two complex entities. Gould's challenge to the prevailing geopolitical logic, together with his rejection of simplistic comparison in favor of the mode he calls "entangled history," has relevance beyond the Atlantic world he takes as his object. Indeed, Gould's assertion that "only in the most general sense . . . can these transatlantic communities be said to have been comparable or distinct" (785) has much in common with the anthropologist Arjun Appadurai's rejection of "the classic idea of comparison [that] relies on the notion that the objects to be compared are distinct and that comparison, therefore, remains unsullied by connectivity" (8).

In translating these ideas into practice, those of us working from disciplines founded on the logic of the nation-state must acknowledge the degree to which "interpretation of the abstract body of the nation depends on acknowledging the experience of the physical body, of the individual caught in this complex network of influences and authorities" (Hooper, *Writing* 33). Such a move is essential to avoid subjecting these bodies to what Peter Linebaugh and Marcus Rediker, quoting Derek Sayer, have called the "violence of abstraction" (7). This is especially the case for cultural scholars working with concepts of mobility, which, as Stephen Greenblatt notes in *Cultural Mobility: A Manifesto*, have too often been placed at the service of macrohistorical frameworks and the desire to "reinforce or confirm the grand narrative" (15), as if "the history of ideas were somehow entirely independent of the history of exile, migration, and economic exchange" (4).[5] Instead, Greenblatt urges cultural scholars to take inspiration from historians and return to empirical work and to take part in "the patient charting of specific instances of cultural mobility" (16), working not with grand narratives but with "microhistories of 'displaced' things and persons [that] represent cultural connections between unexpected times and places" (17). He argues, in the face of the huge growth in scholarship using mobility as a conceptual framework, that "*mobility must be taken in a highly literal sense.*" That is, we must grasp "the physical, infrastructural, and institutional conditions of movement—the available routes; the maps; the vehicles; the relative speed; the controls and costs," which, he affirms, "are all serious objects of analysis." In short, for Greenblatt, "only when conditions directly related to literal movement are firmly grasped [will it] be possible fully to understand the metaphorical movements" (250).

The project to excavate Liverpool's nodal role in the global histories of the nineteenth-century Anglophone and Luso-Hispanic worlds sits at the intersection of these two models—the abstract and the empirical. In order to understand why these connections have remained largely unseen in both versions of the global past, we must first understand the force of the geopolitical logic that has framed them. Liverpool is situated on the northwestern edge of the UK, closer to Wales and Ireland than to London, and so it has always been considered "a city apart" (Belchem, "New Livercool" 217). During the second half of the twentieth century, the metropolitan perspective framed the city as both geographically and culturally peripheral, even if its cultural distinctiveness has at certain points intersected with or even driven the mainstream.[6] Furthermore, like any port city, Liverpool's closest cultural and commercial connections have been not with national capitals or imperial metropolises (and certainly not with its near neighbor and eternal rival Manchester) but with other port cities, themselves by definition located on the geographical peripheries of the nation-states that host them. The Spanish ports whose connections with Liverpool formed the heart of this transoceanic nineteenth-century network were almost without exception in regions from which the center of state power in Madrid was distant not only geographically but also culturally and politically: Bilbao, A Coruña, Vigo, Las Palmas de Gran Canaria, Santa Cruz de Tenerife, Manila, Havana, San Juan de Puerto Rico. Furthermore, their position on the Atlantic seaboard (or, in the case of Manila, on the Pacific) distanced them equally from Spain's second metropolis and its power center on the Mediterranean, Barcelona, a distance that resonates even today in Catalanist suspicion of an Atlantic approach to Hispanic studies.[7]

The cultural and geographical distance of these cities from their respective metropolises intensifies the fact that these networks were forged in the second half of the nineteenth century, precisely at the point when the "grand narrative" of Britain's place in the world and that of Spain's place in the world were at opposite ends of the spectrum. In consequence, the details of the connections between them, not to mention the wider social and cultural implications of these connections, have all but dropped out of both versions of "global" history. In what follows, I begin to consider how we might tease out some of the threads binding these connections together. My analysis takes place in the context of four interlocking dimensions: routes, bodies, ideas, and objects.

Liverpool's Luso-Hispanic Connections (1): Routes

Although it remains largely beneath the radar even of maritime and business historians, the infrastructure that supported Liverpool's Luso-Hispanic connections was considerable. During the second half of the nineteenth century, dozens of shipping companies, large and small, British- and Spanish-registered, traveled the circuits in which Liverpool and the ports of Iberia's Atlantic seaboard were considered local stops on the way to the West African and South American destinations where the real business of empire was to be conducted. Among the oldest of the prominent British-owned companies specializing in South America was the Pacific Steam Navigation Company (founded 1838), which, as its name suggests, connected Liverpool with the Pacific coast of South America, providing a regular passenger service via Galicia and Portugal that was used extensively by Liverpool's Spanish and Portuguese communities. Another long-established company was Lamport & Holt (1845), which pioneered British trading links with the east coast of South America, focusing in particular on the Brazil–New York coffee trade. The African Steam Ship Company (1851), the British and African Steam Navigation Company (1868), and Elder Dempster (1868) pioneered both tourism and the banana trade in the Canary Islands in the 1870s and 1880s, taking advantage of spare capacity on ships en route to West Africa (Abbott 12). Finally, the Booth Line (1863) carried leather and, from 1901, tour parties between Liverpool, Galicia, Portugal, Madeira, and northern Brazil (Hooper, "Spas"; Hooper, *Mondariz*). Short-haul companies that focused primarily on the Europe-Iberia leg included MacAndrews (founded 1770, moved to Liverpool 1850), which specialized in the fruit trade and had offices throughout Spain; T&J Harrison (1853), which specialized in the Spanish and Portuguese wine trade; and Yeoward Brothers (1898), another fruit and tourism specialist that sailed fortnightly to Lisbon, Tenerife, Grand Canary, and sometimes Madeira. Smaller Spanish companies included the Bilbao-based Sota y Aznar (1906), which worked closely with Liverpool's Bahr, Behrend.[8] Of these companies, the only one in business today is Mac-Andrews, which continues to run two weekly services to the peninsula: between Liverpool, Leixões (for Porto), and Lisbon, and between Liverpool, Bilbao, and Santander ("Services").

Perhaps the most prominent of all these companies, however, and the one that, as we will see, had the greatest impact on Liverpool was the Anglo-Basque Larrinaga & Company, founded in Liverpool in 1862 by Ramón de Larrinaga, his brother-in-law Captain Bautista Longa, and José Antonio de Olano, a ship's chandler.[9] From 1870 on, the company ran cargo and passenger steamers between Liverpool and the Philippines under the Spanish flag, and in 1873 it won the lucrative Spanish government contract to transport government and military personnel between Spain and the Philippines, particularly significant given the importance of the islands to Spain's crumbling empire (Borja 94). This contract lasted only until 1879, and in 1881 the company became the agent for the infamous

Compañía Trasatlántica Española, known in Liverpool as the Spanish Line (Borja 95).[10] In 1885, Olano, Larrinaga was reorganized and rebranded as Larrinaga & Company, switching its focus from one end of the Spanish empire to the other with the inauguration of routes from Liverpool to Cuba and Puerto Rico.[11] After the end of the Spanish-American War in 1898, the company was relaunched once more as Miguel de Larrinaga, severing formal ties with Spain and registering all ships in Liverpool. Despite heavy losses in both world wars, the company survived until 1974, when it was absorbed by a Greek company and renamed the Vergocean Steamship Company.

Despite the popularity of Liverpool's maritime history, the Luso-Hispanic dimension of the city's maritime infrastructure has received little scholarly attention.[12] We still know very little about the individuals and communities by, through, and for whom these companies operated, the extensive landside infrastructures that supported them, and the social and cultural implications of their displacement of millions of individuals, families, and other networks around the Atlantic and Pacific basins. A glimpse of the complexity of the landside infrastructure can be seen in the various editions of *Gore's Directory of Liverpool*, which was published at intervals between at least 1825 and 1930 and included information about individuals, associations, and companies ranging from multinationals such as Larrinaga to a surprising number of one-man (or one-woman) bands. From midcentury onward, the directory also included the extensive and ever-changing community of consular staff, who socialized primarily with Spanish merchants, especially the powerful fruit merchants, such as López, Pellicer, and Mahiques. The commercial and maritime infrastructure was supported by commercial travelers, clerks, correspondents, translators, interpreters, ship-owners, boardinghouse keepers, ship's store dealers, ship's butchers, sailor's outfitters, and agents. There were also businesses less obviously connected with the maritime infrastructure, such as Elvira Álvarez's art repository on Liverpool's elegant Bold Street, Martin Basabe's butcher's shop in St. John's market, Eugenio de Naverán's confectioner's shop and wine store on Hill Street, Martín Echave's bakery on Beaufort Street, and at least three general shopkeepers (Bernedo, De la Cruz, and Fernández). Finally, a whole community of tailors and bootmakers on Park Lane (three different Álvarezes, Mrs. María Naya, Joseph Rodríguez, and Bautista Tellería) were probably connected with the otherwise elusive Spanish Club that *Gore's* records at 58 Park Lane in 1900. Further investigation of these shipping routes, commercial connections, and local businesses will reveal a great

FIGURE 1. The derelict site of Liverpool's once-thriving Hispanic waterfront community (Kirsty Hooper, 2012)

deal about the networks of relation holding together the fragile strands of Spain and its fragmenting empire during the difficult decades at the empire's end.

Liverpool's Luso-Hispanic Connections (2): Bodies

A central problem in the reconstruction of these networks is that, unlike the Irish, Welsh, Scandinavians, Italians, Chinese, and West Africans who also settled in the city during the nineteenth century and have retained their sense of collective identity into the twenty-first, Liverpool's Luso-Hispanic communities have seemingly left little trace of their existence. Until very recently they remained on the periphery of the city's official history: unmentioned in scholarly histories, they have no monument like that of the Chinese, no community center like the West Africans, no published histories like the Italians, nor any church like the Scandinavians.[13] In the absence of such resources, the question becomes, as Madge Dresser has argued with regard to community history, how to pursue "the construction of a public history that has emotional resonance but which is decent, honest and fair and which does correspond to some baseline of what we tentatively judge to be historical reality" (n. pag.). In other words, this kind of work requires a balancing act between academic history of the kind that demands evidence and is attentive to every line of the archive, on the one hand, and community memory of the kind that projects affect and demands readings far beyond and between the lines of any written archive, on the other. In the end, though, only careful tracing of the individual circumstances, decisions, connections, and emotions inhabiting these networks of relation can help us understand the living of these individual lives, their place in these networks of relation, and the wider implications of their mobility.

There is much work to be done on the relationship between the material traces of individual lives and the networks of relation that continue to give these traces meaning. Greenblatt's challenge in his manifesto to return to the empirical, the microhistorical case study, provides an impetus for us to begin tracing the flashes of contact with the historical record and so to build up the evidence base to construct thick descriptions of these forgotten lives. Taking into account the need to guard against Linebaugh and Rediker's "violence of abstraction" (7), I carried out a pilot project between 2008 and 2011. It is a detailed empirical survey of individuals, families, and social or kinship networks, drawing on archival sources including the decennial census of England and Wales; parish records of baptisms, confirmations, marriages, and burials; trade and street directories; ships' manifests; seaman's tickets; school records; and local newspapers. The outcome is a biographical database of some two thousand Luso-Hispanic-born individuals who settled in or passed through Liverpool during the long nineteenth century that provides both detailed information at an individual level and a demographic background against which to consider both individual and collective mobilities.[14] Liverpool's first-generation Luso-Hispanic population reflects the city's population growth, more or less doubling in size between the first available census in 1851 (ca. 200 people of a total Liverpool population ca. 376,000) and the last available in 1911 (ca. 400 people of a total Liverpool population ca. 750,000).[15] A survey of birth countries recorded in census returns shows that some 75 percent (1452 people) of all those recorded were born in Spain, followed by around 12 percent (236) born in Brazil and further clusters born in Portugal (79), the Philippines (45), and Cape Verde (23).[16] Meanwhile, a survey of occupation categories across all census returns reveals that the main sources of employment for Luso-Hispanic Liverpudlians were the sea (465 people), commerce (216), trade (209), and domestic service (155).

These figures may be broadly unsurprising, but breaking them down further allows us to assess Liverpool's shifting associations with wider Luso-Hispanic networks and provides a framework within which to map broader changes onto individual biographies. In 1851, fully half of the recorded population were foreign-born British citizens, the majority born in Brazil or the Southern Cone and residing in family groups in the wealthy suburb of Mount Pleasant. This reflects the high level of mobility between Liverpool and British trading communities on the east coast of South America, above all in Pernambuco in Northeast Brazil and in the Montevideo–Buenos Aires region (Sargen). The Spanish-born population was divided between British citizens, with a predominance born during or shortly after the Peninsular War, and a handful of Spanish citizens largely divided between merchants and mariners. There was a single Spanish-run boardinghouse at 32 Drury Lane, in which the Canarian cooper and translator José Romero (later Joseph Rosemary) hosted eight Spanish-born sailors, but otherwise no discernible patterns of association. The picture in 1851 was dominated by Liverpool's role as a gateway for the British trading community and by the aftermath of British involvement in the Peninsular War. It was further conditioned by Spanish government restrictions on emigration, which were partially lifted in 1853 and not dispensed with entirely until 1903 (Shubert 43–46). By 1911, the picture was entirely different: some two-thirds of the recorded population (over 270 people) gave their country of birth as Spain and only a tiny proportion of these claimed British citizenship.[17]

Most strikingly, of the 165 Spanish-born people who also gave a place of birth on the 1911 census, almost half were from the single Basque province of Vizcaya.[18] A Vizcayan population, based largely in the working-class waterfront parish of St. Thomas, first appeared on the census in 1871, just at the point when the Bilbao-based Larrinaga & Company came onto the scene, and it expanded alongside the company throughout the rest of the century. Cross-checking with the Vizcayan diocesan archives those entries for individuals of unspecified birthplace whose surname suggests Basque origin allows us to estimate the overall proportion of Vizcayan individuals in the database at between 35 and 50 percent, with significant subpopulations from the capital and principal port, Bilbao, the Larrinaga family's native Mundaka, and the neighboring towns of Ea, Elantxobe, Gauteguiz de Arteaga, and Ibarrangelu. The resonances of these connections in Vizcaya, as well as in Liverpool itself, remain to be captured.

The demographic shift from a concentrated Anglo-American merchant community to a more diverse, if Vizcayan-dominated, Hispanic working-class community, together with the geographical shift from elegant Mount Pleasant down into the heart of the waterfront, provides a neat if simplistic narrative of Liverpool's shifting place in the postimperial networks of the Luso-Hispanic world. In terms of the macronarratives of commerce and empire, it probably adds little that is not already known. However, the database has great value as a resource because it enables us to trace micronarratives of individual mobility, each of which opens its own doors to understanding the individual choices and decisions that intersect with wider factors to bring these complex networks into being. The example of the Rementería sisters from the tiny village of Ibarrangelu on the north Vizcayan coast is a case in point. All eight sisters emigrated to Liverpool, but they met with quite different destinies in their Liverpool lives. Magdalena (b. 1850), the first to arrive, had made the journey by 1877 with her Vizcayan husband, shoemaker Bautista de Tellería (b. 1851). She and Bautista remained in the city all their lives. Census returns and parish records show them to have been at the heart of the Basque waterfront community alongside their friends Pedro and Carmen Bilbao.[19] Magdalena's sisters all followed her to Liverpool: Josefa (b. 1854, married Paulino Bilbao in Ibarrangelu, 1875), Maria (b. 1860, married Pierre Jerome Pomarel in Liverpool, 1886), and Martina (b. 1862, married Juan Amenzaga in Liverpool, 1890) were there by 1884, 1886, and 1890, respectively, although they and their families subsequently disappear from the record. Four more sisters remain visible: Petra (b. 1856) was in Liverpool by 1879, living with Magdalena and Bautista while her Basque first husband was at sea and then, after her second marriage in 1899 to Catalan greengrocer Emilio Miralles, just next door on Park Lane. Estefania (1866–1939) was in Liverpool by 1900, and by 1911 she was running a boarding house at 1–3 Kent Street with her Galician husband Ramón García, a former steamship stoker. Paula (1868–1940) was in Liverpool by 1899, living with her husband Aquilino Diez on Churchill Street, a marginally better area than the waterfront where her sisters had settled. But the baby of the family, Eduarda (1871–1939), made the most notable match, marrying an Anglo-Irish insurance clerk named James Hall Gerety in 1897 and establishing a household on Upper Huskisson Street in the heart of the city's elegant Georgian Quarter before moving across the water to the upmarket enclave of Wirral.

The case study of the Rementería family allows us to raise a number of questions, both specific and general: Why did the Rementería sisters come

Figure 2. Beaconsfield House, once the home of linguist Manuel López Jonte (Kirsty Hooper, 2012)

to Liverpool while their three brothers remained at home in Ibarrangelu? What brought Magdalena and Bautista to the city in the first place, when he was neither a merchant nor a mariner, nor had any visible connection with any of the city's maritime businesses? What were the consequences back in Ibarrangelu of the departure of eight daughters from one family, and what traces, if any, remain of this collective mobility today? To what extent can the microhistories of the Rementería sisters' marriages with fellow Vizcayans, Galicians, Catalans, Frenchmen, and Anglo-Irishmen allow us to read into the wider network of relations that made up Liverpool's connections with the Luso-Hispanic world?

Liverpool's Luso-Hispanic Connections (3): Ideas

We have rarely been in a position to ask questions of the kind just noted, let alone answer them, and the reason lies in the paradox at the heart of Hispanic Liverpool. The scholarly field of Anglo-Hispanism, itself partly a by-product of Spain's postempire transition (Faber; Mackenzie), has been closely associated for more than a century with the University of Liverpool. However, what has been generally overlooked in accounts of Liverpool's role in the discipline's development is the extent to which this history is overlaid on the vibrant but now largely obliterated network of Hispanic lives, works, and ideas that make up Hispanic Liverpool. The foundation of both university and discipline coincide with the apogee of Liverpool's role as a hub in Luso-Hispanic networks. Liverpool University was founded in 1881, received its charter in 1903, and in 1908 established the Gilmour Chair of Spanish, funded by Captain George Gilmour with the stipulation that the chair should be used above all for promotion of Latin American (and especially Argentinean) culture and language.[20] Gilmour's proviso was ignored, and in 1909, after fierce competition between more than 160 candidates (Ribbans 20), the independent scholar of peninsular Spanish literature James Fitzmaurice Kelly (1858–1923) was appointed Liverpool's first Gilmour Professor of Spanish.[21]

Fitzmaurice Kelly is a useful touchstone for the gulf between various ideas of "Spanish" cultures, tangible and intangible, circulating in a single location. His occupation of the Gilmour Chair, in opposition to the founder's desire to prioritize study of Argentina, exemplifies the multiple erasures that sit at the heart of Hispanism and that underpin Fitzmaurice Kelly's own work. On the very first page of his seminal *History of Spanish Literature* (1898), which would set the tone for almost a century of subsequent scholarship in Spain and France as well as the Anglophone world, Fitzmaurice Kelly had explicitly excised Galician and Basque from consideration, citing Galician literature as "artificial" and Basque as "the spoiled child of philologers, which has not added greatly to the sum of the world's delight" (vii).[22] Fitzmaurice Kelly wrote his history before he came to Liverpool, but his time there did not change his essential intellectual model. He was a key figure in the development from the early twentieth century of an institutional discourse of Hispanism, whose elision of peripheral voices is now, at the distance of over a century, one of its most conspicuous and criticized features. The irony is that his arrival in Liverpool placed him at the center of a city where commerce was king, and, not only this, but also where the everyday experience of "Spanishness" was defined precisely by the cultural and linguistic diversity he sought to obscure.

Of course, nobody would expect an Edwardian university professor to spend time at the Liverpool docks or in the narrow streets of Toxteth Park, and the idea that he could somehow have known the Rementería sisters is absurd. But this familiar gap between "town" and "gown," reflected in the even more familiar strategy of separating intellectual culture from the tangled geopolitical, biopolitical, or material networks out of which it emerges, has wider repercussions. Professor Fitzmaurice Kelly may have remained apart from the working-class masses down by the docks, but, as far as I can tell, he also remained apart from the Luso-Hispanic artists and intellectuals passing through the city. These individuals had their own role to play in the circulation of knowledge and ideas between the Anglophone and Hispanic or Lusophone worlds, even when that role—unlike the professor's—is rarely, if ever, remembered. The most famous of them, without a doubt, was Joseph Blanco White (1775–1841), whose life and work have been thoroughly excavated by scholars even if, as Jo Labanyi has written, "until recently, no national literature has wanted to claim him" (37). His connection with the city, generally considered exceptional, may deepen if we consider it as part of a wider set of interlocking relational influences. Another figure who has been recently incorporated into the historical record is Eulalia Abaitua (1853–1943), the Basque Country's first female photographer, who spent a period of time in Liverpool as a teenager when she fled with her family from the Third Carlist War. Abaitua learned her trade in 1870s Liverpool, and when she returned to her native Bilbao, she took not only her skills and darkroom but an aesthetic as well: she constructed a house there in the Victorian Gothic style, which, although much altered, remains standing today (Jiménez Ochoa de Alda).

Others, whose physical presence in Liverpool is established but whose ideological or cultural connections with the city remain untraced, include the theologian and academic Lorenzo de Lucena (1807–1881), the Andalusian artist Enrique Dastis (1841–1900), the linguists Francisco Quicler (1862–?) and Manuel López Jonte (1855–1918), the Venezuelan consul, novelist and (fleetingly) president José Gil Fortoul (1861–1943), the Catalan anarchist Lorenzo Portet (1870–1917), and the Vizcayan war reporter and academic Teresa de Escoriaza (1891–1968). There were even a small number of Spanish-language books published in the city, the history of whose genesis, production, dissemination, and reception would provide a valuable perspective on the transmission of cultural and political ideas between Liverpool and the Hispanic world.[23] These connections are largely unseen by Hispanists and are also absent from both Anglophone and Luso-Hispanic versions of the global past. There are many reasons for the disappearance of these connections from our collective imagination. By recovering them, we can gain an insight into the microcosmic threads of the individual translocal connectivities (Burton, Appadurai) that make up the thick fabric of global histories.

Liverpool's Luso-Hispanic Connections (4): Objects

Another reason for the disappearance of these microhistories and macrohistories from our collective imagination is that Hispanic studies, like other disciplines originating in the study of language and literature, has historically been focused on the circulation of ideas and (in the abstract sense) the texts that carry them. However, the wider project of understanding global networks of circulation depends on recognizing the material dimension of those networks—that is, following Greenblatt, on reinserting the "history of ideas" into "the history of exile, migration, and economic exchange" (4).[24] The global historian Maxine Berg understands this project as enabling us to pose "open-ended questions . . . over global connections on subjects such as diasporas, the transmission of material culture and useful knowledge, on the connected histories of city life, of embassies and trading missions and religious ideologies" (339). To this end, the closing section of this chapter reflects on the questions we might pose of the Luso-Hispanic objects displayed in the Global City gallery of the new Museum of Liverpool, which opened to the public in the summer of 2011.

The gallery is structured around two stories: Liverpool's place in the British Empire and its relationship with China. The latter, sponsored by Barclays Wealth under the slogan "East Meets West," dominates the user's experience of the gallery. Not only are its display cases placed at the center of the room, but an illuminated ceiling-level surround of Shanghai both draws the eye upward and reflects on the glass cases of other displays, as we can see in Figure 2.3, which shows a Chinese-authored portrait of a member of the Larrinaga family overlaid with the Shanghai skyline. Within this framework, the Luso-Hispanic world is glimpsed only fleetingly and never on its own terms. It appears most prominently in the "Sailing South" panel, located halfway along the left perimeter of the gallery, whose summary of Spanish and Portuguese imperial history is cursory, to say the least: "Spanish and Portuguese exploration brought disaster for indigenous people and their cultures in South America. For 500 years the exploitation of existing communities, mass migration and economic development transformed the continent." In contrast, the panel implies, the British presence in South America brought economic progress: "Liverpool companies saw new opportunities in South America during the 19th century. Trade was initially limited by the region's undeveloped economies and independence wars. By the late 1840s, 63 Liverpool firms had bases in South American ports like Valparaiso in Chile." The panel sits beneath three objects: a carved door surround that once adorned the Lamport & Holt shipping

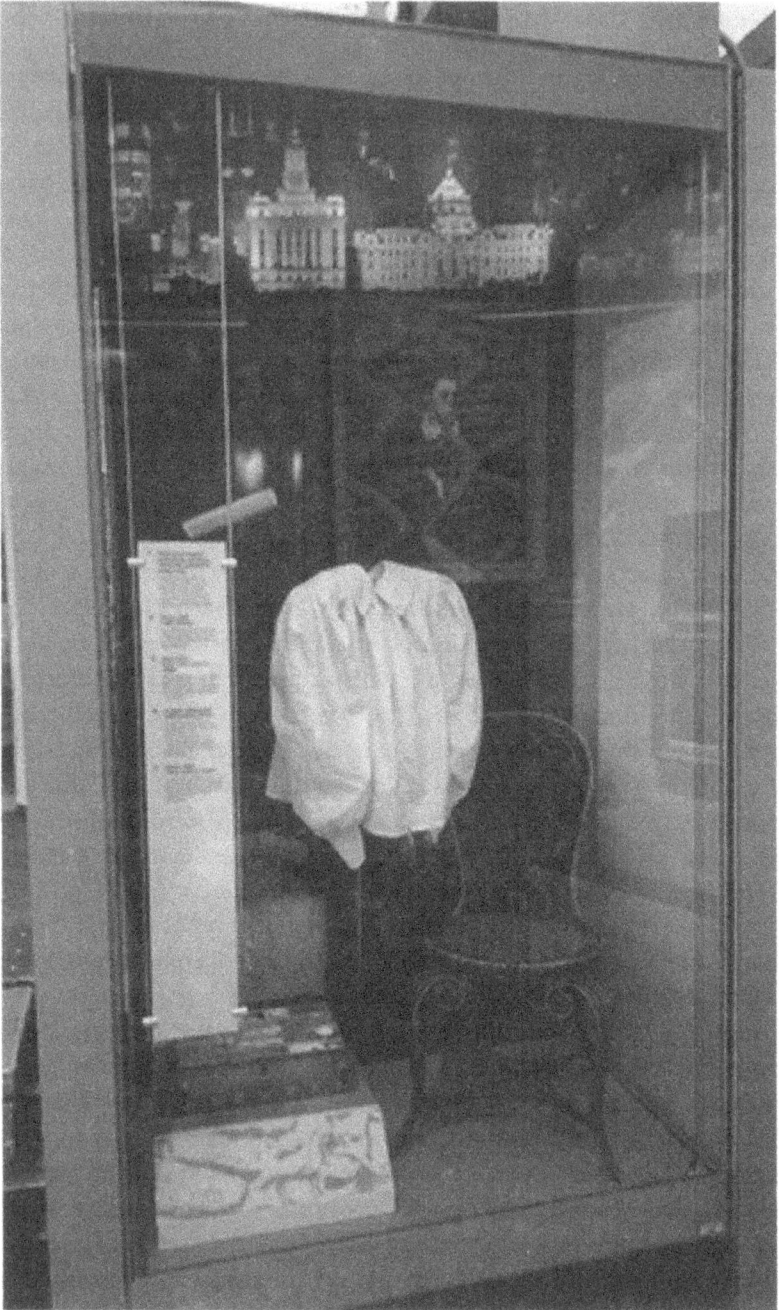

FIGURE 3. Portrait of a member of the Larrinaga family in the Museum of Liverpool's Global City Gallery (Kirsty Hooper, 2015)

offices in Liverpool's iconic Liver Building and two paintings of ships: the *Anselma de Larrinaga* (1898) and the RMS *Oropesa* (1920), two British ships that sailed between Liverpool and South America at the beginning of the twentieth century.

The negative characterization of Spanish and Portuguese imperialism in "Sailing South," combined with the triumphalist economic narrative of British trade with the Luso-Hispanic world, closely echoes nineteenth-century rhetoric designed to cement the place of Spain and Latin America as peripheral territories of the British Empire through the mechanism known as informal empire.[25] As such, it confirms the continued relevance of Ruth Adams's observation that, in the nineteenth century, "Britain's national museums . . . played a role in defining both the 'core' and the 'margins' of the Empire" (64).[26] The marginality of the Luso-Hispanic informal empire to the gallery's projection of Liverpool as global city is emphasized by the quotation that heads the "Sailing South" panel, taken from Ramsay Muir's 1907 history of Liverpool, which gestures toward the emptying-out of Luso-Hispanic specificity in favor of an unmarked, all-encompassing "global": "These busy docks, crowded with the shipping of *every nation . . .* littered with strange commodities brought from *all the shores of the oceans*" (301, emphasis mine).

This stripping out of Luso-Hispanic content in the service of a universalizing but Anglocentric global narrative is also fundamental to the other display with a strong Hispanic presence: "East Meets West," where an entire display case in the center of the gallery, labeled "The Larrinagas—Basque Traders in Liverpool," is given over to the Larrinaga family who, as we have already seen, settled in Liverpool in the 1860s. The Larrinagas, from the small Vizcayan town of Mundaka, were central to the networks connecting Liverpool with the Atlantic and Pacific during the last third of the nineteenth century. Presented only in the context of the "East Meets West" narrative, however, their history is flattened and compressed to fit into the newly prioritized story of Britain's relationship with China. The text from the information panel alongside the display makes this clear: "With great fortunes to be made from trading with China, many merchants came to Liverpool to make money. The Larrinagas, a shipping family from the Basque region in Spain, did just that."

In this narrative, the driving impetus of the Larrinagas' business—Spain's attempt to maintain its power base in the Philippines in the face of significant local and international resistance—is erased, and their story is repackaged as support for a contemporary narrative of Anglo-Chinese history. Three sets of Chinese-influenced items appear in the case: three fans, a lacquered box with the initials DM (for Domingo de Larrinaga), and a Chinese robe and slippers belonging to Domingo's wife Minnie de Larrinaga. Alongside the explanatory panel is a photograph of the Larrinaga family, probably taken in one of the family's residences in the wealthy suburb of Sefton Park—but there is no key, and the photograph is not mentioned in the text. The display is difficult to take in because from every angle the glass is overlaid by the reflection of the giant Chinese dragon that hangs overhead.

While elements of Luso-Hispanic history are present in the Global City gallery, they are doubly refracted: in figurative terms, through British postimperial commemorative practice and contemporary global capital (in the shape of Barclays Wealth), and in more literal terms, through the inescapable reflection of the bright lights of Shanghai. This raises the question of where and how we might best capture the material history of Hispanic Liverpool. Robert Aguirre's careful reading of Victorian collections of Mexican and Central American cultural objects provides a useful starting point. He notes that "we need a more flexible account of the circuits of exchange by which objects moved in both directions across the Atlantic, one sensitive to the role of culture and its complex affiliations with economics and politics" (xxii). Emphasizing the unique and contingent nature of each interaction with a material object, Ayse Caglar provides a useful reminder that such objects need not carry with them the a priori assumptions inherent to the projection of wider collectivities: "One option is to begin our study by exploring person-object relations as these exist in space and time. By plotting the networks of interconnected practices surrounding objects, and the sentiments, desire and images these practices evoke, we can avoid the need to define collectivities in advance" (180).

In other words, Caglar is advocating the inverse of normal museum design, which generally begins with the collectivity—whether of town, region, nation, state, or empire—and fits objects into the resulting story. Instead, by beginning with an object and reading outward through the multiple layers of practice, affect, and meaning it evokes through time and space, we can, she suggests, capture echoes of stories that remain invisible to the eyes of the museum. In this light, the most telling exhibit in the Global City gallery may be the dynamic, illuminated map of shipping routes passing through Liverpool, which draws our attention to the inherent temporal and spatial mobility of Liverpool's maritime networks. Approaching Minnie de Larrinaga's Chinese robe and slippers from this perspective permits us to ask all kinds of questions about their place in her daily life and the social, emotional, or symbolic practices she may have

FIGURE 4. Belem Tower, Liverpool (Kirsty Hooper, 2012)

associated with them. This kind of reading is impossible if we see her possessions only through the museum's eyes as the material residue of contact between a pair of global imperial histories (British and Chinese) within which the Hispanic perspective, let alone Basque or Vizcayan or Filipino, is flattened into nothing. In the end, though, only by stepping outside the space of the gallery will we find and begin to plot the networks of polyvalent objects, practices, and multiple perspectives that generate meanings for what remains of Hispanic Liverpool. There are a thousand and one potential starting points for such a project, but one I have found especially telling is in the once-elegant suburb of Sefton Park, where an abandoned nineteenth-century gatepost inscribed "Belem Tower," lurching before a derelict 1960s tower block bearing the same legend, speaks to the simultaneous fragility and persistence of Liverpool's forgotten but not entirely obliterated Luso-Hispanic past.

Conclusions

I proposed at the beginning of this chapter that uncovering archival, textual, and material traces of Liverpool's role in the forgotten translocal and extraimperial networks connecting the Anglophone and Luso-Hispanic global spaces during the long nineteenth century allows us to use the often devalued lens of the "local" or "peripheral" to reconsider the value of these forgotten networks and their contribution to the entangled histories of the Anglo-Hispanic global past. At the same time, I suggested that the project of recovering these obscured nineteenth-century networks may stimulate reflection on the geopolitical logic underpinning our practice as Hispanists. Madrid barely touches the routes, bodies, ideas, and objects that make up the networks this chapter has begun to thread together, while Barcelona is only marginally more connected. The centrality to these networks of so-called peripheral regions, including Vizcaya, Galicia, and the Philippines, thus teases at the dominant, binomial logic of an academic practice whose geographical and intellectual center can seem inescapably tied to that of the Spanish state.

Of course, there is still much empirical work to be done, details to be recovered and routes and relations to be traced, in order to capture the flashes of contact with the historical record. In so doing, we can build up the evidence base to construct thick descriptions of these forgotten connections, which, as the threads I have begun to pull at here indicate, gain their meaning precisely in the relations between them. In reading through and between these fragments, traces, and absences, we might begin to recover responsibly the networks of relation holding together the entangled histories that are all but invisible within institutional frameworks such as those of the academy and museum. In its potential to open up fresh perspectives on the inherent connection between tangible circuits of mobility and intangibly circulating cultural forms (Appadurai), this project may have profound implications for our understanding of the positioning of

Spain's plural cultures within the transoceanic and global circulation of people, goods, and ideas during the long and inherently, inextricably entangled nineteenth century.

Notes

1. The tagline of the Capital of Culture bid, "Liverpool: The World in One City," was everywhere leading up to and during 2008, even lending itself to an episode of the BBC's popular religious program *Songs of Praise* (14 Sept. 2008). See also UNESCO, "Liverpool—Maritime Mercantile City" and Belchem, "Liverpool." As Belchem notes elsewhere, by the beginning of the twenty-first century, Liverpool's ethnic homogeneity meant that this message "drew upon Liverpool's historical legacy rather than its contemporary complexion" ("New Livercool" 234).

2. On questions of scale and methodology in the particular context of transnational history, see also Struck, Ferris, and Revel.

3. The two colonial projects were articulated according to opposite ideologies. While the British Empire was driven by an economic imperative, the Spanish empire was seen as a civilizing mission, and each depended on the other for its legitimacy. As Christopher Schmidt-Nowara explains, "The counterpoint to Spanish colonial decline was English colonial ascendancy. England was more than an abstract model of colonialism. It was the rival that had hammered Spain into submission over the eighteenth century from the War of the Spanish Succession to Trafalgar and beyond. . . . The writings of Adam Smith . . . were an inescapable reference for any history of European colonialisms and one of the most cogent representations of Spain's shortcomings and England's relative advantages" (25).

4. Gould's key argument is that "if British America was a provincial fragment of Britain proper, it was also, in important respects, part of a Spanish periphery that included much of the Western Hemisphere" (768).

5. See also Elleke Boehmer's reminder that "aesthetic formations" such as the global modernism that is her subject emerge out of "intercultural contacts and clashes, often but not always brought about by trade, capitalism and empire" (604).

6. The best examples of this are comedy, popular music, and football. See, for example, Belchem, *Merseypride*; Leonard and Strachan; and Williams, Long, and Hopkins.

7. See, for example, the Catalan scholar Joan Ramon Resina's dismissal (with heavy use of scare quotes) of "a 'new field' in 'trans-Atlantic studies'" in Hispanism whose intention, he claims, is to "[permit] Peninsularists to reposition themselves nearer the dominant Americanism." For Resina,

"there is nothing particularly 'interdisciplinary' or 'border-crossing' in most of these moves, which in fact reinforce the discipline's traditional reliance on the legacy of the empire" (96).

8. This relationship would have an interesting cultural resonance through the figure of Arthur Behrend (1895–1974), a junior member of the Behrend family who in 1921 was sent to Bilbao for six months to familiarize himself with the Spanish company's operations. Inspired by his stay, Behrend produced the novel *The House of the Spaniard* (1935), which was filmed the following year by Ealing Studios. See Hooper, "Review."

9. For an outline history of the company, see Eccles.

10. This company, founded in Cuba in 1850 and later based in Barcelona, held the Spanish government mail contract for Spain, Cuba, Puerto Rico, and Santo Domingo from 1861, and by 1899 operated an extensive service connecting Liverpool with A Coruña, Vigo, Porto, Lisbon, Cádiz, Las Palmas, Rio de Janeiro, Montevideo, Buenos Aires, Punta Arenas, Coronel, and Valparaíso. A parallel line ran monthly from Liverpool via A Coruña, Vigo, Lisbon, and Cádiz to the Philippines.

11. The Larrinaga line has the dubious distinction of being the victim of the first hostile act of the Spanish-American War, when the *Buena Ventura* (which had been notorious as the first—but was in fact the second—Spanish-owned steamship to pass through the Panama Canal, piloted by the canal's designer Ferdinand de Lesseps himself) was captured by USS *Nashville* off the Florida coast on 22 April 1898 and subsequently sold to a wrecking company.

12. A rare exception is Rory Miller and Robert Greenhill's essay "Liverpool and South America, 1850–1930."

13. Nonetheless, I have discovered that when a native Liverpudlian hears about my project, they will have a story or two about a Spanish family they knew or about their memories of the Spanish clubs and cafés, shops, and boardinghouses that were gathered around the waterfront and the city center. Anecdotal evidence shows that Liverpool's Hispanic communities were a visible and familiar part of city life, especially during the period from the 1870s until the Second World War.

14. Making birth rather than nationality or formal national affiliation the defining criterion for inclusion allows an insight into a range of mobilities while maintaining the focus on the mobile individuals themselves—whether they were economic migrants, seafarers, returning expatriates, trailing spouses, or international businessmen, their families, and retinue. The next phase of the project, which has already begun, captures data about descendants of the first generation of mobile subjects.

15. Note that the census is simply a snapshot of the population on a particular night and does not record everybody who ever passed through the city.

Furthermore, while the database's coverage of the census is comprehensive, it is not exhaustive. At best, it captures greater than 90 percent of the eligible population at each census.

16. A census took place in 1841, but it does not record place of birth beyond "In county," "Out of county," or "Foreign parts." There are smaller clusters from Uruguay, Chile, Mexico, Panama, Argentina, Peru, and Cuba. The following countries are represented only by individuals or single family groups: Colombia, Mozambique, Venezuela, Costa Rica, Dominica, Guam, Guatemala, Honduras, and Puerto Rico.

17. The Spanish-born community in 1911 is spread across the city, with minor hubs in the new and old merchant suburbs at Aigburth and Mount Pleasant and in the new working-class suburbs at Bootle and Toxteth Park and with a major hub at the waterfront, around four large Basque- and Galician-run boardinghouses. The dominant employment sectors among the Spanish-born population are commerce (above all the fruit trade), maritime employment (both land-based and seagoing), domestic service (mostly female), and tailoring/dressmaking (male and female).

18. Analysis of the family names of those who did not record a place of birth suggests that the highest proportions were of Vizcayan or Galician origin. By comparison, just one person recorded a birthplace in the neighboring Basque province of Vitoria. Of the others who recorded a birthplace, twenty-eight were born in Galicia, eleven in Castile and Leon, eleven in Asturias and Cantabria, seven in Barcelona and Valencia, seven in the Canary Islands, and one each in Madrid, Andalusia, and Zaragoza.

19. The two couples seem to have been behind a "Spanish Club" run out of an adjacent property on Liverpool's Park Lane around 1901, of which nothing remains but a passing mention in a city directory.

20. I am grateful to Luis G. Martínez del Campo for the precise information about Gilmour's stipulation.

21. It is worth noting that not one of the six scholars to have held the title to date has specialized in anything other than peninsular Spanish literature.

22. *A History of Spanish Literature* swiftly appeared in Spanish (1901) and French (1904) translation. A second French edition appeared in 1913.

23. Examples include José Antonio Calcaño's *El ruego de la inocencia: Leyenda católica*, published by E. Howell in 1876, a cluster of books published by the Liverpool House of George Philip, Son, and Nephew in 1892 that includes Gil Fortoul's novel *¿Idilio?* and treatise *La esgrima moderna: Notas de un aficionado*, as well as *La balada de los muertos* by his fellow Venezuelan, Luis López Méndez. There were also a range of bilingual books on the Mexican states written by John R. Southworth and published by Blake and Mackenzie between 1899 and 1910. In addition,

Orígenes y tendencias de la eugenia moderna was published by the *Liverpool Daily Post* for the Honduran consul general Joaquín Bonilla in 1916.

24. As I recently argued with regard to Galicia, practicing these new, critical modes of reading implies "taking a snapshot of the relational network within which our subject operates, whether that subject is a text, a discourse, a concept, a life or a moment, and tracing the lines of relation that constitute its process of *positioning*"; in other words, it is to practice "a relational or rhizomatic reading that is attentive to multiple presences . . . and yet is not mesmerised by any of them" (Hooper, *Writing Galicia* 34). With hindsight, it is easy to see that the glaring absence from this list of potential subjects is, of course, the object itself.

25. "Informal empire" is used to describe the situation when an empire exerts influence over a country or region that is not a formal colony, for example, through cultural, commercial, or military ties. Scholars who have discussed this concept in the context of Anglo-Hispanic relations include Aguirre and Brown.

26. As Adams goes on to observe, "Britain has struggled with its reduced status in the postcolonial context and it seems reasonable to suggest that exhibitionary practices were used to maintain the appearance and thus a vestige of colonial power, and to transmit and sustain imperial ideologies, even though, or rather because the political realities had changed" (67).

Works Cited

Abbott, Roderick. "A Socio-Economic History of the International Banana Trade, 1870–1930." Robert Schuman Centre for Advanced Studies Working Paper, RSCAS 2009/22. 2009. Web. 29 Aug. 2012.

Adams, Ruth. "The V&A: Empire to Multiculturalism?" *Museum and Society* 8.2 (2010): 63–79.

Aguirre, Robert D. *Informal Empire: Mexico and Central America in Victorian Culture.* Minneapolis: U of Minnesota P, 2004.

Appadurai, Arjun. "How Histories Make Geographies : Circulation and Context in a Global Perspective." *Transcultural Studies* 1 (2010): 4–13.

Belchem, John. "Liverpool: World City." *History Today* 57.4 (2007): 48–55.

———. *Merseypride: Essays in Liverpool Exceptionalism.* Liverpool: Liverpool UP, 2000.

———. "The New Livercool: History, Culture and Identity on Merseyside." *Thinking Northern: Textures of Identity in the North of England.* Ed. Christopher Ehland. Amsterdam: Rodopi, 2007. 217–38.

Berg, Maxine. 'From Globalization to Global History.' *History Workshop Journal* 64.1 (2007): 335–40. Web. 7 Aug. 2012.

Borja, Marciano R de. *Basques in the Philippines.* Reno: U of Nevada P, 2005.

Boehmer, Elleke. "How to Feel Global: The Modern, the Global and the World." *Literature Compass* 9.9 (2012): 599–606.

Bonilla, Joaquín. *Orígenes y tendencias de la eugenia moderna.* Liverpool: Liverpool Daily Post, 1916.

Brown, Matthew, ed. *Informal Empire in Latin America: Culture, Commerce, and Capital.* Oxford: Blackwell, 2008.

Burton, Antoinette. "Not Even Remotely Global? Method and Scale in World History." *History Workshop Journal* 64.1 (2007): 323–28. Web. 29 Aug. 2012.

Caglar, Ayse S. "Hyphenated Identities and the Limits of 'Culture.'" *The Politics of Multiculturalism in the New Europe: Racism, Identity and Community.* Ed. Tariq Modood and Pnina Jane Werbner. London: Zed Books, 1997. 169–85.

Calcaño, José Antonio. *El ruego de la inocencia: Leyenda católica.* Liverpool: E Howell, 1876.

Dresser, Madge. "Reaching Out from the Archive: Minority History and Academic Method." Paper presented at the first History in British Education conference, U of London School of Advanced Study, 2005. Web. 9 Oct 2012.

Eccles, David. *Larrinaga Line, 1863–1974.* Windsor: World Ship Society, 2005.

Epps, Bradley S., and Luis Fernández Cifuentes, eds. *Spain beyond Spain: Modernity, Literary History, and National Identity.* Lewisburg, PA: Bucknell UP, 2005.

Faber, Sebastiaan. *Anglo-American Hispanists and the Spanish Civil War: Hispanophilia, Commitment, and Discipline.* New York: Palgrave Macmillan, 2008.

Fitzmaurice Kelly, James. *A History of Spanish Literature.* London: Heinemann, 1898.

Gil Fortoul, José. *¿Idilio?* Liverpool: George Philip, Son and Nephew, 1892.
———. *La esgrima moderna: Notas de un aficionado.* Liverpool: George Philip, Son and Nephew, 1892.

Gould, Eliga H. "AHR Forum: Entangled Histories, Entangled Worlds: The English-Speaking Atlantic as a Spanish Periphery." *American Historical Review* 112.3 (2007): 764–86.

Greenblatt, Stephen. "Cultural Mobility: An Introduction." *Cultural Mobility: A Manifesto.* Cambridge: Cambridge UP, 2009. 1–10.

Haws, Duncan. "Lamport and Holt and Booth Lines." *Merchant Fleets.* Vol. 34. Hereford: TCL, 1998.

Heaton, Paul. *Booth Line.* Pontypool: Starling, 1987.

Hooper, Kirsty. *Mondariz-Vigo-Santiago: A Brief History of Galicia's Edwardian Tourist Boom.* Mondariz-Balneario: Fundación Mondariz-Balneario, 2013.

———. "Review (and Fieldtrip!!!): Arthur Behrend's *The House of the Spaniard* (1935)." *Books on Spain: Occasional Thoughts on Books From and About Spain, From the C19 to Today.* 20 May 2011. Web. 2 Oct. 2012.

———. "Spas, Steamships and Sardines: Edwardian Package Tourism and the Marketing of Galician Regionalism." *Journal of Tourism History* 4.2 (2012): 205–24.

———. *Writing Galicia into the World: New Cartographies, New Poetics.* Liverpool: Liverpool UP, 2011.

Jiménez Ochoa de Alda, Maite. *La fotógrafa Eulalia Abaitua (1853–1943).* Bilbao: BBK (Temas Vizcainos), 2010.

Labanyi, Jo. *Spanish Literature: A Very Short Introduction.* Oxford: Oxford UP, 2010.

Leonard, Marion, and Robert Strachan, eds. *The Beat Goes On: Liverpool, Popular Music and the Changing City.* Liverpool: Liverpool UP, 2010.

Linebaugh, Peter, and Marcus Rediker. *The Many-Headed Hydra: The Hidden History of the Revolutionary Atlantic.* 2nd ed. London: Verso, 2007.

López Méndez, Luis. *La balada de los muertos.* Liverpool: George Philip, Son and Nephew, 1892.

Mackenzie, Ann L., ed. *Spain and Its Literature: Essays in Memory of E. Allison Peers.* Liverpool: Liverpool UP, 1997.

Miller, Rory M., and Robert Greenhill. "Liverpool and South America, 1850–1930." *The Empire in One City: Liverpool's Inconvenient Imperial Past.* Ed. Sheryllynne Haggerty, Nicholas J. White, and Tony Webster. Manchester: Manchester UP, 2008. 78–99.

Muir, John Ramsay. *A History of Liverpool.* Liverpool: Williams and Norgate for U of Liverpool, 1907.

Resina, Joan Ramon. "Cold War Hispanism and the New Deal of Cultural Studies." Epps and Fernández Cifuentes 70–108.

Ribbans, Geoffrey. "E. Allison Peers: A Centenary Reappraisal." Mackenzie 19–33.

Sargen, Ian. *Our Men in Brazil: The Hesketh Brothers Abroad.* Lancaster: Scotforth Books, 2009.

Sayer, Derek. *The Violence of Abstraction: The Analytic Foundations of Historical Materialism.* Oxford: Blackwell, 1987.

Schmidt-Nowara, Christopher. *The Conquest of History: Spanish Colonialism and National Histories in the Nineteenth Century.* Pittsburgh: U of Pittsburgh P, 2006.

"Services." *MacAndrews: Europe's Favourite Short-Sea Shipping Service.* Web. 18 Sept. 2012.

Shubert, Adrian. *A Social History of Modern Spain.* London: Routledge, 1990.

Struck, Bernhard, Kate Ferris, and Jacques Revel. "Introduction: Space and Scale in Transnational History." *International History Review* 33.4 (2011): 573–84.

UNESCO. "List of World Heritage in Danger." *UNESCO*. 2012. Web. 18 Sept. 2012.

———. "Liverpool—Maritime Mercantile City." *UNESCO World Heritage List*. 2004. Web. 18 Sept. 2012.

Williams, John, Cathy Long, and Stephen Hopkins. *Passing Rhythms: Liverpool FC and the Transformation of Football*. Oxford: Berg, 2001.

PART II

Racial Theory

From Imperial Formation to
Nostalgic Celebration

3

The Genius of Columbus and the Mixture of Races

How the Rhetoric of Fusion Defined the End and Beginning of Empire in Nineteenth- and Early Twentieth-Century Spain

Joshua Goode
Claremont Graduate University

While it might seem facile to point out that one's attitude to the end of empire entirely depends on one's relation to this empire, reactions to the end of Spain's overseas empire in 1898 proved to be far more complicated than one might presume. For some, especially Spanish intellectuals, the end of empire ushered in a decades-long debate about Spain's future that offered myriad diagnoses of the problem and myriad prescriptions for the cure. For the most part, these reactions all envisioned the reasons for the end of empire and the relative position of Spain in the world as predictable outcomes of the loss of positive components of the Spanish past or as confirmation of the presence of negative forces endemic in the long swath of Spanish history. Yet, while the causes were rooted in history, the actual reasons these historical phenomena were selected reflected far more the presentist concerns of the political writers, scientists, and intellectuals who were performing the diagnosis. As Virginia Santos-Rivero put it recently, the memory of empire in the decades after 1898 represented the "ontological space" to define Spain's history, and, at the same time, the place to define its present decrepitude (8).

Indeed, Santos-Rivero and other scholars have found ample work describing the manifold ideas and concepts that defined the future of the Spanish empire and its legacy for the peninsula's future. Their attention has long been drawn to the decades after 1898 and the animated conversations about a spiritual, racial, and economic bond with the former empire that underwrote the concepts of *Hispanidad, latinidad, raza,* and *hispanismo.* These neonationalist concepts sought either to restitch Spanish nationalism in the face of lost empire or to justify the burgeoning economic liberalism of Spain's middle classes or the political foundations of Spanish conservatism (Mateo Dieste 70–86; Gabilondo; Loureiro). Yet, left out of this discussion are the scientific debates in Spain's anthropological communities that also undergirded attempts to explain the loss of empire in the period just before and after 1898. These debates are particularly illuminating because often the same anthropologists who were puzzling over what caused the end of empire were also charged with identifying the mechanisms for the start of a new empire in Morocco. In other words, the same anthropologists who diagnosed Spain's imperial decline were deployed to write the blueprints for its future expansion. As a result, the explanations for failures of empire in the Western Hemisphere were coterminous with the explanations for success in Morocco.[1]

This chapter analyzes these moments surrounding the end of empire in Latin America and the reanimation of empire in North Africa to show how flexible scientific interpretations of these events were. Importantly, this flexibility allowed these scientific discussions to prefigure later neonationalist discussions in Spain and the former colonies that often were quite self-consciously antiscientific in their rhetoric. The discourses of biology and culture expressed in terms of racial fusion, *mestizaje,* and hispanismo were far more interrelated than the writers who asserted them claimed them to be. The conscious efforts among writers, politicians, and ideologues of the first three decades of the twentieth century to dissociate their ideas from biological notions of race should not be so easily accepted. Instead, one should see in the reactions to the end of empire in 1898 that mixture and racial fusion were compelling ideas deployed in myriad ways in different historical contexts and with myriad political meanings and valences. This chapter concludes with a brief discussion of the portmanteau quality of this anthropological view of racial thought, as the ideas of fusion, mixture, and hybridity traveled across oceans and later connected with a more fulsome celebration of fusion self-consciously divested of any biological or racial content. Ultimately, the idea of racial fusion served as a classic example of a Saidian traveling theory or text. The traveling theory highlights ideas that have appeared in many different contexts and attempts to trace how they have moved across space with the same structural form, like the idea of racial mixture, but have vastly different meanings and purposes in different contexts.[2] This forces scholars to consider who carried ideas across contexts and also to consider how historical contexts shape the political valences of an idea and its application in different places. This chapter examines how the idea of racial fusion became such a portmanteau idea, marked by the contexts in which it landed.

Interest among Spaniards in the peoples of Africa and Morocco, though extant throughout the nineteenth century, was piqued by the losses of 1898. In her recent book, *Disorientations*, Susan Martin-Márquez discusses the ambivalent role that Africa, or at least the image of Africa, played in Spanish cultural, intellectual, and political imagination in the nineteenth and early twentieth centuries. She mentions, for example, how Africa emerged as a counterweight to the sense of doom around the losses of 1898 and to the hand-wringing about the strength of the conquering spirit of the Spanish (32–49). Morocco, in particular, functioned as the stand-in for the continuing promise of Spanish imperial missions (Jensen 210; Balfour 10–11). For Spanish anthropologists participating in this discussion not just as academic and scholarly voices but also as military advisors, Africa and the idea of Spain as the catalyst for racial fusion were important components—indeed, essential elements—of any new Spanish imperial mission. The study of Spain's imperial contexts proved attractive to anthropologists because it not only gave them the authority to assert the "scientific fact" of Spanish racial fusion but also secured their status as specialized experts who could guarantee the careful maintenance of this fusion in any future Spanish imperial enterprise. Ironically, fusion both served as an effective mode for explaining the demise of the overseas empire in 1898 and also proved to be the mechanism for imagining the success of the imperial venture in Africa.

The work of one influential Spanish anthropologist proved particularly important in the unfolding definitions of race that explained the end of empire in Cuba and also the emergence of empire in Africa. Of primary interest were two parts of a triptych of racial studies that Manuel Antón y Ferrandiz delivered at the Ateneo in Madrid in 1891, just before his appointment to Spain's first chair of anthropology at the Central University of Madrid, and in 1900, just at the start of the imperial expansion in Morocco. These lectures, like most of the anthropological lectures at the Ateneo, were among the most popular and well attended in the period (Antón, "Notas" 14; Villacorta Baños 122). Antón was a logical choice in these years to offer comprehensive scientific portraits of the racial makeup of Spain's empires. Prior to his appointment to the chair of anthropology, he had been the director of the venerable Museo de Historia Natural in

Madrid after having trained both in Madrid and in Paris at the Parisian
Anthropological Society, under Armand de Quatrefages. The museum had
functioned in the nineteenth century as the main research center for Spain's
colonial missions and was the repository of the collections culled from
Spain's not very numerous overseas expeditions during that era. Under
Antón's leadership, the museum played the important political function
of projecting and objectifying the imperial power of Spain. The museum's
collections and staff designed and supplied various public exhibitions of
Spanish empire, including the Philippine Exhibition that took place in the
Retiro Park in 1887.[3] Antón also helped begin the formal process of skull
measurements for the Spanish colonial and national cranial collections
that the museum had held (Goode 38–39).

From this position Antón delivered his first lecture to the Athenaeum
when Cánovas del Castillo was president of the body. His paper focused on
the anthropological roots of the peoples of "America before [Columbus's]
discovery" of the Western Hemisphere.[4] Antón's lecture, which exceeded
forty-seven pages, typical for these lectures, was a meandering tour of the
"physical, intellectual, moral characteristics of the inhabitants" and also
a study of the social organization of the groups living there (*Antropología*
7). Synthesizing the existing anthropological renderings of the Americas,
Antón took particular issue with the US anthropologist Samuel George
Morton and his three-volume *Crania Americana* (1839–1849) over Morton's avowal of polygenism, or the multiple origins of different people.
Polygenism departed from the then more commonly accepted biblical,
monogenist account of all humanity emerging from an original pair of
humans, Adam and Eve. Morton and the American school he founded
were most famous for asserting that human races emerged separately and
were thus endowed with distinct and permanent characteristics; his ideas
had always proved appealing to the defenders of the slave trade (Haller
31–34; Gould 82–104). Antón meticulously explained that, despite the
multiple influences on the physiognomy of the various inhabitants, the
clearest explanation for the varieties of peoples in America was the fusion
of European and Asiatic peoples over the previous millennia. He proposed
that there may have been many European characteristics, including dolicocephaly, or long-headedness, in the various populations of the Americas
and suggested a possible Neanderthal influence on American development. Antón's recourse to the possibility of Neanderthals as playing a pivotal, foundational role in human development was also a common move
within Spanish anthropology. Antón had argued that many European
manifestations of dolicocephaly, which according to the anthropological

assumptions of that moment should not have appeared in Europe (like the Basque Country), were the product of Neanderthal intermixture in the past (*Antropología* 8–10).

Yet, this essay is important less because of his anthropological explanation of human origins than Antón's apparent explanation for the end of empire in Latin America. He wrote that "Americans constitute a group of mixed races, and the problem which persists in today's anthropology is in tracing the fundamental crosses and confused mixes that form the basic tapestry of colors that define the American races" (10). However, restitching this fabric through craniometrical and physical measurements was too difficult, according to Antón. Ultimately, he concluded that the only Spanish imperial conquest could be the catalyst for this fusion of distinct American races. Fusions took place over millennia but could be expedited by a strong unifying force. For Antón, the Spanish conquest was an important catalyst. The "genius of Columbus," he wrote, began the process of fusion, but the final fusion was not physical or biological. Instead, it was the product of "the energetic efforts of the Spanish people then who, tempered by 800 years of struggle, had prepared themselves for this, the most daring adventure of colonization, which has long remained one of the most heroic feats and accomplishments in human history" (46). In other words, good racial fusion was always the product of the contradictory acts of fusion and expulsion. What allowed Spanish explorers to prove so effective at stitching the disparate races of America together was a fusionary savvy born of the extraction of negative elements: the expulsion of the Arabs from Spain. At the end of his long discourse on the racial incursions that shaped the peoples in the Western Hemisphere, Antón concluded that the complexity of fusions was proof of the manifold influences of people crossing the Bering Strait and the oceans. The mixture was a cacophony until the genius of Columbus connected the two continents, not biologically but culturally, and the fusionary spirit that underscored the conquest was forged through the final expulsion of Arab invaders initiated eight hundred years prior to Columbus's departure from Spain.

Antón's 1891 speech also demonstrated his tethering of two Spanish imperial contexts. Africa and America both provided a similar justification for Spanish conquest. After 1898 and the loss of the overseas empire, the racial fusionary argument would reemerge from Antón as a justification for the new imperial mission in Morocco. However, by 1908, when Antón was deployed by the Spanish military to the protectorate in Morocco to conduct a wide-ranging study of the races of Morocco, he departed just slightly from the conclusion of his 1891 study. Now, according to Antón, while Spanish imperial strength remained rooted in the fusionary and ex-pulsionary genius of the Spaniard, the traits that produced these qualities were the product of intermixture with Africans in the past. Imperialism was a physical and cultural process, but the impetus was born of physical intermixture. Gone was the focus on Spanish creation of the New World in the Western Hemisphere. The genius of Spanish imperialism and racial strength was very much the product of the Old World, Europe and Africa. This time, however, the Arab influence played precisely the opposite role in Spanish fusionary process.

In Antón's 1909 study of the "races and tribes" of Morocco, he showed the potential cultural and biological links between the North African races of Morocco and the behavioral and physical makeup of Spaniards. Better understanding of the regional populations would both justify the expan-sion of Spanish endeavors in Morocco by helping to quell a protracted period of colonial insurgency and assist the military engaged in this in-surgency. It would also demonstrate, in anthropological terms, the closer affinity of the Moroccans to the Spanish and, therefore, presumably justify Spanish imperial control in the region over their European competitors, the French (Ausejo Martínez 91; Jensen 209–15, 221). For Antón, Spain had a closer ethnic tie to the region, as the Iberian Peninsula had witnessed a racial fusion similar to that which had taken place in Morocco. Spain was the crossroads of two racial incursions. One was European, marked by blond features and long-headedness, or dolichocephalic head shapes, which had left little ethnic mark on the Spanish populace. The other was of North African descent, what Antón called the *libio-ibérico*, or Libyan-Iberian, with roots in North Africa, and the *siro-árabe*, or Syrian-Arab, with roots in the eastern Mediterranean and Asia Minor. The assimilation of these latter groups into the Spanish racial mix, for Antón, provided the basis of the Spanish race. Antón found the roots of the Spaniard among the southern neighbors of Spain, arguing that, based on race and comport-ment, Spain's closest racial affinity lay to the south.

> The first steps in the investigation of the races of Spain which uses the methods of modern anthropology guide us irremissibly to the shores of Morocco. Even the most superficial observation of the Spaniard shows with all clarity that of the two most common and influential races within Europe . . . *Homo europeus*, of Linnaeus . . . and *Homo alpinus* . . . the first has shown very little influence in our population and the second . . . has represented such a large series of infusions that despite its being

so unevenly distributed that no one racial type in particular
is discernible, it is so dispersed that it forms a roughly mixed
corporation of the entire peninsular population spreading
from the Pyrenees to the Strait [of Gibraltar], and from the
Mediterranean to the Atlantic. (*Razas y tribus* 5)

Replete with photographs of both racial types and examples of their
mixtures, Antón's study was meant to provide a template for understanding not only the races of Morocco but also the present-day social and political divisions of Spain. In other words, by studying the peoples of North
Africa, Antón would also be studying the Spaniard; Moroccan racial formation was indeed identical to that of the Spanish.

In addition to the recognizable physical characteristics of these two
groups, there were also cultural and behavioral traits that could be dis-
cerned. The first, the *libio-ibérico*, which he wrote was the "nucleus" of the
racial groups between the Pyrenees and Egypt, was recognizable through
their "regular stature," their moderately long heads, and their "prominent but not excessive noses." In addition, they were "congenial, frank
and resolute, with an independent, egalitarian, democratic and separatist
character." The second, the *siro-árabe*, was tall and very long-headed, with
a prominent, narrow, and aquiline nose and a suspicious, unpredictable,
and nervous temperament (6). Because of the multitude of invasions of
Greeks, Germanic peoples, Moors, Phoenicians, and Romans, Spain had
acquired a mixed bag of these groups' physical and temperamental characteristics, becoming not merely a stronger European race, of which he assumed Spain to form a part, but an intermediate race, one responsible for
the cultural interchange between East and West that, for Antón, marked
the development of European civilization. For Antón, Spain represented
a new racial grouping, the Mediterranean race: "These two racial types
are so intermixed and intertwined in almost all of the Peninsula that they
produced out of this intimate mixture a new race, which one would call
Mediterranean, whose most beautiful expression can be found in Roman
statuary" (6).[5]

In the 1892 study of racial formation in America, Antón had spent
little time detailing the interactive qualities of racial contact. He mentioned nothing at all about the impact of American races on the European. Interestingly, in his 1909 study of Morocco, the anthropologist's
focused on the supposed flow of populations back and forth between
Africa and Spain, Europe and the south. For Antón, the flow always
traveled in one direction, from Spain outward. The process of fusion

involved biological intermixture of peoples, but the effects of cultural fusion usually favored the Spanish contribution. In his 1909 essay, Antón noted that contact with Spain provided the tempering effects of Spanish culture and religion on the racial characteristics of North African tribes (*Razas y tribus* 5). What distinguished the Mediterranean race that emerged from the fusion of the North African, Arab, and Spaniard was that Christianity had galvanized it. What had existed in North Africa prior to its incursion into Christian Spain was a fanatic Islam, bereft of reason or civilization.

> Meditative and dreaming spirit that divined the unity of God, that invented the sensual variety of the Harem, the poetry of David, the knowledge of Solomon on the green hillsides of Jericho, and in the shadows of the trees of Lebanon; but in the desert, the son of Ishmael, in the sun that browned their skin sent into their souls the ardor and delirium of Mohammed with a lazy fanaticism that rejected the reasoned thought of European civilization and instead sent them into the hysterical and often hypnotic convulsions of their religious fanaticism. (10)

Thus, the Mediterranean race, which had tamed religious fanaticism with sober reason, had in part helped to form a distinct race. Racial change was thus the product not only of physical alteration but also of cultural assimilation. But certain elements of the Arab incursions into the Iberian Peninsula still had left their mark within Spanish political and social life. Though the divisive, warlike elements of the Moroccan races had been pacified in Spain, certain remnants of both the independent nature of the *libio-ibéricos* and the warlike behavior of *siro-árabes* continued to express themselves in Spain.

> It is quite clear that the peninsular populations rose up a grade in their racial fusion because of the influence of Christian civilization; but the *physiology of race* still reveals itself in the nationalist separatism of Portugal and certain regions of Spain. It is still all too clear that the Caliph will occasionally reveal the atavistic daggers in his nature, in the fights in Bejar and Calendario, and among the various fighting and brawling one sees between teenage boys and even young men in the streets of our neighborhoods. (12; emphasis added)

Antón's two studies demonstrated racial fusion taking place and offered a model of Spanish contact as tempering different influences. Clearly, biological fusion was only part of the story; cultural assimilation was the real genius of Spain. In the end, Antón and others seemed to anticipate the struggle between spiritual and biological conceptions of race faced by later Spanish intellectuals.

The appeal of mixture and fusion among Spanish anthropologists proved equally enticing to nonanthropological writers who also confronted empire's end and the hopes for its resuscitation in political debates in the peninsula in the years after 1898. Hispanidad, or the literary and cultural movement that envisioned a shared culture emanating from Spain that was then disseminated across the Spanish-speaking world, is a case in point.[6] Hispanidad relied on the presumption that a cultural identity, a system of values, attitudes, and modes of expression, what George Kubler called a family resemblance, linked Spaniards and Latin Americans (Reese 76). Clearly, the idea of Hispanidad is a Spanish idea, but few have tended to place its discussion in a larger framework. For example, considered from a general perspective outside of Spanish historiography, present-day discussions of Hispanidad among historians of Spain appear to mimic debates in Latin America about mestizaje (mixture) and its role in creating contemporary Latin American society.[7] Indeed, even looking at the historical context of the late nineteenth and early twentieth centuries, the differences in definition and use between the concepts of Hispanidad, hispanismo, and mestizaje do not seem very significant.

Art historians, for example, as early as the 1930s and 1940s began to seek out and identify potential cultural artifacts and material remnants of Spanish artistic form in Latin American art.[8] The questions these art historians asked were the same as those posed by historians in Spain debating Spanish legacies in Latin America. What impact did Spanish art have on indigenous art forms? How could one trace the ongoing effects of cultural contact? How does one identify them? US and Latin American art historians considered what was called mestizo art by exploring how indigenous, pre-Columbian art forms intermixed with European forms, not how "primitive" pre-Columbian art was somehow transformed and made sophisticated by European styles. Over time, the tension among these historians intermingled with their own sense of national chauvinism. Different historians argued about whether the fusion of styles grew out of the supposed impact of what Antón called the "genius" of the Spanish conquerors on indigenous artisans—that is, their ability to impose Spanish art forms on indigenous ones—or whether the fusion was more of a two-way interaction.

The same debates have taken place among political and intellectual historians pondering the impact of Hispanidad, hispanismo, and cultural interchange between Spain and Latin America. Some historians, such as Frederick Pike, have argued that the insistence on an undying cultural link between Spain and Latin America in the 1910s and 1920s was really the felicitous expression of Spain's liberal modernizers. Their calls for a discrete Hispanic or Latin world based on natural cultural affinities served as the basis for redeploying and strengthening economic ties and trade relations between Spain and its former colonies (Pike, chs. 3 and 6). Others, looking at the movement as it was promoted within the Spanish right in the 1930s, including by Acción Española and its spokesperson, Ramiro de Maeztu, see Hispanidad as an element of Francoist political and ideological legitimization (González Cuevas, *Maeztu* 288–316). They consider it the ideological glue with which the regime sought to repair wide cleavages formed before and during the Civil War (Pike; González Calleja and Limón Nevado). Quite rightly, they associated Hispanidad not with its expressed international pretensions to bridging different cultures under one Spanish aegis. Rather, they saw it as propaganda deployed for internal uses only, to corral the regional peoples in the diverse Iberian Peninsula into one shared cultural, historical, and even racial unity with the rest of the Spanish-speaking world.[9]

Yet, all those participating in these debates, whether historian or historical actor, shared one basic unexamined presumption. They all agreed that, somehow, peoples and groups encounter one another, come together, form a new entity, and, as a result, express elements of all that compose the new group. They also assume that no matter how or when the process begins, dominant cultures absorb weaker ones. The process is universally described with an imperialist assumption of stronger and weaker groups inevitably conflicting, culminating with the domination of one over the other. Therefore, just as art historians engaged in their debate by unraveling material culture and artistic artifacts to identify the component parts, so too did the promoters of Hispanidad explain the process of cultural fusion in the period when Hispanidad appeared as the new prop of Spanish right-wing and military nationalist ideology. The general consensus about the basic mechanisms that drove cultural exchange or cultural dominance prevalent both among Spanish liberals and conservatives from the 1920s through the 1940s are quite close to the ideas advanced by earlier anthropologists. In fact, as Susan Martin-Márquez has recently argued, Spanish intellectuals and political writers were not actively disavowing biological race but instead were "sublimating" biological definitions of race into the discussion of Hispanidad and hispanismo in the 1910s and 1920s (17). What figures like Ramiro de Maeztu and Miguel de Unamuno were hoping to forge—a nonbiological link, a spiritual family, between the ex-colonial subject and the continuing, if now somewhat subdued, Spanish conqueror—was first presented in Manuel Antón's anthropological excursions. The difference was only that Antón and his colleagues did not share the compulsion to shun physical and biological arguments. In fact, Antón's anthropological discussions did not necessarily conflict with these later intentionally nonscientific views. Tracing these links seems to prove Martin-Márquez's point with one important caveat. The process of using anthropological notions of race was not always sublimated; occasionally it was quite explicit.

For example, historians of the Spanish right usually share an assumption that the Spanish radical, authoritarian, and antidemocratic right had its roots in the late nineteenth century in the crisis and divisions of the Restoration (González Cuevas, *Historia* 15). One of the linchpin figures within this movement was Marcelino Menéndez y Pelayo who, in his authoritative works of history, presented an image of Spain and its empire as the product of the unifying spirit of Catholicism.[10] As has been shown elsewhere, Menéndez y Pelayo was not an intellectual Luddite; religion may have bound Spaniards, but the physical evidence of racial fusion only confirmed the catalyzing and binding role of Catholicism in the formation of a distinct and strong Spanish nation (Goode 61–63). Familiar with Spanish anthropology, Menéndez y Pelayo engaged in an archaeology of Spanish culture, looking for traits like language and art that demonstrated the fusion of difference under the aegis of Catholicism. Though Menéndez y Pelayo originally sought scientific proof of his theories, especially early in his career, he later espoused a nonscientific, indeed antiscientific, theory.

What is more noteworthy is the scientific verification later sought by Menéndez y Pelayo's intellectual progeny. Many gave in to the impulse to modernize Spanish memories of the past and links with its empire by including scientific language and thought. Yet, the impact of doing so often led to quite contradictory, or at least muddled, formulations. Religion alone as a mortar for culture and biology could not support the weight of Hispanidad and its pretensions. A spirit did not just form out of thin air, and whenever thinkers attempted to explain the *process* of cultural fusion, their recourse was to the language of racial or biological fusion. Here the defense of Hispanidad usually broke down in an attempt to explain the

mechanism of cultural fusion and, at the same time, to avoid scientific verification or language associated with race, biological lineage, or hierarchy.

One of the most avowedly nonbiological (or antiracial) expressions of
Hispanidad came from Ramiro de Maeztu, who denied any possibility
that it described more than an ideological link between Spain and Latin
America:

> Hispanidad is not, after all, a race. . . . It can only be understood
> in terms of providing evidence that we Spaniards do not give
> any importance to blood or skin color because what we call
> race is not constituted by those characteristics that can be
> transmitted through protoplasmic obscurities, but rather by
> other characteristics that are the lights of the spirit: language
> and creed. It would therefore be absurd to look for any kind of
> characteristics through ethnographic methods. (22)

However, later in the same book, Maeztu discovers that the lexicon of
race is not altogether inaccurate, as long as the fusion of different peoples
only mimics the cultural fusion brought about by religion. Indeed, the
lights of the spirit actually bring about a biological fusion:

> We have not only brought civilization to other races but
> also . . . a moral unity that has allowed almost all the Hispanic
> peoples to have had some occasion for governors, leaders, poets,
> conductors. And that is not all. An eminent Brazilian doctor,
> Oliviera Lima believes that the Hispanic people are forming into
> a racial unity, thanks to the fusion of races, in which the inferior
> elements will soon disappear, absorbed by the superior elements
> of the race. (108)

Whatever distinction Maeztu may have been drawing was lost in
translation to others attempting to follow his historical discussion. Some
struggled to express Hispanidad as a nonbiological transmission of ideas,
cultures, behaviors, and religion to other people through the generations.
Others merely supplanted the nonbiological rhetoric with biological
mechanisms—in other words, with science:

> There is a hispanic concept of race: "la raza" is constituted by
> language and faith, according to Maeztu, those elements of
> spirit and not protoplasmic obscurities. Race does not represent

an anthropometric unity. Nor is it a pure anthropological category. . . . Over an ancient mosaic of races is painted our consciousness, illustrious and noble, clean and simple, *not only because of blood but also because of Catholicism.* . . . The protoplasmic factor of our race is only religion. Because of it, we are only what we are: Spaniards. (qtd. in González Calleja and Limón Nevado 49, emphasis added)

At first, in these formulations, Hispanidad is intended to subvert racial exclusiveness by basing identity on religion. Unlike their anthropological and biological colleagues, these theorists read the history of Spain not on the bodies of Spaniards but in the history of conversion associated with the Catholic Church. Yet, in explaining *how* the transmission of this conversion becomes hereditary or shared by subsequent generations, the writers turn to the language of biology.

It is possible to argue that the uses of racial or biological language are just healthy examples of metaphor in the imaginations of radical right-wing thinkers in the 1930s and 1940s. But why they would use such a metaphor? One weak point in the defense of Hispanidad is this contradictory rejection of the biological basis driving it and the consistent appropriation of biological and racial language to explain how this nonbiological mechanism operates. However, looking at the available contemporaneous discussions of Spanish heredity in anthropology and popular culture, one finds not only strikingly similar formulations but also strong connections. The idea of heredity, for example, did not only mean the transmission of physical traits. In her book *Organic Memory*, Laura Otis describes how the idea of memory, whether cultural, national, or individual, was explained through various biological and psychological theories of heredity (1–40). Spain, she wrote, was no exception in this process. Looking at the writing of Pío Baroja, Miguel de Unamuno, and Emilia Pardo Bazán, Otis demonstrates the appropriation of various European theories of heredity, including Lombrosian notions of atavism, Freudian notions of residues, and a general trend toward scientific logic and naturalism, in their work (83–92). Indeed, in 1904, Baroja made a plea for sifting through various theories and devising a final understanding of heredity that bridged both physical and moral characters: "At bottom, although physiology cannot appreciate it with exactitude, we have retinas, bronchial passageways, stomachs, livers and skin different from those of a German, and Englishman, or a Russian and *we cannot feel the way they do*" (qtd. in Otis 91–92).

While Baroja might have opened a door for physical characteristics, Unamuno had argued that cultural memories are transmitted through a long series of accumulation, what contemporary social scientists call acculturation and what Unamuno called "intrahistory." According to Unamuno, language, religion, and social patterns are discernible, traceable elements of a nation. Even more, they overcome the physical or racial differences that might otherwise divide people. Unamuno engaged in this debate in 1920, writing about the recently codified celebration of the Fiesta de la Raza on October 12. Unamuno noted that the celebration should not be confused with support for a biological or visible Spanish racial condition. The material conditions of a people, he wrote, even if due to racial iniquities, were transitory, real but fleeting. What defines a nation or the Hispanic race was really its cultural unity:

> There is clearly a racial problem in Spanish America in the natural, animal sense, even though it is much less severe than in other nations. . . . [T]hus, the indian, the black man, the mestizo, the mulatto are a grave problem. There the persistence of different races is also the history of the fusion of all into one human race linked by history, civil society, founded in language. What keeps it going is its culture. (Unamuno 21–22)

Unamuno and Baroja departed from each other on the importance of race to the creation of the Spanish people. Yet, both managed to account for biology and racial difference: Unamuno discounted it in favor of his cultural-linguistic affinity, and Baroja argued for further study. As in Laura Otis's formulation, notions of cultural passage were floating around Spain, appropriated by many of its most famous thinkers and inflected with both biological and cultural notions of inheritance.

To conclude this chapter, it is helpful to consider the end of Spain's empire in Cuba from the perspective of a Cuban ruminating on the anthropological ramifications of imperial demise. Studying the work of a Cuban anthropologist provides a portrait of the transatlantic, or portmanteau, exchange of ideas between Latin American and Spanish scientists. Considering the exchange of ideas also allows the study of racial thought to abide by the recent critiques of Alejandro Mejías-López, who foresees the replication of an imperialist mindset when those studying peninsular thought only study Spanish intellectuals and not the international influences on them (Mejías-López 113–14). Certainly, the exchange of scientific ideas did not rely on a one-way exchange from Spain to Latin America, or vice versa. Analyzing racial thought demonstrates the value of a broad study of the exchange of ideas or of the traveling texts of peninsular and Latin American thought.

Antón and his students trained a few hundred anthropologists, sociologists, lawyers, and others who passed through their classes. From Antón's position in the Natural History Museum, in addition to his more powerful position within the university, he alone trained a large contingent of anthropologists in Spain. Between 1896 and 1898 at the Madrid Athenaeum, he taught postgraduate classes on the anthropological roots of Spaniards to more than 190 students (Villacorta Baños 289–91). Among them was the Cuban anthropologist Fernando Ortiz, who spent much of his later career through the 1960s attempting to define the mechanisms and impact of mixture and transculturation in Cuban and Caribbean populations (Font and Quiroz xiii–xiv). Fernando Ortiz spent about three years in Spain studying in Barcelona and Madrid, and he later served as a consul in the Galician city of A Coruña. In addition to his time studying law and criminal anthropology in Madrid, he also engaged in decades-long correspondence with criminal anthropologists, such as Rafael Salillas and Pedro Dorado Montero, and the sociologist Manuel Sales y Ferré (Naranjo and Puig-Samper 10–16). As some historians with access to Ortiz's letters in the Biblioteca Nacional José Martí in Havana have discovered, Ortiz's early positivist views of the role of Afro-Cubans in Cuban culture and criminology had a deep connection to the ideas of Spanish anthropologists (16).

One particular example of this connection might illuminate how the idea of race was shared across the Atlantic but was also applied differently depending on historical context. In his 1906 analysis of crime in Cuba, entitled *Hampa Afro-Cubana: Los Negros Brujos*, Ortiz intentionally borrowed his anthropological analysis of the roots of crime from his Madrid teacher Rafael Salillas, the Spanish anthropologist and criminologist who had studied under Antón. In his first published work, Ortiz demonstrated his intellectual ties to Salillas. Following Salillas's *El Delincuente Español: Hampa* (1898), which included a prologue from the Italian criminologist Cesare Lombroso, Ortiz also solicited a comment from Lombroso to support his work. He received a short letter from Lombroso that served as a "letter-prologue" for *Hampa Afro-Cubana*. Other similarities were less prosaic. His description of the impact of fusion and the legacy of human mixture in Cuba, especially after Spanish contact centuries earlier, also followed the contours of Salillas's arguments about fusion within the Iberian Peninsula. In particular, Ortiz agreed with Salillas that missteps in the process of fusion, the intermixture of "unhealthy" groups, like the Sinti and Roma peoples (*gitanos* or gypsies in Salillas's and Ortiz's formulations), created crime in Spain. Ortiz also seemed to follow Antón's ideas about the racial composition of Cuban fusion. For Ortiz, the warrior spirit of the Castilian had left an indelible impact on Cuban society. He described how, burnished by eight centuries of warfare, the Spanish introduction of the "white race" into Cuba left a clear tendency toward combat and violence in Cuban society:

> The white race entered Cuba represented by conquering
> Spaniards and by successive immigrants from all regions of
> Spain who all brought their temperament, the level of
> civilization, their customs and their vices. The first colonizers
> came to the Indies as adventurers. They brought with them their
> particular progenitors of civilization, the natural impulsivity
> of the Spanish and the warrior impulses developed over the
> preceding eight centuries of warfare. (*Hampa Afro-Cubano* 3)

Citing Salillas's work, Ortiz noted that the Castilian "warriors" brought with them fighting tendencies and a lack of compassion, forged by the earlier expulsion of Jews and Muslims from Spain and the conversion of infidels across Europe. For Ortiz, like Salillas, history explained a key psychological predisposition. And, like Salillas, Ortiz suggested that a new geographical context would ultimately temper this predisposition.

The trick was to ensure that the racial mixture was well calibrated. In the end, positive, soothing influences of different sectors of the arriving Spanish populations triumphed over the more violent ones, and most Spaniards ultimately worked to becalm the mixed populations of Cuba: "Nevertheless, the nobility and also the Andalucians who arrived in the first few centuries brought all of the gentility and splendor of the Castilian hidalgos, which they transmitted to their descendants and which then formed the basic strata of the character of the oldest Cuban families and, indeed, many of the other characteristics of our psychology" (*Hampa Afro-Cubano* 4–5). Ortiz's view was consistent with Antón's earlier sense of the role of fusion. However, Ortiz's presentation of the social and historical context of colonial Cuba was indeed different from Antón's. The end of empire provided a clearer sense of the role colonialism played in defining Cuba's past and future. The three main racial groups Ortiz had identified as forming contemporary Cuba—the black race, the white race, and the yellow or Chinese races—had all left indelible imprints on social life in Cuba. Ortiz's work also infamously placed much of the blame for Cuban criminality on black populations in Cuba, even though the book explained the process and intricacies of fusion in creating different kinds of criminality. Different population mixes produced specific kinds of criminality. Yet, overall, the mixture of these races, according to Ortiz, led to new cultural and social formations, sometimes to the betterment of Cuban society and sometimes to its detriment. Here, one can see the development of the later formulation of "transculturation" for which Ortiz is best known.[11] Yet, in this early work, focused on the question of the causes of criminality in Cuban society, Ortiz assumed that the positive fusion of different races also deposited "through the various cloacas" of their original racial predispositions certain "pathogenic detritus" on Cuban society; that is, each racial group produced its own type of criminality (*Hampa Afro-Cubano* 15).

Interestingly, each version of this detritus also bore the imprint of the imperial system that formed the social and political context in which fusion was taking place. Set in a slightly different register from Antón's earlier descriptions of the genius of Columbus, Ortiz argued that the imperial system affected the expression of criminality in each of the races that came to dominate Cuban society. Spaniards who had arrived in Cuba saw little impediment to the free exercise of their sense of despotic supremacy or administrative corruption. However, whites born in Cuba were long frustrated by the obstacles Spanish authorities placed in their way (*Hampa Afro-Cubano* 7). The result was that the overall contribution to Cuban criminality of the white race (meaning both creole, or Cuban born, and peninsular immigrants) was the ongoing current of banditry (*bandolerismo*) in Cuban society. Yet, this contribution unfurled differently depending on the influence of particular components of the white race. Banditry was born either of the resentment at professional and intellectual frustration (a manifestation of the creole population) or of too much bureaucratic power (the legacy of the peninsular population). In other words, banditry, though shared across the entirety of the white race in Cuba, was the product of two racial components within the white population, and, more importantly, this racial predilection was the product entirely of one's relation to the imperial government (*Hampa Afro-Cubano* 11).

Ortiz ended on a note of optimism. Over time, he wrote, fusion remained a calming process, allowing negative elements to dissipate. These negative marks of the "white race" on Cuban criminality were dissipating too, presumably now in the age of Cuban independence and the disappearance of the imperial system that exacerbated the racial proclivities of the white population. Of course, he was not entirely optimistic about the speed of banditry's end. He noted that the persistence of banditry, the telltale sign of white criminality, could still be found on the "other side of the Atlantic" (*Hampa Afro-Cubano* 16). Perhaps Ortiz was implying that the conquest at this moment of empire's end was indeed inverted, with the process of racial fusion in Cuba outpacing that in Europe (Mejías-López 15–48). The persistence of banditry was a telltale sign of the state of racial development.

Drawing on the idea of the portmanteau, continued analysis of the study of mixture (mestizaje) or racial fusion could underwrite a wider examination of identity in the latter days of empire in Spain and its former colonies. These conversations across the Atlantic Ocean produced a distinct, nationalist assertion of the Spanish race that was rooted in the loss of empire in Latin America and also served as a justification for the expansion of empire in Morocco. It also appealed to a young anthropologist who would later return to Cuba and become a great formulator of fusionary language related to race. Tracing the links that tie the later explicitly nonracial or biological language of fusion to the earlier more avowedly scientific discussions of race and fusion may allow for a sense of the continuity of ideas across time and a stronger sense of the historical, social, and political contexts that shaped these ideas.

Notes

1. For a fuller account of the anthropological discussion of racial fusion as an explanation for imperial control, see Goode 88–91.
2. Said lays out the importance of context and the shifting meanings of texts in the introduction of his 1978 work *Orientalism* and explores the idea of traveling theories in greater detail in his later work, "Traveling Theory." See *Orientalism* 12 and *The World, the Text and the Critic* 226–47.
3. Antón introduced the exhibition, describing its displays and layout in *El Globo* in 1887. Among the secondary works, the most detailed description of the exhibit appears in Sánchez Gómez.
4. All translations are by the author.
5. The "Mediterranean race" was a term that had then been recently coined by the Italian anthropologist Giuseppe Sergi. On the differences between Sergi's and Antón's definition of the Mediterranean race, see Goode 152. On the racial reliance on a beauty myth and the view of classical Greek statuary as the model of such a myth see Mosse 1–2.
6. Particularly incisive on the development of Hispanidad as a basis of renewed trade between Spain and Latin America is Mateo Dieste 82–84.
7. See Wade; Miller 1–26.

8. Beate Salz first identified mestizo art as something symbolizing Spanish and Latin America artistic fusion in 1944. George Foster continued the project, and George Kubler organized these ideas in an essayistic format. See Reese 76–77; Kubler.

9. For more on this topic, see Gómez Escalonilla; Abellán and Monclús.

10. One should remember Raymond Carr's ascription of Menéndez y Pelayo as the "father" of Spanish fascism (355).

11. First outlined in Ortiz, *Contrapunteo*.

Works Cited

Abellán, José Luís, and Antonio Monclús. *El pensamiento en España desde 1939*. Vol. 1 of *El pensamiento Español contemporáneo y la idea de América*. Barcelona: Anthropos, 1989.

Antón y Ferrandiz, Manuel. *Antropología de los pueblos de America (19 mayo 1891)*. Madrid: Sucesores de Rivadeneyra, 1892.

———. "Notas para la historia de las ciencias antropológicas en España." *Congreso de Granada, 1911: Asociación Española para el Progreso de las Ciencias*. 1912. Madrid: Eduardo Arias, n.d.

———. *Razas y tribus de Marruecos*. Madrid: Sucesores de Rivadeneyra, 1903.

Ausejo Martínez, Elena. *Por la ciencia y por la patria: La institucionalización científica en España en el primer tercio del siglo XX*. Madrid: Siglo XXI de España Editores, 1993.

Balfour, Sebastian. *Deadly Embrace: Morocco and the Road to the Spanish Civil War*. Oxford: Oxford UP, 2002.

Carr, Raymond. *Spain, 1808–1975*. 2nd ed. Oxford: Clarendon, 1982.

Gómez Escalonilla, Lorenzo Delgado. *Diplomacia franquista y política cultural hacia Iberoamerica: 1939–1953*. Madrid: Consejo Superior de Investigaciones Científicas, 1988.

Escudero, María A. "The Image of Latin America Disseminated in Spain by the Franco Regime." Diss. University of California, San Diego, 1994.

Font, Mauricio A., and Alfonso W. Quiroz, eds. *Cuban Counterpoints: The Legacy of Fernando Ortiz*. Landham, MD: Lexington Books, 2005.

Gabilondo, Joseba. "Historical Memory, Neoliberal Spain, and the Latin American Postcolonial Ghost: On the Politics of Recognition, Apology, and Reparation in Contemporary Spanish Historiography." *Arizona Journal of Hispanic Cultural Studies* 7 (2003): 247–66.

González Calleja, Eduardo, and Fredes Limón Nevado. *Hispanidad como un instrumento de combate*. Madrid: Consejo Superior de Investigaciones Científicas, 1988.

González Cuevas, Pedro Carlos. *Historia de las derechas españolas*. Madrid: Biblioteca Nueva, 2000.

———. *Maeztu: Biografía de un nacionalista español.* Madrid: Marcial Pons, 2003.

Goode, Joshua. *Impurity of Blood: Defining Race in Spain, 1870–1930.* Baton Rouge: Louisiana State UP, 2009.

Gould, Stephen Jay. *The Mismeasure of Man.* 1981. New York: W.W. Norton, 1996.

Haller, John S. *Outcasts from Evolution: Scientific Attitudes of Racial Inferiority, 1859–1900.* Carbondale: Southern Illinois UP, 1971.

Jensen, Geoffrey. "Toward the 'Moral Conquest' of Morocco: Hispano-Arabic Education in Early Twentieth-Century North Africa." *European History Quarterly* 31.2 (2001): 205–29.

Kubler, George. *The Shape of Time.* New Haven: Yale UP, 1962.

Loureiro, Ángel. "Spanish Nationalism and the Ghost of Empire." *Journal of Spanish Cultural Studies* 4.1 (2003): 65–76.

Maetzu, Ramiro de. *Defensa de la Hispanidad.* Buenos Aires: Editorial Poblet, 1942.

Martin-Márquez, Susan. *Disorientations: Spanish Colonialism in Africa and the Performance of Identity.* New Haven: Yale UP, 2008.

Mateo Dieste, Josep Lluís. *El "Moro" entre los primitivos: El caso del protectorado español en Marruecos.* Barcelona: Fundació La Caixa, 1996.

Mejías-López, Alejandro. *The Inverted Conquest: The Myth of Modernity and the Transatlantic Onset of Modernism.* Nashville: Vanderbilt UP, 2009.

Miller, Marilyn Grace. *Rise and Fall of the Cosmic Race: The Cult of Mestizaje in Latin America.* Austin: U of Texas P, 2004.

Mosse, George. *Toward the Final Solution.* 1978. Madison: U of Wisconsin P, 1985.

Naranjo Orovio, Consuelo, and Miguel Angel Puig-Samper. "Spanish Intellectuals and Fernando Ortiz (1900–1941)." Font and Quiroz 9–37.

Ortiz, Fernando. *Contrapunteo cubano del tabaco y el azúcar.* Habana: J. Montero, 1940.

———. *Hampa Afro-Cubana: Los Negros Brujos.* Madrid: Librería Fernando Fé, 1906.

Otis, Laura. *Organic Memory: History and the Body in the Late Nineteenth and Early Twentieth Centuries.* Lincoln: U of Nebraska P, 1994.

Pike, Frederick. *Hispanismo, 1898–1936.* Notre Dame: U of Notre Dame P, 1971.

Reese, Thomas F., ed. *The Collected Essays of George Kubler.* New Haven: Yale UP, 1985.

Said, Edward W. *Orientalism.* 1978. New York: Vintage Books, 1994.

———. *The World, the Text and the Critic.* Cambridge, MA: Harvard UP, 1983.

Sánchez Gómez, Luis Angel. *Un imperio en la vitrina, el colonialismo español en el pacífico y la Exposición de Filipinas de 1887.* Madrid: Consejo Superior de Investigaciones Científicas, 2003.

Santos-Rivero, Virginia. *Unamuno y el sueño colonial.* Frankfurt: Verveurt Verlag, 2005.

Unamuno, Miguel de. *Obras Completas.* Vol. 4. Madrid: Escelicer, 1968.

Villacorta Baños, Francisco. *El Ateneo de Madrid, 1885–1912.* Madrid: Consejo Superior de Investigaciones Científicas, 1985.

Wade, Peter. *Blackness and Race Mixture.* Baltimore: Johns Hopkins UP, 1993.

4

Theorizing Racial Hybridity in Nineteenth-Century Spain and Spanish America

Alda Blanco
San Diego State University

Toward the middle of the nineteenth century, new "scientific" theories redefined the concept of "race," creating what Hannah Arendt called "race-thinking." The confluence of natural history, the nascent science of physical anthropology, and, oftentimes, evolutionary theory shaped these novel racial theories, which displayed an obsession with classification and taxonomies, sought to establish the origin of races, and invented racial hierarchies. The result of this race-thinking, according to Arendt, was to divide "mankind into master races and slave races, into higher and lower breeds, into colored peoples and white men" (32). Seamlessly folded into the epistemological principles of the "human sciences," this racialism—which Arendt did not hesitate to call racism—became the cornerstone of European colonialism, the justification for European expansion into "unknown" places and even into those that had been known for centuries. However, if racial discourse was inextricably linked to Europe's imperialist enterprise, it also marked the many meditations regarding the so-called national question in nineteenth-century Europe and postcolonial Latin America.

Race-thinking, then as now, is not homogeneous. Although throughout its modern history its various versions have shared certain theoretical tenets—among which the inequality among races is, perhaps, the most salient feature—beginning in 1749 when Count de Buffon introduced the word "race" into the study of natural history, distinct types of race-thinking have been elaborated to articulate specific racial problematics.[1] Such was the case on both sides of the Hispanic Atlantic at the end of the nineteenth century. During this period a distinct Spanish racial discourse, as we shall see, was deployed both to assert Spain's ability to be a colonizing nation and to contest European notions of race theory, its taxonomies, and its hierarchical classificatory system. In Latin America the governing elites of the recently decolonized nations used racial thought to shape social policy on the terrains of education, health, immigration, and criminal justice (Graham 2).

During the final decades of the nineteenth century, the racial categories of hybridity and *mestizaje*—the name given to the process of interracial mixing in Spanish America—were theorized in Spain and Latin America, given the centrality they were accorded within race-thinking. Yet, in spite of the fact that the national intelligentsias on both sides of the Atlantic theorized the notion of hybridity, rarely did their theories enter into dialogue with each other. With the exception of the Congreso Geográfico-Hispano-Portugués-Americano (Hispano-Portuguese-American Geographical Conference), which I explore in this chapter, Spanish and Latin American racial theorists engaged the ideas that were being disseminated from the centers of scientific knowledge, mainly France, Germany, and the United States. That hybridity and mestizaje became privileged subjects for reflection and, moreover, that Spanish and Latin American racial theorists mostly privileged European racial thinking were inextricably bound to the rise of European racial scientism, which at midcentury had begun to speculate about the wide-ranging consequences of miscegenation resulting from Europe's colonial expansion during what Eric Hobsbawm has called the age of empire. And, because these racial theories intertwined the past, present, and future of nations with their respective racial formations, the Spanish and Spanish American intelligentsias felt the urgent need to theorize hybridity as a critical part of their intellectual and political project of envisioning the future of the nation. Also, the theoretical convergence on the problematics of mestizaje was rooted in a shared history—that of the Spanish empire—as the Spanish colonization of the New World had created the Latin American racial formation in which the hybridization of heterogeneous races was a principal feature.

The first part of this chapter discusses the ways in which the Congreso Geográfico, as an understudied example of Spanish racial knowledge production, postulated the existence of a distinct Spanish or Iberian race constructed on the concept of hybridity as a positive racial attribute.[2] Projecting its positive valuation of mestizaje onto Latin America's racial formations, the conference also exalted hybridity as pivotal for Latin America's future. That the congress sought to extend its racial thinking to encompass the perceived problematics of race in Latin America was congruent with its goal of establishing or reinforcing linkages with the nations on the other side of the Atlantic that, since their independence, had become tenuous at best. The second part of the chapter presents the race-thinking of two key Latin American thinkers, the Argentinian statesman Domingo F. Sarmiento and the Mexican positivist Justo Sierra, whose treatises on race were contemporaneous with the Congreso. By introducing Sarmiento and Sierra into my exploration of the concept of hybridity in Spain and Latin America, I attempt to compare Latin American notions of mestizaje and the Congreso's ideas regarding hybridity within a synchronic frame in order to signal the similarities and differences between race-thinking on both sides of the Atlantic. In a sense, this comparative approach to the issue of racial fusion seeks to depict the dialogue about race that never took place between Spain and Spanish America outside the confines of the conference.

The Congreso Geográfico-Hispano-Portugués-Americano

Madrid's small but active Geographic Society organized a unique transatlantic encounter as a parallel activity to Spain's commemoration of the fourth centenary of the discovery of America. The Congreso Geográfico-Hispano-Portugués-Americano, which took place throughout the month of October 1892, brought together an impressive number of Spanish, Latin American, and Portuguese scientists and government authorities. A myriad of institutions sent delegates to the Congreso, including anthropologists, military geographers, bishops, several admirals, and, interestingly, the marquis of Comillas, owner of the most important and powerful maritime company of the period, the Compañía Transatlántica, which played a major role in the Atlantic slave trade.[3] Although quantity is not necessarily an indicator of significance, in this case the abundant presence of high-ranking politicians reveals the great interest the conference generated among governments on both sides of the Atlantic.[4]

The Congreso displayed extensive geographic and anthropological knowledge, dealt with a wide array of pressing political and scientific issues, and produced a series of conclusions unanimously approved by its participants that established its theoretical tenets and made recommendations for future governmental policies. Because one of the conference's desired outcomes was to shed new light on old problems, throughout its seven sessions the participants discussed the perceived deficiencies of Spain's relationship with Latin America and its colonies in Africa, Asia, and Oceania. These discussions evince Spain's grave preoccupation with the dysfunctional colonial administration in Philippines. Also, proposals were set forth to strengthen the existing but nevertheless tenuous commercial ties between Spain and Spanish America. It is worth noting that whereas the Congreso greatly emphasized the need to develop strategies to deepen and reinforce Spanish and Portuguese colonial enterprises in their overseas dominions with the objective of solidifying Iberian imperial projects, it avoided referencing the contentious struggle taking place between Spain and its Caribbean colonies, which was beginning to reach a breaking point and would culminate in the so-called Disaster of 1898. In fact, no presentations, discussions, or conclusions were entertained regarding this urgent topic.

In an article published in *La ilustración española y americana*, Ricardo Beltrán y Rózpide, who pioneered modern geographic study in Spain, taught at Madrid's Universidad Central, and was also the Congreso's secretary, informed the readers of this elegant high-end transatlantic journal that the first session of the conference "once again demonstrated the value of the Iberian race's potentialities and energies in order to instill in all of the participants the firm conviction that we are still called to do great things in the future destinies of humanity" (458).[5] The singular position accorded to race as an analytic category in the European imperial imaginary, and within the two disciplines that shaped the Congreso's knowledge production, geography and anthropology, accounts for why this conference began its proceedings by seeking to establish that the so-called Iberian race continued to embody the qualities that would enable it to participate in "humanity's future destinies." The link posited between race and empire in Beltrán y Rózpide's summary of the first session reveals that Spain's scientific intelligentsia, like that of other European nations, intimately associated race-thinking with both empire and empire-building even though Spain's empire was clearly on the wane. Although in general the Congreso did not appropriate Spain's imperial past as proof that Spaniards were capable of undertaking future colonial enterprises, some participants did, however, evoke the empire's past "glories" as evidence of Spain's enduring potential as a colonizing nation.[6] The forward-looking scientific intelligentsia privileged the discursive terrain of race to demonstrate the potential of the Spaniards because, within the racial discourse of the period, race was the factor that determined the vigor of the nation.

The proceedings of the Congreso—a rich but understudied archive—reveal that by 1892 a distinct way of thinking and theorizing about race was being articulated in Spain; in other words, there existed a distinct

Spanish racial discourse. One of its theoretical anchors was the certainty that there existed an autochthonous race on the peninsula that was, moreover, unique. To demonstrate this important claim, Federico Olóriz, Spain's most distinguished craniologist and a renowned physical anthropologist, presented a summary of his extensive research in a lecture titled "The Cephalic Index of the Spanish" in which he affirmed that Spain was "a well defined nation from an ethnic point of view," a conclusion at which he had arrived after measuring the crania of 8,368 Spanish men (106).[7]

The other theoretical anchor was the claim that the Iberian race was the product of racial fusion. This manner of conceptualizing the Spanish race contested the central tenet of Arthur de Gobineau's theory expounded in his *The Inequality of Human Races* (1853–1855), which axiomatically stated that the mixing of blood produced racial degeneration and, moreover, the decline of civilization. Although it could be argued that Gobineau was only one among the many racial theorists who had contributed to the development of modern racial thought, his racial paradigm, according to Arendt, had by the end of the nineteenth century become "a kind of standard work for race theories in history" (50), a paramount reference for thinking about and theorizing race. The Congreso thus opened up and presented a singular mode of race-thinking that distanced itself from European racialism.

At the Congreso's first session, Ángel Rodríguez Arroquia, military engineer, general, geographer, and former president of Madrid's Geographic Society, presented a lecture titled "The Spanish Race's Colonizing Aptitudes" premised on the notion that the Spanish race was unique, and he set out to demonstrate not only its singularity but also the way in which it was bound to Spain's colonialist calling. He began by presenting an age-old thesis within Spanish racial thought: "The race that populates the Spanish peninsula has its own characteristics that differentiate it from all the other races, even its closest ones" (83). In his description he represented it as "noble" and "virile" (85) and argued that it had been produced by racial mixing, a thesis he shared with the majority of Spanish racial thinkers who had historically linked the uniqueness of the Spanish race with the supposed racial fusion that had taken place on the peninsula throughout the centuries.[8] According to Rodríguez Arroquia, the Spanish race was "an extremely special, if not exceptional race, not only because all the races that have stepped on Iberian land have been fused into it, but also because when it spills onto the outside, throughout Europe, America, Africa, Asia, and Oceania, it easily fuses with other races without diminishing the virility of its blood and its physical conditions, even inspiring their way of thinking and creating empires or peoples that are eminently Spanish" (75).

The hallmark of the Spanish race, then, was its great expansive strength: when it encountered other races it had always imposed itself upon them, making them Spanish (83). Though he does not prove that the Spanish race's vigor had been able to assimilate other races, he nevertheless proposed that the Congreso adopt his conclusion that "today only the Spanish race can compete with the most powerful for the future superiority in regards to humanity's ethnic destiny" (84). Curiously—or, perhaps, tellingly—the committee in charge of formulating the conclusions for the first session did not include this assertion. In what today would be considered an interdisciplinary presentation, Rodríguez Arroquia combined history and geography to buttress his argument, and ended his lecture by proposing that "history in agreement with the ethnic conditions of the peninsular peoples, demonstrates that they are the most suitable for colonizing" (106).

While it is significant that the Congreso articulated a specifically Spanish modality of racial thought, it is also important to point out that although Gobineau's racial taxonomy did not include the so-called Iberian race, had he applied his classificatory principles to it, he would have classified it among the conquering races that had degenerated through the mixture of blood and consequently died, unlike other races that had maintained their essence and thus lived (23–35). Because one of the Congreso's primary goals was to portray Spain as a European colonial power, it needed to affirm the Iberian race's racial attributes, particularly its resilience—in other words, its ability to survive in spite of being a hybrid and conquering race. The Congreso's belief that the Iberian race had the "energy" and "calling" to participate in "humanity's destiny" (Beltrán y Rozpide 458) is reflected in the following conclusions approved by the delegates:

1. The Iberian race, which has been produced by the physical-geographic conditions of the peninsula, whose climate, land, and flora participate in all varieties that exist on the globe, is able not only to reproduce itself easily in the earth's diverse regions, but can also assimilate even the most diverse races.
2. The study of the Cephalic Index of Spain's contemporary population leads us to conclude that it is the most homogeneous race in Europe. ("Conclusiones" 293)

These two conclusions, buttressed by the authority of the two scientific discourses on which modern racial theories were constructed—natural history and craniology—were the foundational tenets of the Congreso in that they established the existence of an autochthonous Iberian race. The first conclusion derives from the determinism of eighteenth-century natural history, still dominant at the end of the next century, which postulated that terrain and climate determined the race that inhabited a particular place. In spite of being a reiteration of a time-worn theory, the argument took an interesting—and important—turn when proposing, once again through analogy, that the Iberian race, like its natural habitat, included a variety of races and that it was capable of assimilating even the most diverse races while maintaining its essence. Thus, the Iberian race was represented as the product of biological mixture, as being, in other words, the product of miscegenation. It was a hybrid race created by fusion and, as such, had the ability to reproduce itself.

This conceptualization, however, squarely contravened two axioms that shaped the period's racial imaginary: on the one hand, Buffon's stipulation that "individuals of a mixed race were sterile or incapable of generating successive generations" (Niro 99) and, on the other, Gobineau's notion that "purity of blood" was a requisite for perpetuating a people into eternity. Thus, the Congreso's racial theorists refused to link racial hybridity to the supposed decrease of a race's fertility and vitality, a thesis that Charles Darwin had proposed in *The Descent of Man*, published in 1871 (Niro 99). In what can be seen as a curious paradox, the resilience of the biologically hybrid Iberian race was demonstrated using the results of Olóriz's craniological research, which proved that the race was homogeneous. The homogeneity of the Spanish race was thus depicted as the product of biological mixture; its superiority was such, then, that it could assimilate—and indeed already had assimilated—other races that were clearly weaker.

The scientific intelligentsia supported this singular racial notion, which went against the grain of European racialist thinking, for several reasons. On the terrain of international relations, Spain needed to establish scientifically that it should be included among the colonizing nations, an argument that Spain's foremost political leader and so-called architect of the Restoration, Antonio Cánovas del Castillo, had set forth in the *Discurso sobre la nación* (Speech about the nation), his 1882 political roadmap for Spain (131). Moreover, this mode of racial thought sought to refute what the forward-looking intelligentsia believed was the insidious discourse of Spain's decadence and decline, which not only had been firmly ensconced in the Spanish imaginary for centuries but whose pessimism tainted many reflections about Spain's present and future. And, because the Congreso had been conceived as part of the commemoration of the discovery of the New World, this race-thinking attempted to legitimize the history of Spanish colonization in the Americas by exalting, as we shall see, the hybridity between Spaniards and the indigenous peoples of the conquered territory as one of the most salient and significant characteristics of the colonizing process. Furthermore, this positive assessment of the Spanish racial mixture was necessary to prepare the scientific terrain for future sessions of the Congreso that presented the argument that mixed races, particularly the Latin American mestizos, could propagate and prosper.

On the disciplinary terrain of human geography, the Congreso concluded that the vigor of the Iberian race was demonstrable because it had taken both language and religion to the Americas and they had spread throughout the continent. With regard to language, "the amount of people that today speak Spanish and Portuguese induces us to affirm that these languages have spread extensively and will continue to do so as long as the relationship between the American countries and their former metropolis are promoted in a convenient way" ("Conclusiones" 293). Eschewing "scientific" proof regarding religious matters, the conclusion adopted by the delegates succinctly stated that "the Catholic religion took civilization to America and will continue being the main conduit for disseminating and perfecting it on that continent" (293). If the dissemination of Spanish and Catholicism evinced Iberian colonialism's strength and energy, the language used in the two conclusions reveals the lamentable vestiges of colonialist discourse by referring to Spain and Portugal as the "former metropolis" (293) of Latin America's independent nations. Moreover, these conclusions also served as a reminder for the delegates from both sides of the Atlantic that the colonization of the New World had initiated a "civilizing" process, which—surprisingly—had yet to be completed.

Turning his ethnographic gaze toward America, Antonio Blázquez, representing the administrative corps of the Army Academy and the liberal Krausist Asociación para la Enseñanza de la Mujer (Association for the Education of Women), addressed the delegates with a lecture titled "Modern Geological and Geographic Explorations in Mexico and Central America: The Current State and Future of the Indigenous Races of the Americas." Whereas the title suggests that he would discuss the myriad native American races, the text, in fact, explores what he calls the "American race," which he neither defines nor specifies. This racial category seems to comprise peoples of pure blood, that is to say, those native to the Americas, as well as the mestizos that populated the continent. Although Blázquez groups the American natives within the same racial category and at times refers to them as the "raza cobriza" (copper-like race), the rubric used in the majority of European racial taxonomies, one of the Congreso's conclusions nuances his classification by stating that "the American Indians are not a compact and heterogeneous mass in their geographic distribution, their culture nor in their social state because savage tribes live next to those who are in a perfect civilized state" ("Conclusiones" 294). That the scientific intelligentsia ascertained the heterogeneity of the indigenous races and propounded the notion that there existed different levels of civilization among them reveals that the Congreso refuted the prevailing racialism of the period that obsessively elaborated racial hierarchies based primarily on skin color.[9] The significance of this way of conceptualizing America's indigenous peoples becomes evident when comparing it, for example, to the manner in which Spanish Americanistas (Spanish Scholars of the Americas) in 1857 had represented America and its indigenous population: "[America] is not the land of the indigenous tribes but rather is Europe transported to the New World. Everything there is European. The Indian is a growth, a secretion of the social body: he is the pariah of American civilization" (qtd. in López-Ocón 82).

After reviewing the scientific contributions of the European explorers who had traveled throughout Latin America, beginning with Alexander von Humboldt's journey at the turn of the nineteenth century, Blázquez posed the following questions about the American race's future to his colleagues: "Will [the American race] disappear from the surface of the earth? Will it remain in a perpetual state of backwardness and ignorance or will it mix with other races and by acquiring new aptitudes, join the path to civilization and progress?" (257–58). Framed by these questions, Blázquez discussed the polemic surrounding the origin of the American race, spoke expansively about pre-Columbian man's advanced civilization and "marvelous culture," demonstrated the aptitude of the indigenous peoples for progress, compared the colonization of North and South America by characterizing the colonizing efforts of the Anglo-Saxons as brutal and genocidal, and ended by questioning the many negative qualities that were attributed to the Native Americans, such as, for example, their indolence and promiscuity (258). Judging by the applause reported in the *Actas*—a cross between minutes and proceedings—and the unanimous adoption of the five conclusions he had presented, the lecture was a success.

Regarding the American race, two conclusions are worth highlighting here. The first established that the American race's ostensible "state of backwardness" was not because of "its individuals' lack of conditions" but rather because of "historical circumstances" (294). The second ascertained that its perceived "stagnation" was, in fact, an erroneous perception because "it is necessary to add the number of individuals of pure blood to, at least, half of the mestizos, which makes the propagation of the race evident" (294). Blázquez's unwavering belief that the American race had a positive future was anchored in the notion of propagation, which, as we have seen, had also been used to demonstrate the vigor and energy of the Iberian race. If the quantity of mestizos demonstrated the vitality of the race, the second conclusion affirmed that its "betterment" and "prosperity" would be attained "with the mixture of blood" together with reforming the American laws regarding the indigenous peoples, which, as the Congreso stressed, should serve to protect them (294).

Because the conclusions derived from Blázquez's speech included neither his overarching argument nor his vision regarding the future of the American race as presented in his lecture, it is worth restating that vision here.

> Furthermore, if one reflects upon those places where the conquering races mixed with the population of the country because they didn't consider the natives to be different or inferior and, thus, sought in the American tribes their wives, they originated a new race, which has since then become the nucleus of the nationalities called Peru, Chile, Guatemala, Honduras, Paraguay, and the Argentinian Republic. And if one contemplates the progress of these nationalities in the present century, it is necessary to confess that the copper race through racial mixing is destined for greatness, and to greatly serve humanity. (258)

Eschewing the fact that Argentina attempted to eliminate its indigenous and black population, Blázquez nevertheless presents Latin America as an example where mestizaje had engendered a new race that was to be the "nucleus" of its postcolonial nations, once again refuting Gobineau's axiom that conquering races tend to die. Furthermore and more importantly, he recognizes that these nations and their inhabitants had progressed, an acknowledgment that incorporates them into the Western discourse of progress. Yet, stating that the Americans, like the Europeans, had the capacity for progress seems to be insufficient for Blázquez. Thus he makes a bolder proposal: through mestizaje the indigenous race is destined for greatness, and its future is nothing less than to "greatly serve humanity," a providential affirmation that Europeans tended to reserve for themselves.

Therefore, once again, the Congreso posits that mestizaje increases the potentiality of a race rather than leading to its demise. In Spanish race-thinking, then, hybridity is the productive and positive biological result that had produced, on the one hand, the vigorous Iberian race and, on the other, the dynamic and propagating American race, which had resulted from the discovery and conquest of the New World. That Spanish racial thought as articulated in this conference posited mestizaje as an indelible mark of identity contested—or even subverted—dominant European racial theories.

The Notion of Mestizaje in Domingo F. Sarmiento and Justo Sierra

For nineteenth-century Latin American postcolonial statesmen and the intelligentsia—much as for European and Spanish racial theorists—the issue of mestizaje occupied a central place in reflections about the nation for two intertwined reasons. Not only was this racial phenomenon deemed one of the continent's particular characteristics, but, more importantly, it would mark the future of Latin American societies either positively or negatively. According to Lourdes Martínez-Echazábal, mestizaje was both a foundational topic in the Americas as well as "a recurrent trope indissolubly linked to the search for *lo americano* (that which constitutes an authentic [Latin] American identity) in the face of European and/or Anglo-American values" (21). Proof of its privileging is that the most important Latin American thinkers, including Simón Bolívar, José Martí, and José Vasconcelos, have reflected on this subject since the days of independence until the present.[10]

Yet, in spite of the fact that in his day Bolívar argued that mestizaje was a positive racial attribute, which Martí would reaffirm many years later, in the final decades of the nineteenth century there existed within the Latin American intelligentsia a strong theoretical discrepancy that produced opposing interpretations of mestizaje's repercussions for the emergent nations and their futures. Paradigmatic of radically different stances toward mestizaje are the theories of two important thinkers whose visions greatly influenced the way their respective nations were imagined: Domingo F. Sarmiento, Argentine statesman and writer, and Justo Sierra, Mexican intellectual and educator considered the leader of the so-called scientists (*científicos*) during the era of Porfirio Díaz, known as the *porfiriato*. Located on the periphery of knowledge production—much like the Spanish intelligentsia of the Congreso—Sarmiento and Sierra appropriated the methodological tools of the fledgling social sciences developed by Herbert Spencer and Auguste Comte in their textual reflections about their nations' past and present, including the thorny question of mestizaje. Moreover, their theories of race dialogued with the dominant racial theories originating in Europe and the United States, which circulated among the Latin American intelligentsia.

Sarmiento begins his racial treatise *Conflicto y armonías de las razas en América* (1883) by posing the question that frames the book: "What is America?" (63). This question, which goes directly to the heart of the Latin American problematics of identity, is followed by others whose answers purportedly echo the overarching attitudes and opinions held by Argentines: "Are we European? So many copper faces refute this! Are we indigenous peoples? Our blond ladies' scornful smiles perhaps provide us with the only answer. Mixed? No one wants to be this, and there are thousands of people who want to be called neither Americans nor Argentines" (63). If Sarmiento poses the complex question of identity in racial terms by underscoring the skin and hair color of Europeans and indigenous peoples ("blond ladies," "copper faces"), he curiously avoids using racial attributes to characterize the "mixed" race category that seems to encompass both a continental and national identity. Nevertheless, this tripartite racial taxonomy frames his disquisition about the reasons Argentina—and Latin America—had fallen "behind" the "civilized world that marches forward" (45). Presenting himself to his readers as a historiographer, his retrospective analysis mainly focuses on the colonial period: he specifies who had been the conquerors, traces the history of the Argentine town councils (*cabildos*), theorizes the Inquisition as a civil institution, reflects on those whom he calls "horse-riding indigenous peoples" (372), and, finally, tells the story of the English colonization of North America into which he intercalates comparisons with the Spanish colonization, which he considers to have been not only inferior but antiquated—in fact, medieval. In his prologue to the 1915 edition of Sarmiento's text, the Argentine positivist philosopher José Ingenieros insightfully summarizes the two basic ideas that in his opinion "obsessed Sarmiento as the explanation for all of the evils that had weighed upon South America: 1. The Spanish inheritance; 2. The hybridization with the indigenous natives" (37).

In a brief section of *Conflicto y armonías de las razas en América* titled "The Amalgam of Differently Colored Races," Sarmiento turns ethnologist to set forth his argument against mestizaje. Instead of presenting data, observations, or even his own arguments in order to "shape the reader's consciousness regarding the elements that comprise our society, and the influence that these mixed blood people will have . . . in the new society that will be formed when Peninsular Spaniards in turn lose the place occupied by the tyrant class in the Quichua and Aztec empires" (116), Sarmiento assembles a series of lengthy quotes from those he deems authorities on the subject of miscegenation. This narrative strategy perhaps reflects his perception that the "intermediate half breeds"—a nomenclature that restores the colonial racial classification—are "fortunately not very visible in our own Argentine society" (113).

Sarmiento believed, much like the evolutionist Spencer who greatly influenced his thought, that races had the ability to advance on what could be called the spectrum of civilization, with prehistoric man at one end and the civilized man of contemporary society at the other (88). Whereas Sarmiento locates the indigenous natives on the point of the spectrum corresponding to prehistoric man, he does not ascribe a place to the mestizo because "these differently colored races are not . . . a homogeneous whole like the Gauls and Romans . . . or even the Arabs or Saracens, who are ultimately varieties of the same race, the Caucasian one" (116). For Sarmiento, racial hybridity poses a thorny theoretical problem, which he resolves by positing that the racial characteristics and the moral state of the mestizos is determined by the dominant race in what he calls the amalgam. Deploying what he believes to be scientific language, he asserts that Spanish America "would see what would be produced by mixing pure Spaniards, the European element, with a strong sprinkling of the black race, which would be diluted in an enormous mass of natives, prehistoric men of little intelligence" (113). This vision of mestizaje, which reads like a racial recipe, is Sarmiento's sole contribution to the strictly racial aspect of mestizaje—his historical arguments are wholly another matter—inasmuch as this section of the book relies exclusively on his chosen authorities to buttress his negative assessment of this phenomenon.

Sarmiento tethers his argument to the theses he had imported from two sources that he quotes profusely in his text: Harvard professor of anthropology Louis Agassiz's writing on race and the racial-demographic data gathered by Henry Marie Brackenridge, secretary of the 1817 mission sent to South America to study its political conditions, which President James Monroe used to elaborate his famous doctrine. Sarmiento not only reproduces Brackenridge's data in his text but also states in his conclusion that despite the fact that "the proportion of whites to the aborigines, is about one to five . . . the proportion of mixt race must be very considerable; a circumstance that tends to efface the line of distinction between creoles and the natives" (114).[11] Regarding the mestizos, Sarmiento once again quotes the North American statesman: "The next class in numerical terms, is that of mestizos and cholos. The first spring from the mixture of the white and Indian, but not so far removed from Indians, as to be ranked in the class of Spaniards. Although in their dress, manners, and language, no very essential difference is perceived" (114).[12] Sarmiento reproduces what he calls Brackenridge's "curious inventory" (116) in order to highlight the numerous mestizos that inhabit the highlands of Peru, the zone in which the North American had conducted his demographic and ethnographic field study. But, in spite of the fact that the statistics seem important to Sarmiento, his focus is on demonstrating that the proliferation of hybrid races, in which the indigenous race will be dominant because the white one will have "diluted" (113) itself within it, will lead to the inevitable backwardness of America. To support this claim he paraphrases the Harvard anthropologist: "Agassiz does not accept that the progeny of black and white, white and Indian, Indian and black, which produces mulattoes, mestizos, and *mamelucos*, can survive without returning to one of its original types" (113). Thus, he concludes that America's future will no doubt belong to "prehistoric men with little intelligence" (113)—that is to say, the native peoples of the Americas.

Having already predetermined America's future, Sarmiento introduces yet another facet of mestizaje that also seems to have obsessed nineteenth-century racialists: the moral character of this group. Once again he quotes Harvard's "learned" and "wise" professor Agassiz: "Let any one who doubts the evil of this mixture of races, come to Brazil, where the deterioration consequent upon an amalgamation of races, more widespread here than in any other country in the world, and which is rapidly effacing the best qualities of the white man, leaving a mongrel nondescript type, deficient in physical and mental energy" (116). He concludes the section with yet another quote from Agassiz that summarizes their shared ideas regarding hybridity:

> The hybrid between White and Indian called Mammeluco in Brazil, is pallid, effeminate, feeble, lazy and rather obstinate; though it seems as if the Indian influence had only gone so far as to obliterate the higher characteristics of the White, without imparting its own energies to the offspring. It is very remarkable how, in both combinations, with Negros as well as White, the Indian impresses his mark more deeply upon his progeny than

the other races, and how readily, also, in further crossings,
the pure Indian characteristics are reclaimed and those of the
other races thrown off. I have known the offspring of an hybrid
between Indian and Negro with an hybrid between Indian
and White resume almost completely the characteristics of the
pure Indian. (116–17)[13]

Although Sarmiento admits that Argentina has progressed materially
and politically, his perspective on the future of the nation is tainted with
what could be called racial panic, which he forcefully expresses:

Those of us who govern come from a civilized, Christian, and
European race; some of us have accumulated wealth, others
science, and by exercising the sentiment of dignity and personal
freedom we have developed, much like the ambition for
improvement, the glory and wealth of the society to which we
belong. These special conditions in which the most influential
part of society fortunately finds itself should not be modified
through the incorporation of inferior races, in whatever
proportion, or of foreigners, who do not join the whole,
producing a mixed government comprised of whites, blacks,
Indians, mestizos, *zambos* or mulattos, whatever is the result of
the social amalgam of abject peoples. (173)

Thus, according to Sarmiento, Argentina's future depended on excluding
from its political realm both the "inferior races" and the "social amalgam of
abject peoples"—in other words, the vast majority of the population that
inhabited its national geography.

Yet at the other end of Latin America and during the same period in
which Sarmiento was vehemently arguing against the inclusion of mixed
races in the polity, a Mexican voice was posing the issue of mestizaje in a
radically different way. In his essay "México social y político (Apuntes para
un libro)" (1889), Justo Sierra, positivist educator and historian, presents
a panoramic view of Mexico's contemporary population with the objective
of establishing the manner in which the groups that constitute it have par-
ticipated in the creation of the nation.[14] Because, as a follower of Auguste
Comte, Sierra held that the science of society was a branch of the natural
sciences, he elaborates a taxonomy that classifies the Mexican population
into three groups: the "white creoles," the "indigenous family," and the
"mestizo family" (300). Although this classification is clearly bound to

race—white, indigenous, mestizo—what is significant about his taxonomy is that rather than using the term "race" to denote a group, he deploys the term "family," which belongs to the nomenclature of natural history and refers to the main groupings belonging to a class in the natural world. That he chose this terminology to reference a grouping of people in both his demographic statistics and his ethnographic reflections can be seen as a strategy that purposefully resisted the use of a term, "race," that was indelibly marked by the racialism of race-thinking.[15] By eschewing the term "race" and substituting it with "family," Sierra may also have sought to depict the group as bound by the natural, intimate, and affective ties of family rather than by superficial biological and physiological traits, the manner through which race-thinking classified peoples.

In the first section of the essay titled "Ethnology and Demography," Sierra devotes ample space to the "great American family"—the indigenous peoples—describing its present state and geographical distribution, the "social problem" resulting from its poor diet and lack of education, its participation in the creation of the nation, and its predicted future (296). Having already established that the creoles are white, in further discussions of this group he desists from marking them racially, representing the "rich creoles" instead as a "passive" class, a type of "pseudoaristocracy without roots in the past, without tradition, without history, without blood, without a future" and whose place in the history of the nation since independence has been to be "an obstacle (not the counterweight) of innovative tendencies" (299).

After sketching his main arguments regarding the demography, the historic contribution, and the future of the native peoples and the creoles, which he will fully develop in *Evolución política del pueblo mexicano* (1940), Sierra shifts his gaze to the "mestizo family," which he introduces by asserting that "today, the mestizo family constitutes the Mexican family" (297). Sierra, like many of his *científico* colleagues, promoted the "veneration of the mestizo" (Stern 61) and bases his assertion that the mestizo and the Mexican family were one and the same thing on evidence that for him is unquestionable: the growth of the mestizo population, when compared to that of the other two groups that populated Mexico, has transformed it into the nation's most numerically significant group (Sierra 297).[16] Thus, much like at the Congreso, the notion of propagation is the cornerstone of his argument, which he buttresses with demographic data that demonstrate not only that the mestizo population has increased but also that in numerical terms it has exceeded the other two groups. For Sierra, it is evident that the mestizo-Mexican family is growing rather than shrinking.

If the positivist Sierra links the future of the mestizos to demographic evidence, he furthermore contests the race-thinking of "foreign sages" (297) regarding mestizaje on the terrain of sociological logic and methodology, which he finds unequivocally deficient:

> Much has been said for and against mixed-race or mestizo
> families. For a long time foreign sages have accustomed us
> to hearing dogmatic declarations about the antecedents and
> consequences of our political and social situation, and these
> opinions are so distressing that if these conclusions were really
> scientific we would despair about ourselves. . . . But this is
> not the case. Using as our support the same method as these
> infallible condemners of our future, we protest against their
> inductions, which are not scientific because they originate
> in deficient observations of the facts; because given our brief
> national life the prophesy of our impotence can not be inferred
> as a sociological law. (297)

He primarily debates Gustave Le Bon, founder of social psychology and disciple of the anthropologist Paul Broca. In 1888 Le Bon published "The Influence of Race on History" in the French journal *Revue Scientifique*, the study in which he presented his theory on mestizaje. In order to contest Le Bon, Sierra introduces the following quote from the article:

> The mestizos have never advanced a society; the only role
> they can play is to degrade lowering them to their level, the
> civilizations that chance had them inherit. We still have an
> example of this in today's Hispanic American populations. The
> mixture of the passionate sixteenth-century Spanish race with
> inferior races has engendered bastard populations, without
> energy, with no future, and which are completely incapable
> of contributing even with a weak number to the progress of
> civilization. (298)[17]

He refutes Le Bon's thesis that "mestizos have never advanced society" by demonstrating the mestizo-Mexican's material and intellectual progress based on statistical data that he considers to prove Mexico's modernization: the growth since 1869 of schools, railways, and telegraphs. Unlike Le Bon, who had supported his negative evaluation of racial mixing on a historical narrative that originated with the "passionate" Spanish conquest of "inferior races," Sierra strategically elides Mexico's colonial history in his argument and proposes, instead, that the period of independence and that known as La Reforma be studied because they "reveal" that the mestizo family had "constituted the dynamic factor" in Mexican history: it had "moved or had begun to move the stagnant wealth of our land" and had "through peace enabled the advent of foreign capital" (298–99). That is to say, the mestizos had put capital into motion and, with it, the nation's progress. For Sierra, Mexico's economic advance and modernization are evident and, moreover, demonstrable, yet he includes in his argument another index of "civilization's progress" that was essential for nineteenth-century Latin American liberalism: political freedom. Sierra is not quite as adamant about the achievement of freedom as he is about Mexico's modernization. Nevertheless, he expresses no doubt that the mestizo family, having already "established the rule of law," "in one more generation will have established through its actions political freedom" (299). For Sierra, therefore, Mexico's future is unquestionable because it is in the hands of Le Bon's "bastard populations" (298), which had already unleashed their immense energy and begun to produce positive results that set the young nation on its path to progress.

In this chapter I have explored the ways various theories about mestizaje circulated on the transnational terrain of race-thinking during the final decades of the nineteenth century and the meanings that were ascribed to this phenomenon during the age of empire. Whereas for European theorists the question of racial hybridization was intimately linked to colonial expansion, for their Spanish and Latin American colleagues other important considerations were at play. In what was without a doubt a critical moment for Spain's future as a colonial power, its scientific intelligentsia elaborated a singular racial ideology that went against the grain of "European" theories with the objective of reaffirming the Spanish capacity for colonialization. Moreover, the positive valorization of mestizaje also attempted to contest the type of race-thinking that disparaged Latin American mestizo populations. In Latin America, however, this theoretical problematic had concrete consequences; it could even shape national policies. That is, it could influence a nation's future. The importance accorded to the thorny question of mestizaje can be seen in the vehemence with which both Sierra and Sarmiento presented their theories in favor of or against hybridity.

Lest this chapter be seen as merely an exercise in historical inquiry, we should remember UNESCO's declaration on the "race question," published 18 July 1950, nearly a century after Gobineau's treatise on race. The declaration demonstrated the ongoing need to refute the negative assessment of hybridity he expounded in *The Inequality of Human Races*. The UNESCO document clearly considers the issue of "race-mixture" to be of such significance within racial discourse that it not only posits the historical existence of racial hybridity but also provides the scientific proof that racial fusion did not produce "physical disharmonies" and "mental degeneracies":

> With respect to race-mixture, the evidence points unequivocally to the fact that this has been going on from the earliest times. Indeed, one of the chief processes of race-formation and race-extinction or absorption is by means of hybridization between races or ethnic groups. Furthermore, no convincing evidence has been adduced that race-mixture produces biologically bad effects. Statements that human hybrids frequently show undesirable traits, both physically and mentally, physical disharmonies and mental degeneracies, are not supported by the facts. (8)

In spite of being located on the periphery of the modern world (Europe and the United States) that produced and disseminated racial knowledge, Spain's Congreso Geográfico, Mexico's Sierra, and Argentina's Sarmiento nevertheless grappled with the weighty notion of mestizaje and racial fusion and, as we have seen, arrived at differing conclusions regarding its valuation within their distinct race-thinking and racial formations. Regardless of whether they resisted, contested, or (in Sarmiento's case) reinforced the dominant race-thinking that condemned the mixing of blood as producing racial degeneration and civilizational decline, the three examples of racial discourse demonstrate the extent to which the racial ideology of peripheral nations was determined by the racial thinkers at the center of modernity.

Notes

1. In *Imperialism*, Hannah Arendt proposes that certain European nations developed particular types of race-thinking. However, because her primary interest was in identifying the origins of German racism and the way in which Arthur de Gobineau's and Charles Darwin's ideas were inscribed in it, missing in her brilliant analysis is the Spanish "type." This exclusion is not surprising because, according to historian Joshua Goode,

neither thinkers and scholars outside of Spain nor Spanish historiography has paid much attention to nineteenth-century Spanish racial ideas (*Impurity* 1–19).

2. Throughout the Congreso there was a slippage between the use of the terms "Iberian" and "Spanish" race, which are used indistinctly. At the inaugural session Francisco Coello, president of both Madrid's Geographic Society and the Spanish Commercial Geographic Society, explains the reason for the slippage. I would argue that his explanation reflects that of the other participants: "When speaking about the Spanish race I am not leaving aside Portugal, because the origin of both races has been the same. They have both been born in the same way, both have been formed by the fusion of diverse peoples, and have been united by such solid and strong mortar that they have constructed an indestructible conglomerate, taking everywhere the strength of their construction and having been successful in assimilating the other races, of attracting them, of erasing their particular distinctions in order to be fused into one sole race" (*Actas* 1:50).

3. Spain's Royal Academy of History, Madrid's Athenaeum, the Central University, and the Association for Women's Education can be counted among the many institutions that were represented.

4. The Spanish ministers of war, navy, finance, justice, development, interior, and state presided over the Congreso. Represented at the conference were the governments of Guatemala, Santo Domingo, El Salvador, Honduras, Mexico, Peru, and Brazil. At least seven plenipotentiary ministers from Latin American republics were in attendance.

5. Unless otherwise noted, the translations are mine.

6. In his history of Spanish racial thought, Joshua Goode traces the history of the term "race" and demonstrates that, despite originating in the twelfth century, "its ideological meaning in the nineteenth century crystallized around the idea of Spain's legacy as a conqueror, empire builder, and unifier of different peoples" (*Impurity* 20).

7. For an invaluable, but all too brief, intellectual biography of Federico Olóriz, see Goode (*Impurity* 52–57). His lengthy *Memoria* was included in *Actas* (2:301–589).

8. See Goode, "Corrupting" (241–65); Gruzinski also discusses what he calls "hybridization" in medieval Iberia (49, 87).

9. Nineteenth-century European anthropology considered the type and color of hair, the color of the skin and eyes, the cephalic index, the nasal index, and height to be the primary characteristics used for racial classification.

10. See Simón Bolívar, "Carta de Jamaica" (1815); José Martí, *Nuestra América* (1891); and José Vasconcelos, *La Raza Cósmica* (1925). In Brazil, Gilberto Freyre advocated *mestiçagem* in *Casa-grande e senzala* (1933).

11. I have quoted the original rather than Sarmiento's translation (Brackenridge 1: 149).

12. Once again I quote the original (Brackenridge 1: 153–54).

13. I quote the original text rather than Sarmiento's translation (Agassiz 532).

14. This book is a compilation of five articles that Sierra published in Mexico's *Revista Nacional de Letras y Ciencias* in 1889.

15. According to Charles A. Hale, "Like most social commentators of the day, Sierra used the term 'race' freely, both in its anthropological and its historical sense. A race in nineteenth-century parlance could be either a physically non-European group, such as the Indians of Mexico; or it could be simply a nationality or people, such as the 'Spanish race' or the 'Latin race,' developing over time and distinguished from others by geography, language, or religion" (244).

16. In the table he includes in the text, the number of mestizos has grown by 3,153,927 whereas the number of indigenous peoples has increased by 303,933 persons and the "Europeans and creoles" by 887,119.

17. I assume that Sierra is the translator of Le Bon's article, which appeared in *Revue scientifique*, April 1888.

Works Cited

Actas. Papers from the 1892 Congreso Geográfico Hispano-Americano-Portugués. 2 vols. Madrid: Imprenta del "Memorial de Ingenieros," 1893.

Agassiz, Louis. *A Journey in Brazil*. Boston: Ticknor and Fields, 1868. Web. 15 Sept. 2012.

Arendt, Hannah. *Imperialism*. 1951. San Diego: Harcourt Brace, 1981.

Beltrán y Rózpide, Ricardo. "Los congresos del centenario." *La ilustración española y americana* 30 Dec. 1892: 458–59.

Blázquez, Antonio. "Modernas exploraciones geológicas y geográficas en Méjico y en la América central y meridional: estado actual y porvenir de las razas indígenas de América." *Actas* 1: 254–64.

Bolívar, Simón. "Carta de Jamaica." *Doctrina del Libertador*. Caracas: Ayacucho, 2009. 66–87.

Brackenridge, Henry Marie. *Voyage to South America*. Vol. 1. Baltimore: Brackenridge, 1819. Web. 15 Sept. 2012.

Cánovas del Castillo, Antonio. *Discurso sobre la nación*. Madrid: Biblioteca Nueva, 1997.

"Conclusiones." *Actas* 1: 293–94.

Freyre, Gilberto. *Casa-grande e senzala: Formação de família brasileira sob o regime da economía patriarcal.* Rio de Janeiro: Maia e Schmidt, 1933.

Gabilondo, Joseba. "Genealogía de la 'raza latina': para una teoría atlántica de las estructuras raciales hispanas." *Revista Iberoamericana: Otros estudios transatlánticos. Lecturas desde lo latinoamericano* 75.228 (2009): 795–818.

Gobineau, Arthur de. *The Inequality of Races.* New York: Fertig, 1999.

Goode, Joshua. "Corrupting a Good Mix: Race and Crime in Late Nineteenth- and Early Twentieth-Century Spain." *European History Quarterly* 35 (2005): 241–65.

———. *Impurity of Blood: Defining Race in Spain, 1870–1930.* Baton Rouge: Louisiana State UP, 2009.

Graham, Richard. "Introduction." *The Idea of Race in Latin America, 1870–1940.* Ed. Graham. Austin: U of Texas P, 1990. 1–5.

Gruzinski, Serge. *El pensamiento mestizo: Cultura amerindia y civilización del Renacimiento.* Barcelona: Paidós Ibérica, 2007.

Hale, Charles A. *The Transformation of Liberalism in Late Nineteenth-Century Mexico.* Princeton: Princeton UP, 1989.

Hobsbawm, Eric. *The Age of Empire: 1875–1914.* New York: Pantheon Books, 1987.

Ingenieros, José. "Las ideas sociológicas de Sarmiento." *Conflicto y armonía de las razas en América.* By Juan Domingo Sarmiento. Buenos Aires: La Cultura Argentina, 1915. 7–40.

López-Ocón, Leoncio. *Biografía de "La América": Una crónica hispano-americana del liberalismo democrático español (1857–1886).* Madrid: Consejo Superior de Investigaciones Científicas, 1987.

Martí, José. *Nuestra América.* Caracas: Ayacucho. 2005.

Martin-Márquez, Susan. *Disorientations: Spanish Colonialism in Africa and the Performance of Identity.* New Haven: Yale UP, 2008.

Martínez-Echazábal, Lourdes. "*Mestizaje* and the Discourse of National/Cultural Identity in Latin America, 1845–1959." *Latin American Perspectives* 25.3 (1998): 21–42.

Niro, Brian. *Race.* New York: Palgrave, 2003.

Olóriz, Federico. "Índice cefálico de los españoles." *Actas* 1: 106–7.

Rodríguez Arroquia, Ángel. "Aptitudes colonizadoras de la raza española." *Actas* 1: 84–106.

Sarmiento, Juan Domingo. *Conflicto y armonía de las razas en América.* 1883. Buenos Aires: La Cultura Argentina, 1915.

Sierra, Justo. "México social y político (Apuntes para un libro)." 1889. *Evolución política del pueblo mexicano.* Caracas: Ayacucho, 1977.

Stern, Alejandra. "Mestizofilia, biotipología y eugenesia en el México posrevolucionario: Hacia una historia de la ciencia y el estado, 1920–1960." *Relaciones* 81 (2000): 57–92.

UNESCO. "The Race Question." Statement issued 18 July 1950. *UNESCO.* Web. 18 Sept. 2012.

Vasconcelos, José. *La Raza Cósmica.* Madrid: Agencia Mundial de Librería, 1925.

Young, Robert J. C. *Colonial Desire: Hybridity in Theory, Culture and Race.* London: Routledge, 1995.

5

"El color nacional"
Race, Nation, and the Philippine Ilustrados

Joyce Tolliver
University of Illinois, Urbana-Champaign

Christopher Schmidt-Nowara has commented that "for most of the twentieth century . . . while talking incessantly of the loss of the colonies, historians have generally remained mute about the colonies themselves" (8). Schmidt-Nowara makes it clear that historians largely reversed this trend in the last years of the twentieth century, but, in the field of Iberian literary and cultural studies, we continue to find the same muteness regarding Spain's largest and longest-held colony, the Philippines. Every undergraduate who has passed a course in the history and culture of modern Spain knows that in 1898 Spain "lost" Cuba, Puerto Rico, and the Philippines, and yet Philippine studies traditionally have played virtually no role in the research or teaching carried out in Spanish departments of US universities. As Adam Lifshey puts it, "The nation [the Philippines] remains virtually unacknowledged by Spanish departments despite over three centuries of Spanish colonialism; by English departments despite being, according to some measurements, the third or fourth largest Anglophone country in the world; and by Asian departments despite geography, because of all the Western presence in the islands" ("Literary Alterities," 1435). The exclusion of Philippine studies from the teaching and research of Hispanists is explained partially by the complexity of the task: about seven thousand islands compose the Philippines, and over a hundred languages are spoken. Most significantly, even though it was under Spanish rule from the mid-sixteenth century until 1898, Spanish was never the majority language in the Philippines; according to a survey done by the US Census Bureau in 1903, only about 1 percent was literate in Spanish when Spain's control of the colonies was replaced by that of the United States (Rafael 197).[1] Nevertheless, the most geographically and culturally remote part of what was then referred to as "overseas Spain" reflected, even as it tested, the limits of Spain's conception of its empire in the last decades of the nineteenth century.[2]

It is time that US scholars of Iberian literary and cultural studies turned our attention to the literary and cultural production of this colonized nation. As Lifshey has already forcefully argued, in light of a twenty-first-century understanding of world modernity, not only is this area of inquiry urgently needed on its own terms, but it will also lend insights into Spain's modern imperial project. Certainly, scholars of Iberian literatures and cultures who are interested in the nineteenth century will ignore Philippine intellectual and cultural production at their own risk, for this production profoundly complicated and challenged the concepts and practices of Spanish nationhood during this period. The primary aim of this chapter is to contribute to this important yet nascent area of inquiry. My indebtedness to the historians and other scholars—particularly those from the Philippines—who have *not* "remained mute" about this colony is profound and will, I hope, be apparent throughout this study (Schmidt-Nowara 8).

Central to the study of the writings on the Spanish Philippine colony are the Spanish-language writings of a group of elite young Philippine-born men who congregated in Europe's metropolitan centers toward the end of the nineteenth century to claim their right, as *filipinos*, to a place in the Spanish nation. These young intellectuals called themselves "los ilustrados," "enlightened ones." At the center of this group was the Tagalog physician José Rizal, who would become, in the words of León María Guerrero, "the first *filipino*."

In 1896, José Rizal was condemned to death by firing squad, thus immortalizing his status as national hero. Even as he faced martyrdom, the historical narrative goes, he courageously affirmed his solidarity with the people of the Philippines, composing his most famous poem, "My Last Farewell" ("Mi último adiós"), and writing affectionate farewell letters to his family.[3] One aspect of Rizal's martyrdom narrative particularly reveals the project of Philippine national identity on which his status of hero rests. When he examined the official order for his execution by firing squad, he requested that one detail be corrected: where his race had been identified as "chino mestizo" (Chinese mestizo), it should, he insisted, be changed to "indio puro," or "pure Indian" (Coates 312). His attention to this detail in his last moments, so often read as an affirmation of his solidarity with the Philippine nation he imagined, also illustrates the inextricability of the concepts of race and nationhood in the Philippines during the period that Alda Blanco has called the late "modern" empire (2). These categories, of course, are also essential to the construction of an "imagined community" that, perhaps paradoxically, included the so-called overseas provinces that, in theory, formed part of the Spanish nation (Anderson, *Imagined*). In this chapter, I begin to consider the ways these two crossroads—race and nation in the modern Spanish empire, and race and nation according to Rizal and his colleagues in the Philippine reformist movement of the 1880s and 1890s—are, and are not, the same crossroads.

At the end of the nineteenth century, the racial categories imposed in the Philippines by Spanish colonial rule had more to do with legal status than with phenotype or even genealogy, and in fact represented an amalgam of what we would today consider separate categories of social identity. Paul A. Kramer explains that social and racial classification in nineteenth-century colonial Philippine culture depended on a tripartite system that took into account matters of "territorial nativity," genetics (or what was called "blood" in this period), and religion (39). Not surprisingly, whether one was born in Europe or the colonies was a crucial factor in the determination of one's social rights and privileges, with those born in the colonies enjoying fewer privileges than those born in Europe. Obviously, this category interacted with that of ancestry: people whose parents were both European enjoyed a higher position in the hierarchy than either Spanish mestizos, whose ancestors consisted of a Spaniard (usually the father) and a "native," or Chinese ("sangley") mestizos, whose ancestors were Chinese and indigenous. This latter group was far more numerous than the former; in contrast to what occurred in the American colonies, Spanish-indigenous *mestizaje* was relatively rare in the Philippine colonization. But even when "mestizo" was understood to refer to those of Chinese-indigenous ancestry, the matter was complex, thanks to the involvement of the category of religion in racial classifications.

Put simply, the indigenous, "native," or *indio* population was constituted not only by their original inhabitance of the Philippines but also by their acquiescence to Spanish colonial domination through conversion to Catholicism. Of the populations residing in the archipelago when Magellan landed in 1521 at Homonhon Island, not all accepted conversion. The Muslim peoples of the southern islands—whom the Spaniards called *moros*, or Moors——did not convert; neither did the animist nations (collectively referred to as "Igorots") or the so-called Negritos, who occupied the highlands. Only those indigenous nations (in the sense of "birth group") who converted to Catholicism, and thus accepted "civilization," were considered indio. This is a key feature of the intersecting concepts of race and nation in the Philippines.[4] The presence of religion as a factor in the theorization of race is illustrative of the inchoate nature of the concept itself at this time: pseudoscientific racial theories were still fairly new in the 1880s.[5] Further, the term *raza* was used in a variety of ways well into the twentieth century and, in fact, was probably used less frequently to refer to genetic makeup or phenotype than to nation or *pueblo*. As Joshua Goode explains, "Though the term traces its lineage to the twelfth century, its ideological meaning in the nineteenth century crystallized around the idea of Spain's legacy as a conqueror, empire builder, and unifier of different peoples" (20). In terms of both the notion of *raza* and the practices associated with that notion, the case of the Philippines was especially complex. The categories were powerfully hierarchical, and the ways in which they were reflected culturally and legally helped to institutionalize both racial stratification and racism.

Placement in one legal category or another was of vital consequence: indios were obliged to provide the state with six weeks of forced labor every year, a duty from which *mestizos españoles*, creoles, and peninsular Spaniards were exempt; *chinos* paid taxes at a considerably higher rate than did either *mestizos chinos* or indios. Where one could live, and with whom, was also controlled by one's racial classification: as late as the mid-eighteenth century, it was illegal for a "peninsular"—one born in Spain—to live among indios except in the case of intermarriage, and only peninsulars, their children, and their servants were allowed to set up household in the center of Manila, in the walled area of the city known as Intramuros (Kramer 40; Wickberg 63–65). Inhabitants of the archipelago were *legally* required to inscribe obedience to racial hierarchy in their daily personal interactions. For example, obeisance was owed to peninsulars and creoles by their cultural and racial inferiors (that is, everyone else) in any public encounter: the nonpeninsular man was legally obligated to remove his hat. In the presence of a Spanish friar, nonpeninsulars were obligated not only to remove their hats but also to kneel down and kiss the friar's ring (Pardo de Tavera 337; qtd. in Reed 164).

Within the imperial context, the material and cultural construction of race played a different role in the Southeast Asian sector of the Spanish empire than it did in Latin America. As Javier Morillo-Alicea puts it,

"This particular racialization . . . made the colony the object of a 'civilizing mission' similar to that of other European powers in Asia. It is also a crucial factor in explaining why the 'fraternity' with which metropolitan politicians could sometimes embrace the Antillean islands was rarely extended to the Southeast Asian colony" (29). This notion of the Philippines as simultaneously belonging to and being utterly alien from the Spanish national "family" is dramatically illustrated in the writings of peninsular Spaniards who "wrote home" from the Philippine colonies.

Pablo Feced, writing under the pseudonym "Quioquiap," expressed the colonizers' frustration over the seemingly intractable otherness of the non-European inhabitants of the Philippines, whom he alternately called *filipinos* and *indios*. Feced was a Spanish historian who went to the Philippines in 1884 to tend to some property belonging to his brother, who had held a civil servant position there. Before and after his stay in the Philippines, he contributed actively to debates about the Philippines, defending the interests of Spain and attacking Filipino campaigns for colonial reform and independence (García Castellón 107–8). Writing pseudonymously from the Philippines, he published a series of articles in *El Liberal*, which he later edited and collected in the volume *Filipinas: Esbozos y pinceladas* (1888; The Philippines: Sketches and Brushstrokes). Written in the last decade of the empire, this collection of essays laments the "quite impassive, unmoving stuff" of the Philippines—both land and people—and calls for an imperial "resurrection" through racial and economic domination in the Philippines (42, 354).[6] This overtly racist "sketch," as Feced calls it in the title, which Emilia Pardo Bazán blithely praised in print ("La España remota"), makes Morillo-Alicea's claim seem like a bitterly ironic understatement.[7] Far from extending a fraternal embrace to the inhabitants of the Philippines, Feced writes back to his fellow "castilas" in order to illustrate the degree to which the Filipinos are, as he says, "uncolonizable" (7, 347).[8]

In one of the earliest articles, published in *El Liberal* in February 1887, Feced claims that the primary challenge to the success of the colonial project in the Philippines is the racial inferiority of the archipelago's non-European inhabitants. Drawing on the common reductive version of Darwin's theory of evolution, as well as on the ideas of physical anthropologists in vogue at the time, Feced claims that the colonial subject he calls the "indio" is closer to an ape than to a human being and is essentially uneducable: "Cities made of huts, roads made of puddles, bridges made of tree trunks, wild coastlines, fallow fields, bodies without clothing, brains without ideas; in the highlands, nothing but independent, wild tribes, and here, in the flatlands, their brothers . . . an inanimate pile of beings who happen to be human; a civilization in embryonic form and a society still in its diapers" ("Ellos y nosotros" 4; also qtd. in Sánchez Gómez, "Ellos y nosotros" 318).[9] Feced adds that no one has yet done "a careful scientific study of these bodies," but he summarizes the craniological analysis done by Virchow in 1874 of the "ancient settlers of the Philippine Islands," emphasizing the differences between those skulls analyzed by the German anthropologist and the skulls of Caucasians ("Ellos y nosotros" 4). In case the title—"Them and Us"—does not clearly enough position the Philippine colonial subject as Other, Feced ends this essay with an observation about the inherent intellectual and cultural inferiority of the so-called indio, which he compares explicitly to the presumed essential difference between Europeans, on the one hand, and both blacks and "gypsies," on the other: "A longer period of contact and a more vigorous [civilizing] effort have not managed to erase our differences from the black man and from the gypsy. Nor has it done so here, between *them* and *us*" ("Ellos y nosotros" 4).

Throughout the classically orientalized vignettes in the pages of Feced's *Esbozos y pinceladas*, we find a tension between the author's ironic amusement at the antics of the childlike Filipino, on the one hand, and a bitter resentment at the coexistence with the Philippine "sleepwalker" that the colonial situation demands, on the other (8). Because the Filipino is a colonial subject, ironically, he must be considered Spanish, even though he is barely human. The obligatory recognition of the colonial subject's humanity—even though that humanity is merely technical—is what Feced simply cannot tolerate, and he makes his resentment known from the beginning: "Beardless and shapeless, with no surname and sometimes even without clothing, the Filipino is a Spaniard, he is our compatriot. This is something proper Spaniards do not realize until they set foot on the narrow twisted streets of the Pearl of the Orient" (*Esbozos* 8).[10]

Pablo Feced's claim to the right to represent the supposed reality of the colonial situation in the Philippines did not go unnoticed by those who had experienced it as colonized subjects. If Feced reported back to his fellow Spaniards on behalf of the imperial mission, that missive was contested from within the metropolis by both José Rizal and his colleague in the Propaganda Movement, Graciano López Jaena. Along with Isabelo de los Reyes, Mariano Ponce, Marcelo H. Del Pilar, and the brothers Antonio and Juan Luna, Rizal and López Jaena worked from Europe to reform the colonial situation of the Philippines. Their platform was built largely on two overarching causes: a claim for representation of the Philippines in the Spanish Cortes and an end to the system of using Spanish friars (*frailes*) as omnipotent representatives of the empire in the archipelago. They were particularly interested in abolishing the iron control held by the *frailocra-cia* over the educational system. They referred to the reformist movement they founded as the Propaganda Movement, and they reflected their European metropolitan political orientation by referring to themselves collectively as the "Ilustrados."[11] They were, without a doubt, the Philippine public intellectuals of their day: in their attempt to change the political system, all of them preferred the word—or, in the case of Juan Luna, the artist's brush—to the sword. Together, they founded the periodical *La Solidaridad*, which was published between 1887 and 1895; their essays also appeared frequently in intellectually oriented journals published in Madrid and Barcelona.

When the essay that would form the first chapter of Feced's *Esbozos* was published in *El Liberal* in 1887, López Jaena lost no time in responding. His rebuttal, called "Los indios de Filipinas," establishes at the outset that Feced can only get away with such an outlandish portrayal of the islands because they are so far away that few "peninsulars" have ever traveled there. He claims for himself the right to represent the Philippine colonial experience, not from the perspective of the colonizer but from the perspective of the colonial subject, albeit an elite and privileged colonial subject who has been transplanted to the metropolis. López Jaena's essay attacks head-on Feced's characterization of the Philippine male as indolent and, by implication, unmanly. Ironically resituating Feced's characterization of the Philippine male, and quoting "Quioquiap" word for word, he says: "It was *those feeble minds and feeble unclothed bodies, those brains without ideas, that anthropoid race of the Quadrumanus family, that inanimate pile of beings* who once fought with virility at the side of a scarce few Spaniards against Lim Hong's invading Chinese fleet. . . . Jolo, Sipac, Balanguingui, all serve as eloquent testaments to Philippine heroism" (2; also qtd. in Sánchez-Gómez 319–20). But in order to do so, he uses the historical participation of the "indio" in the colonial enterprise itself: the courage and manliness of Philippine mestizo and indigenous men are demonstrated in their service to the Spanish empire against China, in the case of Lim Hong, and against the Islamic populations of the Philippine Islands themselves, in the case of Jolo, Sipac, and Balanguingui. López Jaena's defense of the Philippine male's virility and loyalty to Spain invokes an image of the Spanish empire as the enforcer of Catholicism and supposed purity of blood. Further, López Jaena opens his attack on Feced's outrageous portrayal of the Filipino by exclaiming that, judging from Feced's description, "anyone who has never seen the Philippines would think it's a country of Kaffirs," thus defending the dignity and culture of the Filipino at the expense of the African (2). Ironically, then, in defending the masculinity of those he refers to as "indios," he unwittingly supports the racist framework on which Feced's attack is based and confirms Feced's classic colonial association between masculinity and race.

In López Jaena's eloquent yet flawed essay, there is one apparent exception to the logic of the assimilationist defense he offers: his conclusion. Feced had concluded his essay by claiming that the backwardness of the indio was attributable to biology and was therefore irremediable until that biology could be changed through genetic "whitening." In spite of his earlier defense of the contributions made by the indio to the Spanish imperial cause, López Jaena accepts the premise that the Philippines are "backward" (2). He offers a political explanation: the dominance in the islands of "the friar, who, as a missionary of the Catholic faith and a representative of Spain and of its civilizing enterprise in those regions, has found in the Indio an inexhaustible goldmine of exploitation, plunging him into ignorance and fanaticism" (2). In this, López Jaena pointedly makes the same criticism of the rule by friars—the frailocracia—that José Rizal would later express in his novels *Noli me tangere* (1887) and *El filibusterismo* (1891). But this criticism, which marks a change of topic at the very end of the essay, is undermined by López Jaena's logic up to that point: in helping to fight off armies that would threaten the Church-supported Spanish colony in the Philippines, the indigenous men the author defends were in fact supporting the very frailocracia López Jaena blames for the backwardness of the Philippines.

Rizal strongly attacks the frailocracia of the Philippines in both his novels but does not single out rule by religious orders as the only cause of what López Jaena calls Philippine "backwardness" (2). Like López Jaena, he accepts unquestioningly the precept that capitalism and technological sophistication are the hallmarks of civilization; these are characteristics that he would like the Philippines to develop. All of the Ilustrados, in fact, spent the better part of the late 1880s and the 1890s building a case for the representation of the Philippines in the Spanish Cortes, arguing that the Filipino was entitled to all the rights of citizenship and to representation, based not only on claims of human justice and the discourse of familial colonial relationships, but also on the status granted them in the Constitution of Cádiz of 1812.

The Constitution of 1812 specified that the overseas provinces were to be represented in the Spanish Cortes, a liberal ideal that never materialized for the Philippines, in contrast to the representation eventually granted to Cuba and Puerto Rico. But, in spite of some attempts at liberal reform, by the last decade of the century, Spanish liberals and Philippine reformists alike still found themselves deploring the lack of Philippine representation in the Cortes.[12] As John D. Blanco puts it, "both the Constitutions of 1869 and 1876 (and between them, the project of the Federal constitution of the First Republic in 1873) maintained the need for Special Laws in the archipelago, without ever writing them" (185).

In basing their claim to membership in the Spanish nation on the ideals expressed in the Constitution of 1812, the Ilustrados were on shaky ground. Although the authors of the constitution mandated the representation in the Cortes of the citizens of "overseas Spain," not everyone living in those colonies was automatically granted citizenship. Article 22 specifically excluded from these rights all those "Spaniards who through any lineage are held *and reputed to be* of African origin" (my emphasis; "españoles que por qualquiera línea son *habidos y reputados por* originarios del Africa"), although exceptions could be made in individual cases of meritorious service to the motherland ("Constitución").[13] In his 1889 essay, "The Philippines One Hundred Years Hence," José Rizal obliquely supports this exclusion of the racial Other from representation in the Cortes, even as he exposes the prejudice underlying it. In rebutting the argument that to allow Filipinos to enter the Cortes would inconveniently expose the other *diputados* to "the smell of Igorots," he assures his readers that if that is the real objection, "the *Filipinos*, who in their own country are accustomed to bathe every day, when they become representatives may give up such dirty custom, at least during legislative session, so as not to offend . . . with the odor of the bath" (507). In his ironic reassurance that "Filipinos" practice excellent personal hygiene, he implicitly opposes "Filipinos" to "igorrotes" without questioning the Spanish image of Igorots as uncivilized. His point is not that there is anything wrong with referring to "the smell of Igorots," but rather that *real* "Filipinos"—those who would represent the archipelago in the Cortes—are the Christianized groups, *not* the unassimilated indigenous people. Because they relied on the logic of the 1812 constitution in their campaign for representation in the Cortes, it is perhaps logical that Rizal and other Ilustrados combatted prejudice against "Filipinos" by relying on a rhetoric of essential racial and cultural sameness. Necessarily, this rhetoric insistently elided the striking heterogeneity of the various populations and cultures of the Philippine Archipelago itself. As we shall see, Rizal consistently privileged the Malaysian indios (the group with which he insisted he be identified in the order for his execution) over other demographic groups inhabiting the Philippines.

At the end of the nineteenth century, and well into the twentieth, the Moros (the Muslims of the southern part of the archipelago) and the Igorots, whose settlement in the highland interiors largely isolated them from contact with both the Chinese and the Spaniards, were treated as an internal Other who largely remained outside the economic and social colonial structures. The group that the Ilustrados referred to collectively as "indios," then, were *only* those indigenous peoples—specifically the "malayos"—who had been "Christianized." According to the theory of racial migration waves advanced by Rizal's close friend, the Austrian ethnologist Ferdinand Blumentritt, the indios comprised the third and supposedly most culturally advanced migration wave; it was this group of people, says Blumentritt, that Magellan encountered when he arrived at Homonhon in 1521. Blumentritt claims that while the Spaniards' arrival brought this third migratory wave to an end, it also coincided with a period during which a "religious *conquista* was being carried out by the Moors who spread Islam among the Indians of the Philippines" (*Attempt* 16). "It can be considered a great blessing, as well as luck," adds Blumentritt, "that the Spaniards appeared at the right time before Islam had taken roots deep enough, for otherwise, the European Christian civilization could not have been easily propagated. The people then would have been totally lost to Christianity" (16). As Aguilar explains in detail, Rizal would draw heavily on Blumentritt's theory of the cultural superiority of the indio, compared to the Igorot and the "Negritos" and "Moros," in his own theories of Philippine nationalism.[14]

In his essay "Sobre la indolencia del filipino" ("The Indolence of the Filipinos"), Rizal, like López Jaena, lets the charge of Philippine laziness stand. And, like his colleague, he argues that it is "an *effect* of bad governance and of backwardness, not a cause of them" (231). He places the blame for Philippine lassitude on Spanish colonial rule, but, drawing on *Sucesos de las Islas Filipinas* by the seventeenth-century historian Antonio de Morga, as well as on the studies of his friend Blumentritt, he adopts a scientific perspective to do so. In this, Rizal ironically mirrors Feced's own appropriations of scientific discourse to advance a particular ideology. While Feced argues for the racial inferiority of the Philippine Malaysian indio, Rizal uses Morga and Blumentritt to advance a view of Malaysian superiority. However, in this process, he also assumes the cultural inferiority of other indigenous groups.

Blumentritt posited that the pre-Conquest population of the archipelago arose as the result of three separate migratory waves: first, he says, the "original owners of the land" (Aguilar 612) were the nomadic people called "Negritos," "who were eventually forced to the interior forests." In this, he follows the 1609 account of Morga, who describes the "Negritos" as "a barbarous, dangerous people, who are quick to kill" (259). The second migratory wave, according to Blumentritt, was formed by the Malayans, who invaded from the south and intermarried with the "Negritos." These mestizo populations, says Blumentritt, retreated to the mountains of the interior and produced the contemporary Igorots, Ilogots, and other populations, who would resist colonization. It is the third migratory group that most interests Rizal. When a "second group of Malay invaders" (Blumentritt, "An Attempt" 14) that included the Tagalogs, Visayans, Ilocanos, and others invaded the coastal areas and forced the Igorots and others into the interior, the second group of Malay peoples—that is, the third wave of migration—intermarried with previous Malay occupants, but not with "Negritos" or Igorots. According to Blumentritt, the intermarriage between the two Malaysian migration groups "explains the many similarities, and common bonds, especially in religion, that join the Malays of the archipelago into one" (14). In explaining the ethnographic history of the archipelago, then, Blumentritt fuses religion to racial migration.

It is this population, which Blumentritt claims "had a higher civilization and milder morals as opposed to the first Malay wave" (14), that Rizal and his colleagues identify as "the ancient *filipinos*" (Aguilar 618). Rizal argues at length, in "The Indolence of the Filipinos," that the pre-Conquest rule of the third-wave "original filipinos" constitutes a golden age of Philippine civilization. With the European conquest comes the loss of this great civilization, according to Rizal; the third-wave inhabitants of the islands had developed a rich trade economy based on industry and agriculture, which was still active when Magellan landed in the archipelago: "Back then there was life, there was activity, there was movement" (Rizal, "Indolencia" 236). This rich golden age, however, preceded contact with the Chinese—and, in spite of the fact of his father's Chinese-mestizo heritage, Rizal does not discuss the Chinese contribution to the so-called Filipino race.[15] Certainly, the golden age posited by Morga and invoked by Rizal owed absolutely nothing to the heritage of the "Negrito" or the Igorot, whom Rizal and his colleagues by no means considered representative of the Philippine people. As Aguilar notes, "denigrated by Spaniards and their lowland subjects, 'Negritos' were strangers, an alien race that the Europeans and the 'Malay Christians' placed beyond the reach of civilization. Even the most 'enlightened' considered 'Negritos' inherently primitive" (613).

Alda Blanco, Luis Angel Sánchez Gómez (*Un imperio*), Paul Kramer, and Christopher Schmidt-Nowara have all discussed the ways in which the

1887 Philippine Exposition in Madrid's Retiro Park dramatized the racial and national tensions inherent in the moribund imperial project of the archipelago. Blanco argues that "as a site of imperial consciousness, the Philippines Exhibition served to naturalize empire for its national visitors by producing 'knowledge' about the Philippines and by providing what Tony Bennett has called 'a context for performance'" (58–59). As the studies by Aguilar, Kramer, and Schmidt-Nowara document, Antonio Luna, López Jaena, and Rizal were equally appalled that the Philippine Islands were represented by the very populations they themselves considered savage and backward; their colleague Isabelo de los Reyes caused quite a sensation when he called himself, in a way that Aguilar calls "mischievous" (616), a brother to the forest dwellers. To be fair, the initial repulsion provoked in the Ilustrados by the inclusion of the Igorots and Jolós in the exhibition turned to compassion and outrage at the inhumane conditions provided for the human beings who formed part of the spectacle, which was intensified when a Joló woman died of pneumonia during the exhibition. Still, this did not prevent López Jaena from angrily complaining that the organizers of the exhibition failed to distinguish between "chinos, chinitos, negros, igorrotes"—and Filipinos (Aguilar 620). Such a sentiment would seem to undercut the Ilustrados' eloquent and vigorous condemnation of the vile racism of Feced and others. Indeed, their very defense of the intellectual, cultural, and *human* value of the Filipino rested on a notion of Filipino-ness that subtly yet perversely upheld the racist logic of Feced's representation of "them and us," a logic based on a narrative of cultural and racial origin, one that contrasted sharply with the civil and legal notions of racial identification as mutable and contingent.

The group of Philippine Ilustrados was composed of young men who were all members of the privileged class, but not all of the same ethnic or racial background. Isabelo de los Reyes identified himself primarily as an Ilocano. Rizal explicitly identified himself as an "indio," even though both his maternal and paternal ancestors were Chinese mestizos. And Evaristo Aguirre, while born in the archipelago, was the son of two peninsular Spaniards. The differences of background sometimes caused tensions among the members of the Philippine expatriate intellectual community in Madrid. In March 1887, Evaristo Aguirre wrote from Madrid to Rizal, who was living in Germany at the time, to tell him about the most recent conflicts within the group. An unnamed colleague, according to Aguirre's summary, was trying to sow dissension in the group of Ilustrados by writing a letter to Rizal telling him that a division in the group had been formed between real Filipinos and aristocrats; that "we don't see ourselves as *filipinos* but

rather as indios or mestizos or castilas" (246). Aguirre dismisses the letter
from the colleague as ill-willed troublemaking, assuring Rizal that "there's
no division among us at all, unless it's on the part of two or three who
consider themselves authentic, and who, in spite of everyone's best efforts,
have obstinately separated themselves from the majority in order to do
them as much harm as possible" (247). In a rhetorical move that signals
the changing use of the term *filipino* to refer not to creoles like himself
but to members of the Philippine community as the Ilustrados imagined
it, Aguirre asserts that, at least among the group of Ilustrados, racial and
social classification is meaningless: "We do not, nor should we, have any
name except for *filipino*s, which is the name of our Common Mother: who
is making up categories, who is setting up differences?" (247).

Aguirre's appeal to Rizal is profoundly ambivalent. To classify the
group into "the authentic" and "the aristocrats" would necessarily place
Aguirre in the latter category, when he really preferred to stake a claim
to the former. He expresses what comes close to envy of those colonial
Filipinos whose heritage is readable on their bodies. Without a doubt,
they are "genuinos," according to his own reading: "I feel more satisfaction when I see a paisano of color, and I feel a greater affinity with
him than when I see a paisano who is not like that, because the former
immediately reminds me of our common origin, and the latter does not
so obviously carry the mark of our blessed birthplace" (248). Aguirre is
acutely conscious that, in contrast, his own phenotype features no overt
markers of this "blessed birthplace," and, for that reason, others may
not identify him as a true Filipino. He fears, in other words, that others
may think that he is unsuccessfully trying to pass for Filipino: "Since I'm
being frank, I'll tell you that I can't help feeling mortified when I am in
public, among our paisanos, or in any event when we're being noticed,
and I realize that people might think I am an intruder into the group,
because my features do not have that physiological characteristic that is
most visible and most particular to our land—the national color" (248).
Aguirre's discomfort was likely based on ample experience; few inhabitants of the metropolis would imagine that a fair-skinned man could be
Rizal's *paisano*. In a report on the banquet honoring the artists Juan Luna
and Félix Resurrección Hidalgo on the occasion of their winning national
prizes, one Madrid newspaper refers, first and foremost, to the skin color
of their fellow Filipinos in contrast to that of "illustrious personages":
"The dark faces of the sons of the Philippines were mixed in with those
of the most illustrious personages of Spanish politics, oratory, arts, or
letters" ("Banquete" 1). Although he might reject its validity on ideo-

logical grounds, the color line was in fact a divisive barrier, even among the Ilustrados who worked so hard to articulate the dimensions of what would later be called "filipinidad."

Aguirre acknowledges the power of racial divisions, as well as the desire Rizal shares with him to erase those divisions: "Just as you despair of not being able to combine in your own veins all the different blood [*sangres*] that might separate us, as a common bond, I despair of the fact that my own blood might make people not think of me as authentic" (247).[16] A month later, Rizal himself would echo this theme of racial unity in a letter to Blumentritt, emphasizing the necessary reconciliation of differences of background and race among the Ilustrados, as well as the personal sacrifices they made in service of their notion of national and racial unity: "Our young people should not devote themselves to love or to those exciting speculative sciences, as the young people of happier nations do; we must all sacrifice something in the name of politics even if we have no desire to do so. This is something that our friends who edit our Madrid journal understand; they are young criollo youth of Spanish background, Chinese mestizos, and Malaysians, but we refer to ourselves simply as Filipinos" ("Carta" 115).[17] Aguirre represents Rizal as desirous of incarnating, in his own body, "all the blood," the multiple races that constitute, for him, the Philippine nation (Aguirre 247). The choice of metaphor is not arbitrary, given the importance played in the Philippine national narrative by the *pacto de sangre*, the blood compact supposedly made in 1565 by the Bohol indigenous leader Sikatuna and the Spanish trader Miguel López de Legazpi. According to this legend, the Spaniard and the indigenous leader each made an incision in their arms and then poured the blood from their wounds into a cup of wine, from which they then both drank. Kramer explains that this compact was interpreted by the Ilustrados of the Propaganda Movement as a symbol of the racial union of Spaniards and "nativos":

> According to their accounts, as well as those of Spanish historians, it was ancient Philippine custom to seal treaties of alliance or friendship by mixing the blood of leaders. . . . Unlike many elements of Propaganda argument, the blood compact subverted rather than sought recognition. Recognition required two parties: if Spaniards and *filipinos* were indistinguishable, then the former could not "recognize" the latter; if anything, the compact was a moment when Legazpi had been forced to recognize native tradition (59).

The literal mixing of blood was such a powerful metaphor for the members of the Philippine intellectual elite that Juan Luna commemorated it in one of his most famous works, "El pacto de sangre" (The blood pact), which was hung in the courthouse of Manila. Luna painted "El pacto" in 1886, the year before Aguirre wrote to Rizal of their mutual anxiety about the "blood" of Filipinos (Aguirre 247). Luna's model for the indigenous leader Sikatuna was none other than José Rizal (Kramer 60).

According to the fusion of blood evoked by Aguirre (247), the "authentic" Filipino was not the child of Spaniards born in the archipelago but the mestizo whose ancestors included Christianized indios. In terms both of nation and of race, what Aguirre called the "authentic" Filipino (247) was, for Rizal and Aguirre both, the descendant of Blumentritt's third migration wave; membership in the nation was inextricably intertwined with skin color. Rizal, in other words, seemed to celebrate a certain "impurity of blood," to use Goode's term, that, for Rizal, was essential to the imagined community of Filipinos. But "all the blood" (Aguirre 247) of those that Rizal would mix in his own veins to represent the union of the Filipinos did *not* include the blood of all the inhabitants of the Philippine Islands: the Filipino—that is, the indio—may have included the blood of the *castila*, but *not* that of the Igorot, the Joló, or the "Negrito." As Aguilar puts it, the worldview of the Ilustrados "impelled them to demand equality with the colonizer but concomitantly eschew 'savages' from their imagined community" (631). Like their nemesis Feced, then, Rizal and other Ilustrados saw the hope for Philippine advancement in a carefully controlled *mestizaje*. Whether through a proposal for a new genetically engineered future—as Feced advocated—or through recourse to a narrative of exclusionary racial origin—as Rizal invoked—both the Ilustrados and supporters of the empire advocated for a notion of Filipino nationhood that assumed that membership in the nation was reflected in the skin color of its members. Ultimately, the project of nationhood that Rizal and his fellow reformers advanced rested on a notion of purity of blood that, as Goode has shown, has always been a fiction. Ironically, that fiction was also foundational for the imperial rule that Rizal and his contemporaries struggled valiantly to abolish.

Notes

1. It is important to remember, however, that the figures reported by the 1903 Census were neither infallible nor objective. Fernández argues for a more nuanced understanding of the distribution of Spanish at the beginning of

the twentieth century, suggesting that it may have been significantly wider than the often-cited figure of 1 percent (369).

2. Schmidt-Nowara's seminal *The Conquest of History* explores the complications of this view of the colonies as overseas provinces, which were simultaneously part of and radically different from Spain. Other key studies of the Spanish colonial Philippines include the books by Cushner and Fradera. The anthology edited by Pan-Montojo and Alvarez Junco is also an excellent resource.

3. Rizal's fraudulent trial and subsequent execution play a central role in Philippine historiography. See Retana for accounts of this event published within a few years of its occurrence, including one by Unamuno, included in the epilogue to the Retana volume. Horacio de la Costa, SJ, has translated Retana's transcription of the Spanish documentation of the execution. Also see Tolliver, "El heroísmo del escritor," for a discussion of Unamuno's epilogue.

4. In addition to Kramer's *The Blood of Government*, key contemporary sources for an understanding of the intersections of race, nation, and social category in the colonial Philippines include the studies by Chu, Fradera (*Colonias*), Reyes, Schmidt-Nowara, Thomas, and Wickberg. Chief among those who advanced theories of Philippine race during the late nineteenth century was Ferdinand Blumentritt. Aguilar's "Tracing Origins," which provides a firm foundation for the present essay, is a groundbreaking study of these intersections as they are reflected in the writings of the Philippine Ilustrados, and in particular of the influence on Rizal of Blumentritt's racial migration theory.

5. Joshua Goode's *Impurity of Blood* provides essential reading for an understanding of the development of the notion of "raza" and race in nineteenth-century Spain. For a cogent and thorough discussion of the development of racial theory in the Philippines during this same period, see chapter 2 of Thomas (47–96).

6. Unattributed translations are my own. Page numbers refer to the original Spanish.

7. For a discussion of the polemic created when Pardo Bazán published her positive review of Feced's book, see Tolliver's "Over Her Bloodless Body."

8. "Castila" was the term used in the Philippines for peninsular Spaniards.

9. Sánchez Gómez reproduces the entire essay, "Ellos y nosotros," which was first published in *El Liberal*, 16 Feb. 1887. The first two paragraphs of this essay were included in the collection *Esbozos y pinceladas*, but the section quoted here appears only in *El Liberal*, not in the volume.

10. For a different view of the Filipinos' membership in the imagined Spanish community, see Pardo Bazán's short story, "Página suelta," which Tolliver analyzes in "Framing Colonial Manliness."

11. Schumacher provides the most authoritative account of the Propaganda Movement and the work of its leaders. Benedict Anderson discusses the Ilustrados in both *The Spectre of Comparisons* (227–62) and *Under Three Flags*, with a particular focus on Isabelo de los Reyes (in *Under Three Flags*) and Rizal (in *The Spectre of Comparisons*). Both Mojares and Thomas provide thoughtful analyses of the importance of the Ilustrados Pedro Paterno, T. H. Pardo de Tavera, and Isabelo de los Reyes in the formation of today's concept of the Philippine nation. The most complete account of the life and works of Rizal is still Retana's *Vida*; in contemporary times, the definitive biographies are those written by León María Guerrero and Austin Coates.

12. Miguel Morayta's 1891 speech to the Asociación Hispano-Filipina provides an excellent example of the defense of Philippine representation in the Cortes on the part of a peninsular liberal, while also offering a firsthand account of liberals' attempts at colonial reform.

13. Rieu-Millán summarizes the debates held in Latin America about Article 22 and the role played by race in the conception of Spanish citizenship reflected in the Constitution of 1812 (157–73).

14. Blumentritt's 1890 ethnographic map of the Philippines charts sixty-three different ethnic groups, divided into three categories according to the territory they occupied: "cristianos hispano-filipinos," "cristianos nuevos e infieles," and "moros" (*Mapa etnografico*).

15. Wickberg demonstrates that, according to both custom and the legal code, the Chinese were segregated in Spanish colonial Philippines: they did not have the right to participate in local government, were obligated to live outside the city walls of Manila, and paid the highest taxes of any group (62–66). Rizal's own grandfather was a "mestizo sangley" but legally changed his tax status to the lower-paying *indio* category, so legally both Rizal and his father were considered *indios* (Craig 54). Aguilar suggests that Rizal may have been ambivalent about his own Chinese heritage (626).

16. Aguilar cites the English translation of the first part of this passage without specifying that it was Aguirre who was writing to Rizal (627). The translation glosses over Aguirre's reference to the potential division among the Ilustrados caused by racial classification: "Rizal was said to have deplored 'not having in [his] veins all the blood that could serve as a common bond'" (National Heroes Commission 2: 99, qtd. in Aguirre 627).

17. Rizal refers here to the short-lived periodical *España en Filipinas*.

Works Cited

Aguilar, Filomeno, Jr. "Tracing Origins: *Ilustrado* Nationalism and the Racial Science of Migration Waves." *Journal of Asian Studies* 64.3 (2005): 605–37.

Aguirre, Evaristo [Cauit]. "De 'Cauit' a Rizal." Carta 123, 10 marzo 1887. *Epistolario rizaliano*. Vol. 1 (1877–1887). Ed. Teodoro M. Kalaw. Manila: Biblioteca Nacional de Filipinas, 1930. 5 vols. 234–49.

Anderson, Benedict. *Imagined Communities: Reflections on the Origin and Spread of Nationalism*. New York: Verso, 1983.

———. *The Spectre of Comparisons: Nationalism, Southeast Asia and the World*. New York: Verso, 1998.

———. *Under Three Flags: Anarchism and the Anti-Colonial Imagination*. New York: Verso, 2005.

"Banquete en honor de los pintores Luna e Hidalgo." *El Imparcial* 26 June 1884: 1–2.

Blanco, Alda. "Spain at the Crossroads: Imperial Nostalgia or Modern Colonialism?" *Contracorriente: A Journal of Social History and Literature in Latin America* 5.1 (2007): 1–11.

Blanco, John D. *Frontier Constitutions: Christianity and Colonial Empire in the Nineteenth-Century Philippines*. Berkeley: U of California P, 2009.

Blumentritt, Ferdinand. *An Attempt at Writing a Philippine Ethnography: With an Appendix, the Spanish Maritime Discoveries in Philippine Archipelago (with a Map of the Philippines): Translated from the Original German Text*. Trans. Marcelino N. Maceda. Marawi City: University Research Center, Mindanao State U, 1980.

———. *Mapa etnográfico del Archipiélago filipino*. Madrid: Boletín de la Sociedad Geográfica de Madrid, 1890. Map.

———. *Las razas del archipiélago filipino por Fernando Blumentritt*. Madrid: Estab. tip. de Fortanet, 1890.

Chu, Richard. "The 'Chinese' and 'Mestizos' of the Philippines: Towards a New Interpretation." *Philippine Studies* 50.2 (2002): 327–70.

Coates, Austin. *Rizal: Philippine Nationalist and Martyr*. London: Oxford UP, 1968.

Constitución Política de la Monarquía Española. 1812. Web. 18 March 2015. *www.congreso.es/docu/constituciones/1812/ce1812.pdf*.

Costa, Horacio de la, SJ. *The Trial of Rizal: W. E. Retana's Transcription of the Official Spanish Documents*. Manila: Ateneo de Manila UP, 1961.

Craig, Austin. *Lineage, Life, and Labors of José Rizal, Philippine Patriot*. Manila: Philippine Education Company, 1913. Web.

Cushner, Nicholas P., SJ. *Spain in the Philippines: From Conquest to Revolution*. Quezon City: Ateneo de Manila U, 1971.

Feced, Pablo ("Quioquiap"). "Ellos y nosotros." *El Liberal* 13 Feb. 1887: 3.

———. *Filipinas: Esbozos y Pinceladas*. Manila: Ramírez, 1888.

Fernández, Mauro. "The Representation of Spanish in the Philippines." *A Political History of Spanish: The Making of a Language*. Ed. José del Valle. Cambridge: Cambridge UP, 2013. 364–79.

Fradera, Josep María. *Colonias para después de un imperio*. Barcelona: Bellaterra, 2005.

———. *Filipinas, la colonia más peculiar: La hacienda pública en la definición de la política colonial, 1672–1868*. Madrid: Consejo Superior de Investigaciones Científicas, 1999.

García-Castellón, Manuel, ed. *Estampas y cuentos de la Filipinas hispánica*. Madrid: Libros Clan, 2001.

Goode, Joshua. *Impurity of Blood: Defining Race in Spain, 1870–1930*. Baton Rouge: Louisiana State UP, 2009.

Guerrero, León María. *The First Filipino*. Introd. by Carlos Quirino. 1963. Manila: Guerrero, 2010.

Johnson, Courtney Blaine. *Rewriting the Empire: The Philippines and Filipinos in the Hispanic Cultural Field, 1880–1898*. Diss. U of Texas, Austin, 2004.

Kramer, Paul A. *The Blood of Government: Race, Empire, the United States, and the Philippines*. Chapel Hill: U of North Carolina P, 2006.

Lifshey, Adam. "The Literary Alterities of Philippine Nationalism in José Rizal's *El filibusterismo*." *PMLA* 123.5 (2008): 1434–47.

———. *The Magellan Fallacy: Globalization and the Emergence of Asian and African Literature in Spanish*. Ann Arbor: U Michigan P, 2012.

López Jaena, Graciano. "Los indios de Filipinas." *El Liberal* 16 Feb. 1887: 2.

Matibag, Eugenio. "'El verbo del filibusterismo': Narrative Rules in the Novels of José Rizal." *Revista Hispánica Moderna* 48.2 (1995): 250–64.

Mojares, Resil B. *Brains of the Nation: Pedro Paterno, T. H. Pardo de Tavera, Isabelo de los Reyes and the Production of Modern Knowledge*. Quezon City: Ateneo de Manila UP, 2006.

Morayta, Miguel. "Discurso pronunciado en el banquete dado por la Asociación Hispano-Filipina el 23 de diciembre en honor del señor Becerra." 15 Jan. 1891. *La Solidaridad*. Trans. Guadalupe Fores-Ganzon. Manila: Fundación Santiago, 1996. 3: 10–14.

Morga, Antonio de. *Sucesos de las Islas Filipinas, Obra publicada en México en 1609. Nuevamente sacada a luz y anotada por José Rizal y precedida por un prólogo del profesor Fernando Blumentritt*. Paris: Garnier, 1890. Web. 18 March 2015.

Morillo-Alicea, Javier. "Uncharted Landscapes of 'Latin America': The Philippines in the Spanish Imperial Archipelago." *Interpreting Spanish Colonialism: Empires, Nations and Legends*. Ed. Christopher Schmidt-Nowara and John Nieto-Phillips. Albuquerque: U of New Mexico P, 2005. 25–54.

National Heroes Commission. *Rizal's Correspondence with Fellow Reformists*. Vol. 2, Book 3. Manila: National Heroes Commission, 1963.

Pan-Montojo, Juan, and José Alvarez Junco, eds. *Más se perdió en Cuba: España, 1898 y la crisis de fin de siglo*. Madrid: Alianza, 2006.

Pardo Bazán, Emilia. "La España Remota." *Nuevo Teatro Critico* 1.3 (Mar. 1891): 75–81.

Pardo de Tavera, T. H. "History." *Census of the Philippines, 1903*. Washington, DC: U.S. Bureau of the Census, 1905. 1: 309–418.

Rafael, Vicente L. *The Promise of the Foreign: Nationalism and the Technics of Translation in the Spanish Philippines*. Durham, NC: Duke UP, 2005.

Reed, Robert Ronald. "Hispanic Urbanism in the Philippines: A Study of the Impact of Church and State." *University of Manila Journal of East Asiatic Studies* 11 (1967): 1–222.

Retana, Wenceslao Emilio. *Vida y escritos del dr. José Rizal*. Madrid: Librería General de Victoriano Suárez, 1907.

Reyes, Raquel A. G. *Love, Passion, and Patriotism: Sexuality and the Philippine Propaganda Movement, 1882–1892*. Singapore: NUS Press in association with U of Washington P, 2008.

Rieu-Millán, Marie Laure. *Los diputados americanos en las Cortes de Cádiz (Igualdad o independencia)*. Madrid: Consejo Superior de Investigaciones Científicas, 1990.

Rizal, José. "Carta 15." *Cartas de Rizal a Blumentritt en alemán, 1886–1888*. Vol. 5, part 1, of *Epistolario rizaliano*. Ed. Teodoro M. Kalaw. Trans. Emilio Natividad. Manila: Biblioteca Nacional de Filipinas, 1938. 110–16.

———. "Filipinas dentro de cien años / The Philippines a Century Hence." 15 Dec. 1889. *La Solidaridad*. Trans. Guadalupe Fores-Ganzon. Manila: Fundación Santiago, 1996. 1: 505–13.

———. "Sobre la indolencia del *filipino*." *Escritos políticos e históricos*. Manila: Comisión Nacional de Centenario de José Rizal, 1961. 227–61.

Sánchez Gómez, Luis Angel. "'Ellos y nosotros' y 'Los indios de Filipinas,' artículos de Pablo Feced y Graciano López Jaena (1887)." *Revista Española del Pacífico* 8 (1998): 309–21.

———. *Un imperio en la vitrina: El colonialismo en el Pacífico y la Exposición de Filipinas de 1887*. Madrid: Consejo Superior de Investigaciones Científicas, 2003.

Schmidt-Nowara, Christopher. *The Conquest of History: Spanish Colonialism and National Histories in the Nineteenth Century*. Pittsburgh: U Pittsburgh P, 2006.

Schumacher, John N., SJ. *The Propaganda Movement, 1880–1895: The Creation of a Filipino Consciousness, the Making of the Revolution*. Rev. ed. Quezon City: Ateneo de Manila UP, 1997.

Thomas, Megan C. *Orientalists, Propagandists, and Ilustrados: Filipino Scholarship and the End of Spanish Colonialism*. Minneapolis: U Minnesota P, 2012.

Tolliver, Joyce. "Framing Colonial Manliness, Domesticity, and Empire in 'Página Suelta' and 'Oscuramente.'" *Revista de Estudios Hispánicos* 46.1 (2012): 3–24.

————. "'El heroísmo del escritor': Unamuno, Rizal, y el heroísmo incorpóreo." *Perfiles del heroísmo en la literatura hispánica de entresiglos (XIX–XX)*. Ed. Luis Alvarez Castro and Denise DuPont. Valladolid: Verdelis, 2013. 201–10.

————. "Over Her Bloodless Body: Gender, Race, and the Spanish Colonial Fetish in Pardo Bazán." *Revista Canadiense de Estudios Hispánicos* 34.2 (2010): 285–301.

Wickberg, E. "The Chinese Mestizo in Philippine History." *Journal of Southeast Asian History* 5.1 (1964): 62–100.

PART III

Slavery, Empire, and the Problem of Freedom

6

Spanish Prisoners
War and Captivity in Spain's Imperial Crisis

Christopher Schmidt-Nowara
Tufts University

Between 1808 and the mid-1820s, Spaniards struggled to liberate their country from French rule while also fighting to retain their control over the American colonies, with mixed success. The War of Independence eventually led to France's evacuation of the Iberian Peninsula and the restoration of the Bourbon monarch Ferdinand VII in 1814. The wars in the Americas were much more tortuous. While the monarchy was frequently able to rally supporters to its cause in the early phase of the Spanish American revolutions, the reactionary policies of Ferdinand and his advisors drove a wedge between the metropole and the colonies. Riego's uprising in Cádiz in 1820, Iturbide's declaration of Mexico's independence in 1821, the military defeat at Ayacucho in Peru in 1824, and Britain's recognition of the new republics' independence spelled the end of Spanish dominion, even though the metropole refused diplomatic recognition and mounted several ill-fated invasions. Of the vast American empire only Puerto Rico and Cuba remained after the 1820s, as did the Philippines on the other side of the world. However, while territorially miniscule compared to the continental colonies, the two Caribbean islands, especially Cuba, were undergoing plantation revolutions that paralleled those taking place in the deep south of the United States and the Paraíba Valley in southeastern Brazil.[1] Cuba became the largest slave society in Spanish American history and the source of great wealth for the Spanish state and Spanish investors. Thus, while Spain's American empire was greatly diminished, it was by no means at an end, as retrenchment around the slave trade and sugar plantations in the Caribbean provided a new imperial core (Fradera). The complex and unpredictable restructuring of empire involved not only new economic and spatial contours but also significant ideological adjustments. Spaniards fought to free themselves from foreign domination while also seeking to justify continued rule over millions of American subjects. Even as they sought to establish legal equality among white Spaniards on both sides of the Atlantic in the 1812 constitution, they tried to uphold colonial inequalities by disenfranchising those of African descent. Moreover, the small but vibrant imperial core that emerged by the 1820s relied on the enslavement of hundreds of thousands of African workers forcibly transported across the Atlantic.[2] How did Spaniards negotiate these apparently contradictory aspirations that joined the urge for liberty and equality with the demand for colonial submission and mass slavery?

To explore this question, this chapter addresses the theme of captivity, specifically the experience of prisoners of war, both Spaniards and American royalists, in Europe and the Americas. The literature on captivity in the Hispanic world is extensive,[3] though the work that has most immediately influenced my approach is Linda Colley's study of the shifting meanings of colonial captivity in the British Empire between the seventeenth and nineteenth centuries. As she argues, captives on the edges of empire "mark out the changing boundaries over time of Britain's imperial aggression, and the changing boundaries of its inhabitants' fears, insecurities, and deficiencies" (12). I believe that we can understand how Spaniards responded to the profound changes taking place during the lengthy imperial crisis in similar fashion, as they fought wars, suffered imprisonment, and sought freedom across the European and American continents. In addressing these situations, what I believe will emerge is not the reconstruction of a coherent ideological project but, rather, insights into distinct visions of what it meant for Spaniards to be free and unfree during the Spanish empire's contraction and Cuban slavery's expansion. My conclusions, especially regarding the consequences of captivity in the Americas, are still hypothetical, but I believe they open up an avenue of research into Spanish colonial mentalities in this period of flux and retrenchment, emancipation and enslavement.

Captivity and Antislavery

At least one Spanish author made explicit the connection between Spanish captivity and the burgeoning slave complex in Cuba. Joseph Blanco White was a former Catholic priest who fled his native Seville in 1810 before the invading French troops. He settled in London, converted to Anglicanism, and, with assistance from the British Foreign Office and powerful patrons such as Lord Holland, published the widely read periodical *El Español* (1810–1814), which provided news and commentary on Spanish and Spanish American politics, history, and ideas.[4] In London, Blanco came into contact with a wide range of intellectuals and politicians, including the leading British abolitionist William Wilberforce, whom he greatly admired. He published excerpts of Wilberforce's writings and speeches in *El Español*. He also agreed to translate into Spanish one of his pamphlets, a work that he effectively rewrote to be more in tune with a Spanish reading public. Wilberforce, like most of the leading British abolitionists of the day, was an evangelical Christian who sought to redeem Britain morally by suppressing the trade from Africa to the West Indies (Brown). Though Blanco agreed wholeheartedly with this goal and even shared aspects of this religious outlook during his early years in London, he was well aware that an evangelical argument for abolition would have little purchase among Spaniards.

However, there was other material in Wilberforce's *Letter on the Abolition of the Slave Trade* (1807) that he could inflect and translate into a more familiar idiom (Schmidt-Nowara). Wilberforce's condemnation of the slave trade drew heavily from the work of the explorer Mungo Park, who had traveled through the slaving regions of West Africa. Wilberforce, citing Park, drew attention to warfare—including wars between states and the feuds that divided particular societies—as a means by which Africans fell into captivity in their homelands. Though Park found these situations to be long-standing, Wilberforce, and later Blanco White, emphasized the role of Europeans in directly and indirectly fomenting wars for the sole purpose of reaping yet more captives for the transatlantic slave trade. To those defenders of the slave trade who argued that warfare, feuds, and slave raiding ("village breaking" in Wilberforce's words) were endemic in Africa and took place quite independently of the transatlantic trade, Wilberforce argued that the voracious European and American market for human cargoes had transformed venerable practices: "Though we cannot fairly lay to the charge of the Slave Trade all the wars of Africa, we yet may allege that to the causes which produce wars elsewhere, the Slave Trade superadds one entirely new and constant source of great copiousness and efficiency, while it gives to the wars, which arise from every other cause, a character of peculiar malignity and desolation" (26).

Blanco White was able to make great use of the themes of war and prisoners of war. In discussing how European slavers procured captives in

Africa, described in the first section of his work, he noted: "A great part of the slaves purchased by Europeans are prisoners of war. . . . The desire to capture prisoners to sell to the Europeans is a powerful incentive to war among the Africans" (75). Like Wilberforce, and Thomas Clarkson, who had carried out wide research on the business of the British slave trade among veterans of the traffic, Blanco White insisted that the presence, demands, and outright interference of European factors and ship captains routinely influenced warfare and slavery in Africa:

> The case of two substantial towns on the banks of the Calabar River will serve as an example. These towns had been in conflict for some time but tired of the evils of war they tried to make peace and to confirm it with marriages between young people from either town. Unfortunately for them, slaving vessels arrived on the coast. . . . The prospect of peace made the captains desperate so they tried to block it. Through the most diabolical means they incited both towns and taking the side of one of them they killed many of the inhabitants, and they took many others as the prize for their services. (79)[5]

Warfare and prisoners of war figured significantly in Blanco's depiction of the slave trade not only because they did in the writings of Wilberforce, Clarkson, and Park, but also because he hoped that the Spanish war against the French might turn Spaniards against the slave trade. Just as the Africans had suffered enslavement at the hands of European intruders, so Spaniards had fallen prisoner to and been marched far from their homes by the French invaders. Blanco White made this connection explicit in his final plea to Spanish readers:

> Do not forget that you too have seen foreigners set foot in your homeland. Leave in peace that of others. Leave those unhappy Africans the scarce portion of goods that Heaven has bestowed on their land. Leave them in peace so that they can advance little by little along the road of civilization. Just because they are poor and ignorant, can you treat them worse than you would the beasts in the wilderness? They are poor and ignorant. But the same blood runs in their veins that runs in yours. The tears that their eyes shed are just like yours. Like you, they are parents, children, and siblings. Martyrs of Spanish patriotism! . . . From this day forward stop the *Spaniards* from going to the coast of

Africa where they surpass in cruelty and injustice those invaders
that destroyed your soul. You, who know what it is to have [your
families] ripped from your homes by foreign soldiers, leave to the
father his children, and to the husband his wife. (195–96)

Even as he drew a broad parallel between the condition of Spaniards
and Africans, Blanco White spoke from quite immediate and intimate
knowledge: his own family's experience of warfare, exile, and captivity
brought about by the French occupation of the Iberian Peninsula. The
most stunning development for the Blancos was the capture of Joseph's
younger brother Fernando in Madrid in 1808. Fernando joined a unit of
Seville volunteers and marched to Madrid, which the French had evacuated
after unexpected setbacks during the early months of the invasion. However, in the autumn of that year, the French, led personally by Napoleon
Bonaparte, routed Spanish forces in the capital's environs and retook the
city on December 4. Fernando was one of the many Spanish soldiers and
officers taken prisoner that very day.[6] He would spend the next five years
of his life as a prisoner of war in the environs of Dijon and Chalon-sur-
Saône, among the nearly sixty thousand Spaniards held prisoner in France
by the end of the war (Aymes 109–16). Not until the allied armies invaded
France in early 1814 would he find an opportunity to escape. Then, under allied protection, he and several other Spanish officers crossed eastern
France, Switzerland, Germany, and the Netherlands before finally reaching
England, where Fernando was reunited with his brother Joseph.

During his long captivity, Fernando wrote regularly to his parents and
to his brother. Though the correspondence is regular, uncertainty and
anxiety fill the pages as he asked if his letters had arrived, if there were
letters that he should expect from the family but somehow missed, and,
most importantly, if they were sending funds to support him. These letters
convey the account of his capture, the forced march from Madrid to Bur-
gundy, his hunger, disorientation, and sense of abandonment, all elements
that would reverberate through Joseph's depiction and attack on the slave
traffic. In one of his letters home Fernando tells his family that in the first
months of his captivity he was "dying of hunger" until they were able to
supply him with funds. He also described the hard march to eastern France
after being captured in Madrid:

They would give us bread and meat when there was some, and
we would cook it with water and some times with salt. Everyday
we walked seven leagues on foot . . . and on the days when the

march was long they would not allow us any rest on the road
so that it was necessary to eat a piece of black bread, like *pan de
munición*, while walking. The cold was insufferable, as strong as
here, and the ice so hard that we stumbled with every step. To
sleep on the ground was now customary.[7]

Only the family's support saved him from the most abject suffering:
"My brother wrested me from misery though not from slavery, by sending
me aid from his own pocket. . . . Every hour of the day that I look from my
window and see myself surrounded by snow and ice and then turn my eyes
to my stove, finding myself free from the cold, I feel myself moved upon
thinking that this and so much more I owe to you who have given me the
means and to my brother who has sent them to me."[8]

Fernando's captivity was clearly not the same as capture in Africa or enslavement in Cuba: he was not sold as property, and his captivity, though
protracted, was temporary, not hereditary. His letters and diary say nothing of physical abuse at the hands of his captors, but he did express fear
that he might suffer the same fate as that of Spanish officers who tried to
escape: imprisonment in the Fortress of Joux in the Jura Mountains (the
place where Napoleon imprisoned Toussaint Louverture, who perished
there in 1803).[9] Since he had given his word of honor that he would not
seek to escape, he was at liberty to rent a room in the home of a local family
and was free to move within a certain radius from the town. He received
letters and financial support from his family so that he could purchase
food, acquire clothing, and pay his rent, though, as the uncertain and at
times desperate tone of the letters indicates, such contact was tenuous under the circumstances of war.

Rather than drawing a literal comparison between Fernando's captivity
and African slavery, I am arguing that Fernando's experience of captivity,
and Joseph's own exile, made Joseph more receptive to abolitionism and
provided him a means by which to translate imaginatively Wilberforce's
evangelical outlook into a parallel situation more immediately comprehensible to Spanish readers struggling against the French. Blanco reworked
materials already present in the *Letter* to establish connections between enslaved Africans and imprisoned Spaniards. Wilberforce's work relied extensively on Park's reports that described the mechanics of the West African
slave trade in vivid detail: warfare, long overland marches, the separation
of captives from their families and homes, and the want and uncertainty
that they endured. In Blanco's hands, these stories of capture and enslavement merged easily with his attacks on the French occupation of Spain. He

was betting that the many Spaniards with personal knowledge of invasion, war, exile, and captivity could share his outrage that because of other Spaniards, Africans were "torn from their homeland, deprived of their parents, children, and siblings, and transported to a remote region, without hope of returning to the country where they were born!" (91).

Blanco White gambled that equating the plight of Spanish and African captives would sway the views of Spaniards against the slave trade, a more likely impetus than the evangelical Christianity that motivated Wilberforce, Clarkson, and the mass antislavery movement in Britain. After all, thousands of Spaniards found themselves taken prisoner by the French invaders between 1808 and 1814. At the same time, Spaniards were falling prisoner to American armies in the independence wars on the other side of the Atlantic. Thus, he appealed to an experience that was widespread throughout the Hispanic world during those years. But would that experience of captivity provoke empathy with the enslaved, as Blanco White hoped? And was it likely to resonate in the Americas, where prisoners of war would undoubtedly have direct knowledge of slavery (and might have been slave owners), unlike most peninsular Spaniards? A brief glance at Spanish accounts of captivity during the Spanish American revolutions suggests that quite different sentiments were taking shape.

Captivity and Barbarism

When Fernando finally reached safety in England in 1814, he showed little inclination to return to Seville. He enjoyed the company of his brother and his circle of friends. He was also interested in earning his living and learning his trade in Britain, which was more promising than in war-torn Spain. Fernando insisted to his parents that his prospects were much brighter working in a commercial house in England. In Spain, he could only hope to stagnate as a junior officer in the Spanish army or, even worse, "go to America to wage a horrible war, that is, if it is still being fought."[10] Fernando clearly knew that his fate as an officer, or prisoner, in the Americas would have been quite different from the one he met during his captivity in France and his sojourn through Napoleon's crumbling European empire.

One reason for this divergence was that the movements for political independence in Spanish America, sparked by the overthrow of the Bourbon monarchy in 1808, became thoroughgoing social revolutions. Historians of Latin America once treated the Spanish American revolutions as essentially conservative movements that left the social structures of colonialism intact;

they now see the wars of independence as deeply disruptive and radical, challenging in several ways the forms of servitude, legal discrimination, and political disenfranchisement that had characterized the Spanish colonial regimes, inequalities that Spaniards sought to uphold even in the liberal Constitution of 1812. For example, it is clear that the independence movements spelled the death knell of slavery in the colonies that successfully broke from Spain (but not in Cuba and Puerto Rico, which remained loyal). The widespread participation of enslaved people, amply documented recently by Peter Blanchard, forced leaders such as Simón Bolívar not only to free large numbers of slaves but also to pass abolition laws in the new republics, though gradual in nature, and to ban the slave traffic. By the 1850s, slavery was abolished in almost all of independent Spanish America.[11] Politically, the broad social participation in the protracted military struggles led to regimes that were nominally committed to racial democracy and the suppression of the legal racial handicaps of the colonial era, though the goal of republican equality and "harmony" was more often an ideal than a reality.[12]

Spanish loyalists thus found themselves in a world being turned upside down, as the norms and privileges that had governed colonial life came under attack, not only through legal and political changes but also through direct physical violence as revolutionaries and counterrevolutionaries struck at one another with remarkable cruelty.[13] In the early phases of the conflict in Venezuela, Mexico, the Río de la Plata, and Nueva Granada, both sides committed massacres, not only of military prisoners but also of civilians, as a form of political terror intended to ensure loyalty, quiescence, or flight. Simón Bolívar explained this dynamic of violence and terror to the British governor of Curaçao who was urging him to exercise clemency toward his Spanish prisoners: "I resolved to put in effect a war to the death, in order to deprive the tyrants of the incomparable advantage of their organized methods of destruction" (40).[14]

Even those Spaniards and royalist Americans who avoided executions nonetheless experienced a form of captivity quite different from Fernando's.[15] Fernando, like many officers in Europe, had given his word of honor that he would not escape from his imprisonment so was permitted to lodge with a family close to the main depot of Spanish prisoners. Other officers lived under similar conditions, though their range of movement contracted as the war turned against France. At one point in his captivity, Fernando even asked his parents for money to study in Paris! Though those possibilities soon diminished, he still read widely, studied mathematics, played music, took long walks, and fraternized with other Spaniards, several of whom were old friends from Seville.

While he spoke the language of enslavement and liberation, his captivity was mild when compared to that of a group of royalist officers in the Río de la Plata,[16] who related their experience to Spain's ambassador in Rio de Janeiro, which, along with Montevideo, was the nerve center of Spanish royalism and counterrevolution in the region.[17] Captivity was not novel in this region of Spanish America; since early colonization, settlers had routinely suffered captivity by Indians and continued to do so well into the independence period in the vast open lands of the Argentine frontier (Socolow). Settlers understood Indian captivity as the triumph of barbarism over civilization; Spanish officials and soldiers held prisoner by revolutionary forces described their experiences in like terms. In contrast to Fernando Blanco White's sedentary residence in the vicinity of Chalon-sur-Saône, Ambrosio del Gallo, Juan Michelana, and Antonio Fernández de Villamil recounted forced marches through the interior of Argentina, processions through towns where the populace mocked and beat them, and internment in prisons and camps, most notoriously Las Bruscas, located to the south of Buenos Aires in the wilderness, where almost one thousand Spanish and American royalist prisoners were held, many of them captured at the battles of Chacabuco and Maipú in Chile in 1817 and 1818, though others, including Ambrosio del Gallo, had been prisoners for much longer. The authors of the account told of the struggles at Las Bruscas to build shelters and to forage for fuel to cook their meager rations. Like the Blancos on the other side of the ocean, the escapees from the camp equated imprisonment with enslavement. The prisoners "were groaning under a hard slavery" at Las Bruscas, while many Spanish and American captives "still moaned under the terrible iron yoke that oppressed them." After more than a decade of war and turmoil, the Buenos Aires revolutionaries continued to "ridicule them, injure them, [and] degrade them, especially with blows from the lash."[18]

Fear of beatings, summary executions, and massacres permeated the account, this anxiety accentuated by rumors of a large Spanish expeditionary force destined for Buenos Aires and the belief that the revolutionary government would execute all possible allies of the Spanish invaders (Mariluz Urquijo 59–74; Galmarini). Such fears were far from idle. In February 1819, the *Gaceta de Buenos Aires* reproduced reports of a massacre of royalist prisoners held in San Luis in Chile by the commander Vicente Dupuy.[19] Dupuy informed his superiors that the "European Spaniards have presented a new scene of horror, ingratitude, and barbarism." Six officers gathered before Dupuy and after cordial greetings denounced him and pounced on him, knives in hand. Dupuy managed to escape their initial attack, killing one of his assailants. Though he suffered wounds, he was saved by the people of San Luis, who, when they detected the assassination attempt and the simultaneous attack by prisoners on the barracks, responded "as if by an electric explosion, and armed themselves." They burst into Dupuy's quarters, at which point his would-be assassins implored him to protect them from the wrath of the mob. Instead, "I ordered that their throats be cut on the spot." The same fate befell Spanish officers who were in their barracks or who were lodged in the town. Dupuy included a list of more than twenty-five Spanish prisoners killed in the reprisal and promised a thorough investigation of the plot, whose origins he believed lay in prison camps in Mendoza and beyond that in Montevideo, where Spaniards plotted the counterrevolution. News of the events at San Luis reached the prisoners at Las Bruscas (Galmarini 119–20), who anticipated a similar fate when their guards rousted them for a long march to another camp in Mendoza on March 3. The prisoners were sure they would never reach Mendoza alive, perishing either because of hunger, cold, and weakness or because their captors would "never allow us to reach [Mendonza] but instead execute their vengeful intentions during our journey."[20] However, as they awaited their fate on the road to Mendoza, some unknowable twist of government policy in Buenos Aires led them back to Las Bruscas, where they were once again plunged into miserable suffering.

The violence and uncertainty of captivity lodged in the memories of those who survived the ordeal, if the later account of Ambrosio del Gallo is any indication. Del Gallo recalled his travails again some twenty years later when he was a senior officer in Manila, where he served the crown for more than fifteen years. In his *hoja de servicio*, the record and narrative of his military service, dated 25 May 1841, del Gallo described at length his experience as a captive in the Río de la Plata.[21] Born in Extremadura of noble status in 1779, del Gallo started his military service as a cadet in 1795 and was almost immediately thrown into action against the French. He served the patriot cause during the War of Independence and then shipped to Montevideo in 1813 as an officer in the Second American Regiment. The city was besieged by insurgent forces and surrendered in June 1814. Del Gallo and other officers, instead of being shipped back to Spain as they expected, were held as prisoners by the Buenos Aires government and moved about the vast region for the next six years. In an itinerary that covered hundreds, if not thousands, of miles, del Gallo was moved to the town of Salto and then to the distant western provinces of Cuyo and Córdoba. In 1817, while being held near the Abipones reduction, he made his first escape, to Santa Fe on the Paraná River, whence he fled by boat to

Montevideo but there was returned to his captors, who took him practically naked to Buenos Aires and held him for "42 days in a dungeon," after which he and a group of other prisoners were interned in Las Bruscas. His attempt to escape from the camp in 1818 was short-lived, and, as punishment, he "was taken to Buenos Aires and held for 22 days in shackles" before being returned to Las Bruscas where his captors put him and other officers in "chains and collar." He finally escaped in 1820 to Montevideo, where he would pen the urgent pleas to the Spanish minister in Rio de Janeiro, but he would not return to Spain until 1824, and then only briefly before being shipped out to Manila in 1825.

Captivity, Slavery, and Empire's End (and Renewal)

These admittedly highly selective accounts of captivity during war in Europe and the Americas offer some insight into how Spaniards responded to the profound political, social, and economic transformations to the imperial order taking place in the early nineteenth century. Joseph Blanco White, ensconced in the reformist and abolitionist milieu of London, could use his brother Fernando's imprisonment as a means to defend natural freedom and equality. Fernando's—and, by extension, all of Spain's—captivity under the French was an exact parallel to the escalating enslavement of Africans in Cuba. In this case, captivity during the imperial crisis led to abolitionism and an attack on the slave traffic to Cuba and the thriving plantation complex: freedom for Spaniards meant freedom for all. Other Spaniards shared Blanco's hatred of the slave traffic to Cuba, but their objections, voiced in pamphlets like Blanco's *Bosquejo* and in parliamentary debates during the resistance to the French, lost out to slavery's defenders in Cuba and in Spain. Indeed, as the empire crumbled and the slave trade burgeoned, Cuban and Spanish proslavery advocates began to voice robust defenses of the new colonial order taking shape in the Caribbean; by the end of empire in continental America in the 1820s, proslavery thought was ascendant. Proponents of slavery and the transatlantic slave trade, such as the Cubans Francisco de Arango y Parreño and Juan Bernardo O'Gavan, argued that slavery as practiced in Cuba was humane and civilizing and that African captives transported across the ocean were in fact being rescued from a worse fate in their native lands. Perversely, they presented captivity and slavery as a form of emancipation.[22]

Yet, we should not take this ideological victory for granted even though it represented the views of powerful economic and political forces on both sides of the Atlantic, as planters, merchants, and slavers reaped great fortunes from the developing Cuban plantation complex and the suddenly diminished Spanish state found ample colonial revenues. For centuries, Spain had resisted full-blown involvement in the transatlantic slave trade for a variety of institutional, geopolitical, and ideological reasons. The newly deregulated traffic (inaugurated in 1789) to Cuba upset a colonial equilibrium formed since the sixteenth century.[23] Blanco's attack on the slave trade gave voice to the many Spaniards who saw this change in the colonial order as noxious.

Nonetheless, many Spaniards adapted to the new order in the Caribbean, and I believe that warfare in the Americas helped them to do so. We know that many of the leading Spanish military figures in nineteenth-century Cuba and Puerto Rico hailed from the group called the Ayacuchos, in reference to the decisive military defeat in Peru in 1824.[24] Governors such as Miguel de Tacón and Gerónimo Valdés were defenders of constitutional government in the peninsula and agents of despotism in the colonies who oversaw a flourishing illegal slave trade to Cuba. They accommodated themselves to this situation, and helped to bring it about, because of their desire to defend Spain's last, and economically vital, colonial territories. However, I would suggest that the experience of war and captivity also shaped Spanish views and decisions in the last colonies, not just among the most elite politico-military figures but also among the many soldiers, officers, bureaucrats, and planters who concentrated on the islands from the 1820s onward. They had lived through the inversion of the colonial order and witnessed slaves struggling to free themselves, free people of color aspiring to equality, and creole elites, their supposed brethren, declaring war to the death against peninsular Spaniards. Some who had experienced captivity by revolutionary forces had seen their privileges and status stripped away and claimed that they were reduced to slavery.

For this reason, I believe that the accounts from the Río de la Plata and Chile are significant, as they show us something quite different from Blanco's antislavery perspective, though I admit to making something of a stretch by connecting the diverse regions of the empire. The authors of the "Breve resumen," in describing their harsh internment at Las Bruscas and recounting the possibility of sudden death at the hands of their captors, as had occurred at San Luis, understood their captivity as a descent into barbarism, a state of affairs engendered by the revolutions in the Americas. The revolution of Buenos Aires sanctioned violence against Spaniards and American royalists, and no one felt the revolutionary fury more than the prisoners of war: "Toward [the prisoners] their barbarism and cruelty have been taken to the extreme. They have taken pleasure in subjecting them to every kind of grief, beating them and degrading them through methods unknown to even the most savage tribes."[25]

In this account, captivity led not to an emancipatory perspective on the upheavals of the era but rather a counterrevolutionary fear of political violence and social turmoil that included a strong subtext of humiliation and dishonor. My hypothesis, admittedly tentative, is that as Spain renewed colonial rule after its military and political defeat in the mainland American colonies, this attitude toward colonial subjects, grounded in experiences of terror and dishonor, would prevail among the rulers. Maintaining a new order of colonial absolutism, plantation slavery, and other regimes of forced labor in the Caribbean and the Pacific became a matter not only of fomenting colonial and metropolitan prosperity but also of protecting civility and honor against the forces of revolution and barbarism confronted and recounted by Spanish captives during the long years of brutal warfare and social change in Spanish America.

Notes

My thanks to Billy Acree and Akiko Tsuchiya for their invitation to take part in the symposium "Empire's End" and to Jeremy Adelman, Iver Bernstein, Peter Blanchard, and Álvaro Caso Bello for their comments on an earlier version of this chapter. Thanks also for the helpful comments from the participants at the American Historical Association's annual meeting in New Orleans and the University of Buffalo's Humanities Institute. Support for research and writing came from two Spanish government grants, numbers HAR2009-07103 and HAR2012-32510.

1. On the expansion of slavery in the nineteenth century, see Moreno Fraginals; Berlin; Tomich, *Prism*; Bérbel, Marquese, and Parron; and Fradera and Schmidt-Nowara.
2. The 1820s and the 1830s were the peak decades of the slave trade to Cuba. According to the Trans-Atlantic Slave Trade Database, the 1820s saw some 136,381 slaves disembarked on the island, the 1830s 186,179. See the estimates at *www.slavevoyages.org*.
3. See Amelang for an overview in the context of early modern Spanish "ego documents." For a recent treatment of this genre, see Buscaglia Salgado.
4. The bibliography on Blanco White is extensive, but the best starting point is Murphy.
5. Blanco White culled this anecdote from Clarkson.
6. On the military situation in Spain, see Esdaile.
7. Letter to Guillermo Blanco y Morrogh and María Gertrudis Crespo y

Neve, dated Dijon, 28 Feb. 1810, Blanco White Family Collection; 1713–1930 (mostly 1798–1841), Manuscripts Division, Department of Rare Books and Special Collections, Princeton University Library (hereafter BWFC), box 7, file 4.

8. Letter dated Chalons SS Enero de 1813, BWFC, box 9, file 6.

9. Fernando related to his family how his friend Juan María Maestre was imprisoned at the fortress after an escape attempt: "El pobre Juan María emprendió un viage muy arriesgado que le ha costado su total libertad. Irá a un castillo, y lo peor es que no tiene un quarto. Al momento le he mandado lo que he podido." See letter dated Chalons SS 10 November 1812, BWFC, Box 9, File 6.

10. Letter to his parents dated London, 23 April 1814, BWFC, box 9, file 6.

11. Among independent republics, the outlier by mid-century was Paraguay, which had abolition imposed from outside by the Brazilian Empire, the greatest slaveholding regime in the history of Latin America, at the end of the Paraguayan War in 1869. For perspectives on Spanish American independence and slavery, see Andrews; Blanchard.

12. For a cogent synthesis, see Andrews chs. 2 and 3. For a careful local study of these political and social dynamics, see Lasso.

13. Adelman makes an effort to explain and explore the uses of violence. See also Thibaud; Racine; and Fradkin.

14. See also the comments in O'Leary (64–65) on Bolívar's decision to have eight hundred Spanish prisoners executed in La Guaira and Caracas in 1814.

15. The fact that many prisoners taken by the independence forces were Americans, not Spaniards, raises the interesting question of identity and loyalty during the revolutions, a theme that Colley explores in her study of the American revolution (ch. 7).

16. "Breve resumen de los padecimientos de los oficiales realistas prisioneros bajo el gobierno subversivo de Buenos Aires," Montevideo, 5 Oct. 1820, Archivo Histórico Nacional (Madrid), Estado, legajo 3769, box 1.

17. An excellent study of Spanish plotting in the region is Mariluz Urquijo.

18. "Breve resumen."

19. *Gazeta de Buenos Ayres* 22 Feb. 1819, extraordinary issue.

20. "Breve resumen."

21. Archivo General Militar de Segovia, Sección Primera, legajo G-319.

22. See Berbel, Marquese, and Parron chs. 2 and 3; and Fradera chs. 2 and 3. See also Tomich "Wealth"; and González-Ripoll and Álvarez Cuartero.

23. Explained in Delgado. See also Russell-Wood on Spanish theological

and legal qualms about the Portuguese slave trade in the sixteenth century.
24. The classic account is Pérez de la Riva. See also Fradera ch. 2; Navarro García; and Sobrevilla Perea.
25. "Breve resumen."

Works Cited

Adelman, Jeremy. "The Rites of Statehood: Violence and Sovereignty in Spanish America, 1789–1821." *Hispanic American Historical Review* 90.3 (2010): 391–422.

Amelang, James S. "L'autobiografia popolare nella Spagna moderna: Osservazioni generali e particolari." *Memoria, famiglia, identità tra Italia ed Europa nell'età moderna.* Ed. Giovanni Ciappelli. Bologna: Il Mulino, 2009. 113–30.

Andrews, George Reid. *Afro-Latin America, 1800–2000.* New York: Oxford UP, 2004.

Aymes, Jean-René. *Los españoles en Francia (1808–1814): La deportación bajo el Primer Imperio.* Trans. Araceli Ramos Martín. Madrid: Siglo XXI, 1987.

Bérbel, Marcia, Rafael Marquese, and Tâmis Parron. *Escravidão e política: Brasil e Cuba, c. 1790–1850.* São Paulo: Hucitec/FAPESP, 2010.

Berlin, Ira. *Generations of Captivity: A History of African-American Slaves.* Cambridge, MA: Harvard UP, 2003.

Blanchard, Peter. *Under the Flags of Freedom: Slave Soldiers and the Wars of Independence in Spanish South America.* Pittsburgh: U of Pittsburgh P, 2008.

Blanco White, José María. *Bosquejo del comercio de esclavos y reflexiones sobre este tráfico considerado moral, política y cristianamente.* Ed. Manuel Moreno Alonso. Seville: Alfar, 1999.

Bolívar, Simón. *Selected Writings.* Ed. Vicente Lecuna and Harold A. Bierck Jr. Trans. Lewis Bertrand. Vol. 1. New York: Colonial, 1951.

Brown, Christopher Leslie. *Moral Capital: Foundations of British Abolitionism.* Chapel Hill: U of North Carolina P, 2006.

Buscaglia Salgado, José Francisco. Introduction. *Infortunios de Alonso Ramírez.* By Carlos de Sigüenza y Góngora. Madrid: Consejo Superior de Investigaciones Científicas, 2011. 11–106.

Clarkson, Thomas. *The History of the Abolition of the African Slave-Trade.* 2 vols. London: L. Taylor, 1808.

Colley, Linda. *Captives: Britain, Empire, and the World, 1600–1850.* New York: Anchor, 2002.

Delgado, Josep M. "The Slave Trade in the Spanish Empire (1501–1808): The Shift from Periphery to Center." Fradera and Schmidt-Nowara 13–42.

Esdaile, Charles. *The Peninsular War: A New History*. Basingstroke: Palgrave Macmillan, 2003.

Fradera, Josep M. *Colonias para después de un imperio*. Barcelona: Bellaterra, 2005.

Fradera, Josep M., and Christopher Schmidt-Nowara, eds. *Slavery and Antislavery in Spain's Atlantic Empire*. New York: Berghahn Books, 2013.

Fradkin, Raúl O. "Los usos de la violencia: la campaña de Buenos Aires durante la década de 1810 vista a través de los sumarios y partes militares." *Illes i Imperis* 15 (2013): 11–27.

Galmarini, Hugo Raúl. "Los prisioneros realistas en el Río de la Plata: breve historia de sus desventuras." *Revista de Indias* 179 (1987): 103–22.

González-Ripoll, Ma. Dolores, and Izaskun Álvarez Cuartero, eds. *Francisco Arango y la invención de la Cuba azucarera*. Salamanca: Ediciones Universidad de Salamanca, 2009.

Lasso, Marixa. *Myths of Harmony: Race and Republicanism during the Age of Revolution, Colombia, 1795–1831*. Pittsburgh: U of Pittsburgh P, 2007.

Mariluz Urquijo, José María. *Los proyectos españoles para reconquistar el Río de la Plata (1820–1833)*. Buenos Aires: Perrot, 1958.

Moreno Fraginals, Manuel. *El ingenio: Complejo económico social cubano del azúcar*. Barcelona: Crítica, 2001.

Murphy, Martin. *Blanco White: Self-Banished Spaniard*. London: Yale UP, 1989.

Navarro García, Jesús Raúl. *Puerto Rico a la sombra de la independencia continental: Fronteras ideológicas y políticas en el Caribe, 1815–1840*. Seville: Escuela de Estudios Hispano-Americanos, 1999.

O'Leary, Daniel Florencio. *Bolívar and the War of Independence*. Trans. and ed. Robert F. McNerney Jr. Austin: U of Texas P, 1970.

Pérez de la Riva, Juan. Introduction. *Correspondencia reservada del Capitán General Don Miguel Tacón con el gobierno de Madrid, 1834–1836: el General Tacón y su época*. Havana: Consejo Nacional de Cultura, 1963.

Racine, Karen. "Message by Massacre: Venezuela's War to the Death, 1810–1814." *Journal of Genocide Research* 15.2 (2013): 201–17.

Russell-Wood, A. J. R. "Iberian Expansion and the Issue of Black Slavery: Changing Portuguese Attitudes." *American Historical Review* 83.1 (1978): 16–42.

Schmidt-Nowara, Christopher. "Wilberforce Spanished: Joseph Blanco White and Spanish Antislavery, 1808–1814." Fradera and Schmidt-Nowara 158–75.

Sobrevilla Perea, Natalia. "From Europe to the Andes and back: Becoming 'Los Ayacuchos.'" *European History Quarterly* 41.3 (2011): 472–88.

Socolow, Susan. "Spanish Captives in Indian Societies: Cultural Contact along the Argentine Frontier, 1600–1835." *Hispanic American Historical Review* 72.1 (1992): 73–99.

Thibaud, Clément. "'Coupé têtes, brûlé cazes': Peur et désirs d'Haiti dans l'Amérique de Bolívar." *Annales. Histoire, Sciences Sociales* 58.2 (2003): 305–31.

Tomich, Dale. *Through the Prism of Slavery: Labor, Capital, and World Economy.* Lanham, MD: Rowman and Littlefield, 2004.

———. "The Wealth of Empire: Francisco Arango y Parreño, Political Economy, and the Second Slavery in Cuba." *Interpreting Spanish Colonialism: Empires, Nations, and Legends.* Ed. Christopher Schmidt-Nowara and John Nieto-Phillips. Albuquerque: U of New Mexico P, 2005. 55–85.

Wilberforce, William. *A Letter on the Abolition of the Slave Trade: Addressed to the Freeholders and Other Inhabitants of Yorkshire.* London: T. Cadell and W. Davies, 1807.

7

Empire's End, Long Live the Empire
The Rise and Fall of Empires in the Spanish Caribbean in the Nineteenth Century

William Luis
Vanderbilt University

I

The title of this chapter parodies the words pronounced by the duc d'Uzes upon the death of the French king Charles VI and the coronation of his son Charles VII in 1422. This now-famous phrase was uttered to indicate a change of government, but also to ensure a succession of power. Since then, many monarchies have followed this tradition of change and continuity. I draw a similar relationship between the decline in power Spain exercised over the Spanish Caribbean and the rise of the United States at the end of the nineteenth century to fill a power vacuum in the same region. While my analogy refers to two different powers, I want to underscore how the rise of one empire replaced the decline of the previous one, and how each contributed to the formation of Caribbean culture and identity forged in the colonies but also in the empire. The death of Charles VI invokes the downfall of Spain's colonial rule, and the ascension of Charles VII represents the newfound authority of the United States as a neocolonial center. The change in power structure closes the nineteenth century and opens the twentieth century, or, in Viconian terms, ends one cycle and begins a new one.[1]

Though Spain was the primary colonial authority of the New World, measured by the size of its overseas territories and the number of countries that speak Spanish or Castilian, its supremacy began to wane at the start of the nineteenth century. The decline was precipitated by the Napoleonic Wars, the deposition of Ferdinand VII, the disintegration of the "Supreme Central and Governmental Junta of Spain and the Indies," and the ratification of the liberal Constitution of 1812.[2] This chain of events produced local juntas and independence movements that spread throughout the Spanish American colonies, one falling after the other in rapid succession and emerging as independent republics.

Not all the colonies followed the trend evident on the American continent. The exceptions were the Caribbean territories of Cuba, Puerto Rico, and the Dominican Republic. Cuba had a fledging independence movement that coincided with similar uprisings in Cuba's sister territories: Cuban historians point to Joaquín Infante and his valiant effort to propose an early constitution and to declare Cuba a sovereign state. Moreover, during the Aponte Conspiracy of 1812, blacks with some whites were accused of plotting to turn Cuba into another independent and black nation like the neighboring country of Haiti to the east. The leaders of the first insurrection were imprisoned and deported; those of the second were hung and decapitated, and their heads were displayed in public spaces. There were other movements, such as the Soles y Rayos de Bolívar, founded by José Francisco Lemus in 1821, whose list of distinguished members included the Cuban poet José María Heredia, and Narciso López's annexationist movement of 1848, which made incursions into Cuba with the participation of the Cuban novelist Cirilo Villaverde.[3]

Puerto Rican scholars point to later events, and they underscore the collaboration of Ramón Emeterio Betances and Segundo Ruiz Belvis in Betances's Secret Abolitionist Society of 1856 to fight slavery in Puerto Rico. They also highlight El Grito de Lares of 1868: in exile, Betances and Ruiz Belvis organized an uprising in which opponents of the colonial government occupied the town of Ponce but later abandoned their plans when they met with severe resistance from colonial authorities (Wagenheim). In both Cuba and Puerto Rico, the Spanish government fought to protect the remnants of a glorious empire and the valuable sugar production and markets they controlled. The case of the Dominican Republic was different. The Spanish colony shared the island of Hispaniola with the newly created black Republic of Haiti, but its territorial status was altered when President Jean-Pierre Boyer invaded the eastern part of the island and unified the country under one rule in 1822, a period that is best captured by the closing moments of Alejo Carpentier's *The Kingdom of This World* (1949). Therefore, the Dominican Republic does not celebrate its independence from Spain but from Haiti, in 1844. To preserve its "independence" from Haiti, Dominican leaders sought reannexation to the flagging Spanish empire in 1861.

The end of the Spanish empire coincided with the beginning of US dominion over Spanish territories in the Caribbean. However, the process started much earlier. As I have mentioned, the nineteenth century witnessed movements for independence in Spanish territories, spearheaded by Simón Bolívar and José de San Martín. With Spain weakened, the United States and European nations looked beyond their geographic borders to maximize their gains during this period. To counter foreign incursion in the New World, the celebrated Monroe Doctrine of 1823 proclaimed America for the Americans. Indeed, there were common interests between the United States and its immediate neighbors to the south.[4] The south and southeastern regions of the emerging power, despite linguistic differences, shared commercial, social, economic, political, racial, and cultural interests with other slave territories of the Caribbean. The Knights of the Golden Circle, under the direction of General George Bickley, proposed in 1846 to acquire a "circle" of land with its capital in Havana and whose rim encompassed Mexico, Central America, the Caribbean, and the southern part of the United States, all designated to be slave territories (Crenshaw). The bold plan included gaining control of Mexico and dividing it into fifteen new slave states, thus shifting the balance in Congress to favor slave-holding states growing crops such as cotton, sugar, tobacco, and coffee (May).

The transfer of power from Spain to the United States unfolded gradually toward the second half of the nineteenth century as the US government spread its sphere of influence to become a continental and world power, an idea made popular by John O'Sullivan's Manifest Destiny, a God-given right to spread democracy (Sampson). Texas's declaration of independence from Mexico in 1836 and the US annexation of the State of Texas in 1845 were the first steps in obtaining land from Mexico. The Treaty of Guadalupe Hidalgo of 1848 added more than half of Mexico's national territory to the United States; the land was divided into the present-day states of California, Nevada, and Utah, as well as large portions of Arizona, New Mexico, Colorado, and Wyoming (Griswold de Castillo). And after its Civil War, the United States emerged as a strong world power and set its sights on the islands of the Caribbean.

Presidents of different administrations, dating back to the presidency of Thomas Jefferson (1805) and including that of James Polk (1848), favored a geopolitical strategy that incorporated the island of Cuba. James Monroe's secretary of state, John Quincy Adams, considered the acquisition of neighboring islands a natural outcome of political events.[5] The long-overdue plan was finally accomplished during McKinley's tenure, when the United States moved swiftly to control Cuba and Puerto Rico, as well as the Philippines and Guam. At the conclusion of the Spanish-American War, which for Cubans lasted from 1895 to 1898, Puerto Rico became a colony of the United States and Cuba an economic, political, and military dependency, as the Platt Amendment to Cuba's Constitution of 1901 indicated. In so doing, the Treaty of Paris placed the final nail in the coffin of the Spanish empire and sent Spanish cultural pride into a tailspin. The Generation of 98, a group of Spanish writers, was marked by the loss of these possessions, which produced a need to promote Spanish isolationism (Carr).

Cuba was the prized possession of the Spanish empire, and the island also became an important asset for the emerging empire of the United States. As the largest island in the Caribbean, Cuba played a fundamental geographic and strategic role; it was located near the US coast, and any country controlling the island could also gain access to the United States. In addition, Cuba was Spain's most profitable colony at a time during which Cuban sugar was the most valuable commodity in the world. An increased slave population guaranteed cheap and steady production of sugar with enormous profit margins, which brought unprecedented progress and wealth to all promoting sugar, slavery, and the slave trade. To sustain the world's demand for sugar, the sugar machine fueled the plantation machine (Benítez Rojo). Illegal trafficking in slaves continued, and by the early part of the nineteenth century the number of enslaved people and free blacks surpassed the number of whites.[6] As a result, colonial authorities feared that Cuba was in danger of becoming another Haiti, whose history was all too well known. The population of enslaved people in Haiti, under the leadership of Boukman—who presided over the ceremony at Bois Caiman in 1791—Toussaint Louverture, and others rebelled against their French colonizers and founded the Republic of Haiti in 1804, the first independent black country in the world. This unprecedented event led many whites to fear blacks; among such whites was Simón Bolívar, who, though he fought for independence, refused to emancipate slaves.[7] The fear of black people affected Caribbean psyches and culture, and the terror of the past continues to resonate in the present.

In Cuba, the Aponte Conspiracy of 1812 to liberate the island and free those who were enslaved was followed by the Ladder Conspiracy of 1844, in which Captain General Leopoldo O'Donnell accused the unsuspecting mulatto poet Gabriel de la Concepción Valdés (aka Plácido)

of masterminding an overthrow of the colonial government to impose a
black republic. The act recalled Napoleon's reaction to quell the uprising
in Saint Domingue but also the Spanish defeat of the Aponte Conspiracy
some thirty years earlier, exploiting a generalized white fear of blacks,
their culture, and their religions. Though scholars continue to debate
whether the conspiracy was real or contrived, British consul to Cuba
David Turnbull was a feared abolitionist, and the captain general used
Turnbull's presence to eradicate a growing black middle-class population
of musicians, writers, tailors, and other professionals and to exile white
creoles who opposed colonial rule, slavery, and the slave trade.[8] It was
clear that O'Donnell's target was the free population of color. Of the
3,066 charged in the conspiracy, an overwhelming 71 percent of them
were *libres de color* (Paquette 229).

Captain General O'Donnell's actions proved deadly for Cuba's emerging culture. The prosecutor of the commission interrogated Plácido, and
under duress the poet implicated many visible Cubans who had become
dissenters against slavery and the colonial regime. He incriminated the
poet, autobiographer, and former slave Juan Francisco Manzano, who was
later imprisoned for one year; Manzano's own verifiable testimony contra-
dicted information Plácido provided, but he was not considered a credible
witness (Friol 195–97). Plácido also identified Manzano's patron, Domingo del Monte, Cuba's most important cultural promoter, as a principal
conspirator, and he accused Del Monte of working with the British consul David Turnbull and other presumed dissenters such as Santiago Vom-
balier, Juan Manuel de Castro, and Julián Aguiar (Friol 189). In addition,
Plácido accused Del Monte's colleague, José Antonio Saco, who supported
the abolition of slavery and opposed the annexation of Cuba to the United
States. For fear of retribution, Del Monte and Saco did not return to their
native island to answer charges levied against them; Del Monte died an
exile in Spain, and Saco did not return to Cuba until many years after.

As the number of enslaved people diminished after the Ladder Conspiracy, increasing waves of Chinese contract workers and Canary Island-
ers fueled the sugar machine; and under these conditions many Chinese
workers were treated like slaves. By the end of the first war of independence, known as the Ten Years' War (1868–1878), the United States had
significant economic interests in Cuba, with US businesses purchasing
sugar plantations abandoned by Spanish landowners. With the overthrow
of the Spanish empire, US creditors acquired lands and sugar mills at a low
cost, and they became the new economic masters, controlling more than
80 percent of the island's sugar production (L. Pérez). These actions offered

a different interpretation of the Monroe Doctrine: indeed, America was for (or belongs to) the Americans (that is, the United States).

II

Cuban culture emerges during the colonial period and coincides with the birth of national cultures in Spanish America, even though Cuba would not become a republic until almost a century later. Cuban intellectuals in the early part of the nineteenth century began to envision a country distinct from the colonial empire, with its own landscape, flora and fauna, language, tropes, cuisine, and concerns. The birth of Cuban literature revolves around sugar and slavery, and Domingo del Monte's insistence that his author friends, in the words of the enslaved Cuban poet Juan Francisco Manzano, "pintase en ellas la hermosura del país Cubano, su feracidad y costumbres nobles de sus habitantes" (Friol 196; to paint the beauty of the Cuban country, with the fertility and noble customs of its inhabitants). For Félix Tanco y Bosmeniel it entailed abandoning the habit of "painting a chosen society: white, alone, isolated, because *blacks discolor* and *dirty* that society. It is essential to see it with the grime left by their touch, that is, it is necessary, indispensable to see the blacks" (qtd. in Luis, *Literary Bondage* 44; emphasis in original). Del Monte transformed the Comisión de Literatura of the proslavery Sociedad Económica de Amigos del País into the Academia Cubana de Literatura but encountered opposition from the president, Juan Bernardo O'Gavan, and Captain General Tacón suppressed it. Del Monte kept the idea alive with his literary circle, which first convened in Matanzas in 1834 and then met in Havana one year later. Del Monte was also known for his vast library with the most recent books published in Europe, which he shared with friends.

Del Monte commissioned many of the early works, which he gathered in an antislavery notebook, and in 1839 he gave the notebook to Richard Madden, the arbiter in the Mixed Court, to present before the next meeting of the Anti-Slavery Convention, to be held in London in 1840. These works included Juan Francisco Manzano's slave autobiography and poems, Félix Tanco y Bosmeniel's *Escenas de la vida privada en la Isla de Cuba*, Anselmo Suárez y Romero's *El ingenio o las delicias del campo*, and José Morilla's "El ranchador," among others.[9] Madden translated Manzano's autobiography and a selection of his poems; he published them, with some of Madden's own slave compositions, interviews with Del Monte, and his own essay on the conditions of those enslaved in Cuba, as *Poems by a Slave in the Island of Cuba, Recently Liberated*, in the same city and year in which the convention was held and Madden was a prominent speaker. These and other works form the center pillar of Cuba's burgeoning literature and culture.

While Manzano has the distinction of being the only enslaved person in Spanish America to write his autobiography, he was a visible poet before Del Monte commissioned him to write his life story in 1835. Many years before the 1830s, when Del Monte helped Manzano circulate his poems in the periodicals of Matanzas and Havana, Manzano published *Poesías líricas* (1821) and *Flores pasageras* (1830). His early compositions documented images of Cuba and its nascent culture years before Del Monte encouraged the members of his literary circle to do the same. He wrote about Cubanness before José María Heredia, José Jacinto Milanés, and Gertrudis Gómez de Avellaneda, among other notable writers, published their works. Manzano must be considered a foundational writer of Cuba's literature and culture.

Early Cuban narrators were diligent about documenting the reality unfolding before them. Of paramount importance were the unjust suffering of the enslaved and the sexual exploitation of the *mulata*, whether free or in bondage. The topics were linked to the theme of incest, which was alluded to in many literary works. The early versions of Cirilo Villaverde's short story and novel *Cecilia Valdés* (1839) allude to incest between the unsuspecting half brother and sister, and in Anselmo Suárez y Romero's *Francisco* (written in 1839) there are intimations of incest between the slave Dorotea and her master Carlos, who were "hermanos de leche" (milk brother and sister). In Tanco y Bosmeniel's "Petrona y Rosalía" (1838), in which son and daughter are half-brother and half-sister, the master and his son abuse mother and daughter, respectively. In this story, the violence created by sugar and slavery also impacts the family. Incest is used to address the conditions created by a slave society in which powerful white men exploit the vulnerability of black and mulatto women, a concern Manzano had already addressed in the poem "A la esclava ausente" (1823; Luis, *Autobiografía del esclavo poeta y otros escritos* 170–74). The white attack on black produces the racial mixture evident in Cuba's population in which many are related in some way. From this perspective, the core of Cuban culture is based on a taboo, the incestuous relationship between brother and sister. Though Avellaneda did not belong to the Del Monte's literary salon, she followed similar guidelines and wrote from Spain about the same topics that island writers had narrated several years earlier, suggesting a love the enslaved Sab felt for his landowning cousin, Carlota.

In this early period, Cuban literature was born with social, political, racial, and gender intents. Its main goal was to educate and expose readers to a different reality, not the one taking place in a different geographic space, the empire, or in the empire's colonial center, but at the margins, among the lettered sector of creoles, who questioned the power of those who supported slavery and the slave trade. In this other version of "historical events," slaves were not commodities but people with human feelings and with whom the reader could identify. This Cuban-style literature exposed the immoral and evil intentions of whites, whether the unsuspected mother, who spoiled her son by looking the other way when he abused mulatto women, or the vicious master or slave trader, who considered his needs or profits over the life of those enslaved, as described in *Cecilia Valdés*.

My reading of this early period is different from the readings of critics and historians because I analyze literature alongside historical events and consider the narrative strategies in literary texts indispensable for understanding history. As I have argued elsewhere, these early works represented a counterdiscourse to history and offered a perspective that historical writings could not and did not portray. Literature revealed the underside of slavery and narrated accounts from the point of view of the victim, the enslaved person, his agony and pain, a position denied to other types of writing. Literature attempted to destabilize the dominant discourse and indeed was a threat to the colonial power. For this reason, early works were censored, and writers such as Manzano, Plácido, and Del Monte were considered dangerous and were implicated in the Ladder Conspiracy, an uprising to end slavery and overthrow the colonial government. From its inception to the present, literature in the Spanish Caribbean assumed its rightful place to narrate history, culture, and society. Literature represents a counterdiscourse to the discourse of power.

III

Cuban literature, politics, and identity were also crafted outside of the island, in the empire. As Cubans sought to influence how Spaniards and the Crown envisioned the island and its culture, they, in turn, were also affected by unfolding events. Cuban deputies were sent to represent island interests in the Spanish court, and residents from the colony traveled to and lived in the empire. The deputies pressed for reforms for the island, and several even offered the court their own constitutions. This was indubitably the case with Francisco de Arango y Parreño in 1792, José Agustín y Caballeros in 1811, Joaquín Infante in 1812, Gabriel Claudio Zequeira in 1822, and Félix Varela in 1823. Arango y Parreño supported the agricultural interests of Cuban growers, but Infante, Zequeira, and Valera promoted a more independent state. Varela pressed for economic and political autonomy for Cuba and acknowledged the independent countries of Spanish America. However, upon Ferdinand VII's return to power, Varela was forced to flee to Gibraltar and then made his way to what would later become the nascent empire of the United States.

In 1813, the same year Ferdinand regained his absolutist powers and returned to the throne, Gertrudis Gómez de Avellaneda was born in Camagüey, Cuba. At the age of twenty-two she left her native island for the Spanish peninsula, from where she envisioned a literary career and wrote about the familiar topics of her youth. Gómez de Avellaneda's works include the much-celebrated autobiographical poem "Al partir," which describes her parting for Spain in 1836. The poetic voice describes the sadness that besets her upon leaving the island against her will, represented by the mournful color of the dark sky. Like a delicate flower, she is uprooted from her Eden, her island paradise. Cuba aids in her journey and destiny, as the hot wind emanates from the interior of the island and fills the ship's sails. She ends the poem with the following lines:

> ¡Adiós, patria feliz, edén querido!
> ¡Doquier que el hado en su furor me impela,
> tu dulce nombre halagará mi oído!
>
> (Farewell, my Eden, land so dear!
> Whatever in its furor fate now sends,
> Your cherished name will grace my ear!) (Harter)

The poem captures the main concern of Avellaneda's work, to write about her native Cuba, but from her adopted country, Spain; in so doing, she became an important writer of Cuban and Spanish literatures. Some years later, she incorporated themes developed in poems such as "Al partir" and "A El" into the writings of her "antislavery" novel, *Sab* (1841), about events taking place on the island. The novel refers to the prevalent slavery system, though the characters respond not to the brutal social and political system known to the authors of the Del Monte salon but to a romantic notion of unrequited love, for true love remains unfulfilled. So, slavery is used to heighten the true feeling of love because Carlota would not and could not be interested in Sab, who was enslaved. This is also the case with Teresa, a poor white woman; when she confesses her desire to be with Sab, he responds that his love belongs to someone else. They are the only two characters that experience true love in the novel. Carlota, who marries Enrique, becomes a tragic figure; her indifferent husband casts her to one side. Sab and Teresa, whose social position defines them as marginal characters, are the novel's true heroes. I should underscore that Teresa, not Carlota, frees herself from the traditional role of women and declares her feelings for Sab, the slave.

The novel's time of writing was, I argue, influenced by events taking place in the colony and in the seat of empire, from which the author wrote. Though Carlota is destined to marry Enrique Otway, a British citizen interested in gaining a financial stake in the island, the enslaved Sab emerges as the sacrificial figure and moral leader the reader embraces. Critics continue to overlook the blood relationship between Carlota and Sab, the suggested incest attraction between the two cousins, the enslaveds' rights to equality and even citizenship as a result of their fathers' privileged status, and the extended family's symbolic representation of Cubanness, issues already addressed by antislavery narratives. In Gómez de Avellaneda's novel, moral superiority, represented by a benevolent position toward slavery—and those enslaved are considered members of the Cuban family—occupies a higher plain to the much-coveted successful business interests.

Moreover, the same year Gómez de Avellaneda departed the colony for her new home, changes were taking place in the empire. When she arrived in A Coruña, the liberal revolution of 1836 was underway. Based on the ideas of the revolution of 1810 and the liberal Constitution of 1812, it led to the establishment of the Constitution of 1837, which called for a parliamentary system of government, freedom of the press, and suffrage (though mainly for a wealthy minority). Equally important, she arrived in a country that had abolished slavery. Other events were unfolding in the turbulent Spain of the period. A few years before her arrival, the crown was in turmoil. With the death of Fernando VII in 1833 and the regent's morganatic marriage a few months later to a palace guard, María Cristina became involved in the Carlist Wars, defended a woman's right to the throne, and ensured the succession of her daughter Isabela II to the crown—all of which could only be accomplished with the support of liberals (Bahamonde and Martínez 202). The changing events form the backdrop to *Sab* and Gómez de Avellaneda's own life. However, efforts to address issues of race and gender were already connected to and supported by the women's suffrage movement in the United States.

Gómez de Avellaneda contributed to literature and culture in her birth country, but she also influenced the development of romanticism in the empire. She was unorthodox for her time and, like the regent, tested the limits of social conduct expected of women of her society. Her relationships with men and contributions to literary circles also helped to produce writings that shaped Spanish literature. *Cartas de amor*, written to Ignacio de Cepeda, and the play *Alfonso Munio*, about Prince Don Sancho of Castilla's love for Munio Alfonso's daughter Fronilde, one representing the classic hero and the other the romantic heroine, are but two examples of her vast work (Mata-Kolster 175–80).

IV

As the transfer of power was initiated from the collapsing Spanish empire to the growing US empire, just as there were significant political and cultural contacts between Cuba and Spain that contributed to the formation of a Cuban culture at home and abroad, there were also other exchanges developing between the United States and Cuba, Puerto Rico, and the Dominican Republic that further influenced the development of each island's sense of national identity. I argue that national identity is not singular but multiple and that it also includes the culture of the country from which the author resides and writes.

In this period of transition from the fall of the Spanish empire to the birth of US dominion in the Spanish Caribbean, New York, Philadelphia, Tampa, and other US cities were transformed into Caribbean spaces where intellectuals contributed to both the culture unfolding in their country of origin and that of their place of residence. For example, after fleeing from Spain, Varela lived in Philadelphia and New York and became involved in the Spanish and mainstream communities of those metropolitan cities. He published newspapers in Spanish, such as *El Habanero* (1824–1826), which supported Cuban independence from Spain, and *El Mensajero Semanal* and *El Mercurio de Nueva York* (both in 1828), and in English, such as *The Protestant's Abridger and Annotator*.[10] A devoutly pious person, Varela was intimately involved in the religious life of his adopted homeland, and he was named vicar general of the Diocese of New York in 1837 (Rodríguez).

With impending signs of the Ten Years' War, Cuban tobacco factories left the volatile conditions of the island for the United States, to cities such as Key West, Tampa, and New York. Many tobacco workers followed their jobs and joined the most liberal sectors of US and Cuban societies. As Fernando Ortiz pointed out in his seminal work, *Contrapunteo cubano del tabaco y el azúcar* (*Cuban Counterpoint, Tobacco and Sugar*, 1940), to-bacco was grown in small parcels, required skilled workers, and supported independent thinkers. The *tabaqueros*, or cigar rollers, with the help of the *lector*, became knowledgeable about current events and also literature, cul-ture, history, and even philosophy. Araceli Tinajero's *El Lector* studies the contributions made by this fascinating person to the education of tobacco rollers, from this figure's beginnings in medieval monasteries and convents to its further development in nineteenth-century Cuba, the Dominican Republic, Mexico, Puerto Rico, and the United States. The transfer of tobacco readers and rollers to the United States during the Ten Years' War is important for understanding Cuban history, politics, and culture. These same workers supported Cuban life and culture in the growing empire and, with their money and actions, embraced the independence move-ment to free Cuba and Puerto Rico from Spain's colonial authorities.

Puerto Rican literature on the island and mainland also documents the role played by the tobacco reader. In *A Puerto Rican in New York, and Other Sketches* (1961), Jesús Colón explained the significance of the to-bacco reader, just as his compatriot Bernardo Vega, a fellow tobacco roller whose life was illustrated in *Memorias de Bernardo Vega* (1977; Andreu Iglesias), did. Both followed in the tradition of nineteenth-century liberal thinkers. In "A Voice through the Window," Colón recalls his childhood in the town of Cayey, Puerto Rico, where he lived next to a cigar factory. One morning, he peeked through the window and saw some 150 cigar makers sitting in front of a table covered with different types of tobacco leaves. They listened intently to the voice emanating from a man at the front of the room, known as "'El Lector'—the Reader." In the morning, Colón tells us, the man read the daily newspaper or some working-class publications, and in the afternoon "he would read from novels by Zola, Balzac, Hugo or from a book by Kropotkin, Malatesta or Karl Marx. Famous speeches like Castelar's or Spanish classical novels like Cervantes's *Don Quixote* were also read aloud by 'El Lector'" (11). This early scene impacted Colón so profoundly that he continued to hear the same voice in the United States; he recalled the themes sometimes in Spanish but most of the time in English. The voice appeared to say that if tobacco rollers continued the struggle, the workers of the world would win.

The emerging empire provided a haven for insurgent groups. New York housed José Martí's Partido Revolucionario Cubano (1892–1902), which drew its members from other New York City groups, and Las Dos Antil-las (1892–1898), founded by Puerto Ricans Arturo Alfonso Schomburg, Rosendo Rodríguez, and Rafael Serra, whose political aim was the independence of Cuba and Puerto Rico (Sinnette 21). There were also news-papers whose collaborators actively supported the independence of Cuba and Puerto Rico. José Martí's *Patria* (14 March 1892 to 31 December 1898), the official newspaper of the Partido Revolucionario, was published in New York. Its registry from 14 March 1892 to 3 August 1895 included luminary Cuban figures such as Máximo Gómes, Antonio Maceo, Father Varela, Gonzalo de Quesada, and the first president of Cuba, Tomás Estrada Palma; Puerto Rican patriots such as F. Gonzalo Marín and Sotero Figueroa; and Dominican heroes such as S. I. Massenet.[11] The Comité Revolucionario de Puerto Rico, founded by Juan Ríus Rivera, Ramón Emeterio Betances, and José Francisco Basora in Santo Domingo, sup-ported Puerto Rico's El Grito de Lares. Betances and Segundo Ruiz Belvis, with Juan de Mata Terreforte as vice president and Gonzalo Marín and Schomburg in attendance, founded and led the New York City chapter.

New York became a Caribbean cultural and geographic space that wel-comed writers like Heredia, who wrote his romantic "Oda al Niágara" in 1824. The majestic and powerful waterfall reminded the romantic poet of the palm trees in his native Cuba. As I have illustrated, this city also affected Martí. Most of his work was written from abroad, and from his vantage point in this other geographic center he considered the new em-pire a threat to the newly established nations of the once-powerful Spanish empire. During the time of Martí's writings, these adolescent nations of Spanish America were susceptible to the growing menace from the United States, a warning he described in his well-known essay "Nuestra América" (1891). Like his countrymen, Cirilo Villaverde wrote about his native Cuba from the United States, where he completed the definitive version of Cuba's national novel, *Cecilia Valdés* (1882). While Cuban scholars con-sider these and other writers living in and writing from the United States to be national writers of their country of origin, their works were greatly influenced by life and events in their country of residence and could not have been written in the same manner from the island. If the Spanish em-pire contributed with its language and culture to the Spanish Caribbean, the US empire provided a home for writers, workers, and politicians in the nineteenth century. This tradition has continued into to the twentieth and twenty-first centuries, for the literature and culture of the Spanish Ca-ribbean is also forged in the United States. Just as Gómez de Avellaneda's works were influenced by events taking place in the Spanish empire, these other writers living in the US empire were impacted by the actions unfold-ing in the adopted country, and those writing in English also contributed to US literature and culture.

In the mid-nineteenth century Villaverde relied on the geographic space of New York to denounce slavery in Cuba by describing in the second part of *Cecilia Valdés* life on the Gamboa sugar plantation, where those enslaved were treated like animals. He also attributed to the owner of a coffee plantation, Isabel Ilincheta, not only the benevolent attitude associated with the cultivation of this crop but also a stance that appears to reflect the women's rights movement in the United States. The movement had gained attention during the 1840 London Anti-Slavery Convention, the same one at which Madden was to present the antislavery notebook Del Monte gave him before he departed the island in 1839, which contained Manzano's autobiography and poems. At the convention, Elizabeth Cady Stanton, Lucretia Mott, and other US women delegates were refused representation. In the United States these and other women worked hard to change the dominant perspective on women and slaves, as their position during the Women's Rights Convention at Seneca Falls, New York, in June 1848 indicated. Isabel treats her slaves with benevolence and as her equal, but her actions seemed somewhat unusual and anachronistic for Cuba of the period. Her disposition can best be explained by associating her actions with those seeking women's suffrage in the United States. Villaverde lived in New York, the same city in which Susan B. Anthony encouraged women in the typesetting and sewing machine trades to unite under the Working Women's Association; they demanded equal pay for equal work, a platform she pressed as a delegate to the National Labor Congress in 1868. Earlier that same year, Anthony founded the weekly journal *The Revolution,* and Elizabeth Cady Stanton worked as her editor. Through the journal, Anthony continued to support the rights of women and African Americans, a position she made clear when addressing the Ninth National Women's Rights Convention of 12 May 1859 (Lutz 200–45).

Villaverde's novel incorporates the ideas expounded by Anthony, in particular those pertaining to the suffrage of women and African Americans. Equally important, the Cuban writer living on the mainland uncovers additional information about the historical period he describes. Set between 1812 and 1834 to refer to the Dionisio Vives years, from 1823 to 1832, the novel reminds the reader that during the early part of the nineteenth century, and certainly during the narrative time of the novel, the Cuban counterpoint was not between sugar and tobacco, as Ortiz would have us believe; rather, it was between sugar and coffee. The numerous coffee plantations gave way to the aggressive and more powerful sugar machine, supported by an ever-increasing number of people who were enslaved. The two crops engaged in a battle that the sugarocracy won. Though there were independence movements that dotted the historical landscape of the first half of the nineteenth century, as mentioned above, the dominant societal dialogue was not about ending slavery and achieving independence but, according to Villaverde's narration, about the type of slavery that was best for Cuba: a ruthless and centrally controlled system sugar demanded or a compassionate and decentered one coffee supported.

Toward the end of *Cecilia Valdés*, Isabel agrees to marry Leonardo, thus showing the historical control sugar had over coffee. However, Villaverde's novel closes with an unusual and unexpected twist. Though Leonardo abandoned Cecilia and married Isabel, Pimienta disregards Cecilia's instructions; instead of killing Isabel, he assassinates Leonardo and escapes from justice. Is Villaverde's José Dolores Pimienta, I wonder, the same Santiago Pimienta who was executed for his alleged participation in the Ladder Conspiracy, an event Villaverde records in his novel? With the novel's ending, Villaverde takes another stand against sugar and the sugar machine's exploitation of blacks, slaves, and women: Leonardo will not be physically present to control Isabel's motives and intentions. As a widow, Isabel is predisposed to continue her independent behavior, which includes a critical stance against a ruthless form of slavery, without the supervision of a male authority figure that represents sugar. In the novel, Villaverde depicts the historical unfolding of events; he was aware that by the time he finished the novel, sugar had become the most important and powerful crop in Cuba. But he recognized its danger and, in his own way, contested the sugar machine and supported independence by concluding his novel with Pimienta's escape. During the second half of the nineteenth century, when Villaverde researched his work, tobacco became the counterpoint to sugar, as Ortiz's book proposes, and many Cubans, both on and outside of the island, supported "independence" during the Machado and post-Machado dictatorships. Ortiz promoted the ideals of an independent republic, one that was already suggested in Villaverde's actions critical of the Spanish colonial authorities and slavery.

As I have mentioned here and elsewhere (Luis, *Literary Bondage*), Villaverde is the first writer to describe the audacious assassination of a white by a black who also escapes from justice and at the closing of the narration remains on the loose. While staying true to the historical period that highlighted the counterpoint between coffee and sugar, Villaverde disagreed with the events visible in Cuba during the time he was writing, in which sugar triumphed over coffee first and tobacco later; rather, he reveals the sentiment of those who opposed slavery, slave trafficking, the sexual and racial exploitation of mulatto women, and, through Isabel, the sexual exploitation of all women, regardless of race. In so doing, he incorporates into his narration the conditions of a postslavery society: not the actual Cuban society in which slavery continued until four years after the publication of the novel in 1886, but the one in the United States after the Civil War and the proclamation of the Thirteenth Amendment, which granted freedom to slaves. With Leonardo's death, Villaverde closes a cycle of exploitation by whites, empowers a black person, and supports that person's subsequent flight from justice. Though Cándido will continue to have a strong economic foundation, he and his wife have been dealt the most painful blow any parent can receive, the death of a son and heir to the family name, business, and fortune. Just as Spain influenced Cuban society in the island and Spanish culture impacted Cuban writers living in Spanish empire, US society and mores also contributed to the development of Cuban culture, which is intricately interwoven with events in the writer's country of residence.

V

Like the earlier empire, the new one endeavored to exert political and economic control over the Spanish Caribbean. After the Spanish-American War, in 1901, Puerto Rico became a colony of the United States; Puerto Ricans were granted citizenship in 1917, just in time to enlist for World War I; and in 1952, under Luis Muñoz Marín, Puerto Rico became the oxymoronic Free Associated State. Operation Bootstrap, which began in 1948, had an adverse impact on the Puerto Rican economy and produced an unexpected and unprecedented wave of migrants from the countryside to the capital city of San Juan, and from that city to New York City. The US presence on the island marked Puerto Rican history, society, and literature, both at home and abroad, for generations to come. René Marqués was one of the first to write about the displacement of Puerto Ricans during the post–World War II period. His play *La carreta* (1950) captures succinctly the journey confronting many Puerto Rican families of humble origins, who traveled from their towns to the capital city and later abroad in search of a better life. However, this other life came at a high cost evident in the disintegration of the Puerto Rican family, culture, and values. In the play, Juanita and Doña Charo return to Puerto Rico following Luis's death, at a time others were abandoning the island in unparalleled numbers. Marqués's play indicates that Puerto Ricans are treated with hostility on the mainland and should return to their country of origin; however, this romantic vision of the home country does not account for the reasons these families left in the first place. Though living on the mainland, they continue to suffer. As US citizens, Puerto Ricans are treated as outsiders. This perception of Puerto Ricans is portrayed in *West Side Story*, when the Italian and Polish members of the Jets accuse the Puerto Rican Sharks of being foreigners, when in fact the Jets were the outsiders. Puerto Ricans, with their distinct accent and skin color, were easy to identify and discriminate against.

Marqués's *Cuentos puertorriqueños de hoy* (1959) gathers the voices of writers who best narrate the period during which a disproportionate number of island Puerto Ricans in general and Afro-Puerto Ricans in particular were displaced. José Luis González's "En el fondo del caño hay un negrito," Emilio Díaz Valcárcel's "Sol negro," and Edwin Figueroa's "Aguinaldo negro" dared to uncover the racial conditions in an island that considered all Puerto Ricans to be equal. Each of these stories highlights the Afro–Puerto Rican experience and describes unfair racial suffering. Pedro Juan Soto's *Spiks* documents the continual discrimination and unwarranted treatment Puerto Ricans must endure.

VI

Indeed, the new empire exercised control over the political and economic conditions on the island and over those who made the adopted country their new home. The effects had significant consequences on Puerto Rican culture on the island and in the United States. But Puerto Rican culture in the United States has also influenced mainstream politics and culture. This is also the case for Cubans and Dominicans who left their country of birth for economic or political reasons and made the United States their new home. As a result of Castro's takeover of the island, Cubans left in four waves, spanning a thirty-five-year period, from the first two waves of exiles (1959–1961 and 1965–1973) to the Mariel boatlift (1980) and lastly to the *balseros* (1994). They continue a long tradition of Cuban migrants and exiles that date back to the time the Spanish empire ruled the region. Many Dominicans left their homeland a few decades earlier, while others came after Trujillo's execution or, in greater numbers, after the US occupation of the country and the Family Reunification Act of 1965; they traveled mainly to Caribbean cities such as New York. In a ten-year period, from 1990 to 2000, the number of Dominicans in the United States doubled, from 520,121 to 1,041,910 inhabitants, and they became the fourth-largest Hispanic and Latino national group on the mainland.[12]

Puerto Rican, Cuban American, and Dominican American authors living and writing in the United States are at the forefront of a new literary boom that questions the viability of a singular concept of identity. These Latino Caribbean writers create hybrid, layered, and fluid spaces that explore notions of distinctiveness. This observation is significant, as Hispanics and Latinos have transformed the United States into the second-largest Spanish-speaking country in the world. There are more Spanish speakers in the United States than in Spain, Argentina, or Venezuela; it is second only to Mexico. By the middle of the century, Latinos will be one-third of the US population. Some Latino authors write in Spanish, but most in English, though some choose to express themselves in Spanglish. They move freely from previous notions of boundaries and transgress fixed notions of space. Tato Laviera's *La Carreta Made a U-Turn* is a response to Marqués's well-known drama that proposed a return to the place of origin. With his title, Laviera questions homecoming and informs readers that the destiny of Puerto Ricans is not to return to their native island but to remain in the United States, where they must confront the harsh reality in their adopted country. Though Laviera writes Nuyorican-style poetry, one that is closer to performative spoken word, not all Puerto Rican American writers can be classified in the same manner. Others, such as Judith Ortiz Cofer and Julio Marzán, who lives in the same city as Laviera, prefer a more standard expression known to many mainstream poets and writers.[13]

Cuban American writers such as Oscar Hijuelos, Cristina García, and Gustavo Pérez Firmat weave in their narrations the Cuban past with the US present. Each revisits a past of which they have little or no memory, and the act of writing becomes a way of exploring, interacting with, and reliving a culture that has become distant and only accessible through writing and from the perspective of a US resident. Writers like Pérez Firmat and Carolina Hospital have no memory of the past and resort to either inventing it or, as in the case of Pérez Firmat, transforming a longing for Cuba into a yearning for Miami.[14]

VII

The Dominican Republic's unique history, declaring its independence not from Spain but from Haiti, produced under Pedro Santana an unprecedented movement for Spain to annex its former colony. While all the countries in Spanish America, including Cuba and Puerto Rico, fought to gain a much-deserved status as republics, the Dominican Republic stepped backward in history by asking to be recolonized by the fledgling Spanish empire. Dominicans feared another Haitian takeover of the eastern part of Hispaniola and embraced Spain's dominion in the region. Boyer unified the island in 1822, Dominican patriots reclaimed their country in 1844, and the legal maneuver to become part of Spain was accomplished in 1861. But Queen Isabela II annulled it four years later because of opposition from rebels during the War of Restoration. Gregorio Luperón and Santiago Rodríguez led the rebellion that defeated Spain, which would also launch a period of political instability in Dominican history.[15]

The early period of Dominican history is best described by Dominican American literature, which allows women and blacks to occupy their rightful place in Dominican society, a place previously denied to them. Julia Álvarez's *In the Name of Salomé* (2000) narrates the birth of the Dominican nation through the life of her protagonist, Salomé, who was born six years into the founding of the republic—her life reflects the history of the young homeland. Álvarez begins the first chapter, "El ave y el nido: Santo Domingo, 1856–1861," with the following description of her country:

> The story of my life starts with the story of my country, as I was born six years after Independence, a sickly child, not expected to live. But by the time I was six, I was in better health than my country, for la patria had already suffered eleven changes of government. I, on the other hand, had only endured one major change: my mother had left my father. . . . We had fought off an invasion from Haiti, and soon we would fight a war with Spain. Now we were fighting among ourselves. (13)

Salomé is a metaphorical representation of this burgeoning but sickly nation. Though the alternating blue and red parties signal the father's exile or return, by the time the chapter ends, the Dominican Republic has returned to its previous status as a colony of Spain (1861–1865). The poem "El ave y el nido" (Bird and nest), the first one Salomé wrote in 1867 and the one that gives the chapter its title, is a poetic conversation the speaker has with a bird frightened because she approached her nest. The poetic voice reassures the bird not to be alarmed and explains that the adornments she brings are meant to decorate the nest. The speaker ensures the bird that she knows how to respect innocence and the bird's sense of home. As the poetic voice departs, she encourages the bird to return to the nest and explains that when the speaker reappears in the future to visit the bird's progenies, she will want to adorn the free nest or independent home. Certainly, the poem can be read alongside the historical changes taking place in the Dominican Republic; the concept of home for the bird and the poetic voice becomes an important symbol that the bird and the poetic voice protect. The phrase "free, independent home" (*libre hogar*) is repeated three times in a six-stanza poem. The bird should return to its home just as Dominicans are entitled to have a free homeland.

The novel interweaves two alternating time periods and female perspectives. One begins in the present with Camila Henríquez Ureña and the other during the early years of her mother, Salomé Ureña. The one with Camila is narrated backward in search of an origin; it commences with her teaching experiences at Vassar College, then describes her relationship with Marion and her stay in Cuba, and concludes with her childhood in the Dominican Republic. The other narrative, with Salomé, is chronological and starts with the life of the country's national poet, Salomé Ureña, before chronicling her marriage to Francisco Henríquez y Carvajal, his rise to the presidency during the US occupation, and Salomé's last pregnancy with the soon-to-be-born daughter Camila. Álvarez is interested in underscoring the paths taken by the mother and daughter, and the final chapter examines the women's common origin during the mother's pregnancy and the lessons the mother passed on to her daughter: "'You listen to me,' I said, stroking my belly. Sensing I might not have much time with my daughter, I'd begun to raise her before she was even born. 'Wherever we end up, remember, *this* is your patria!'" (302; emphasis in the original). The lesson is tied to the concept of homeland. The second part of the final chapter is titled "Bird and Nest: Departing Santo Domingo, 1897." In this section, the family leaves for the Cape, in Haiti, but not before Salomé dies of tuberculosis and Camila is asked to recite the poem "El ave y el nido," which gave title to the first chapter and here appears in translation, "Bird and Nest." Home as a concept, in whichever language it is articulated, will always be with her.

There is another lesson to be learned equally as important as the idea of home: Camila should be cautious of men who are unfaithful to their wives, a lesson Salomé did not appear to learn from her mother. Francisco, while married to Salomé, had a second family when studying in France and later began to court Tivisita when his wife was on her deathbed. Salomé's grandeur as a woman and a poet serves to narrate the unfaithful actions of Dominican men and to explain why Camila was attracted to and had an intimate relationship with her companion, Marion. My interpretation of Álvarez's reading of "El ave y el nido" takes into account that Camila is the *prole* mentioned in the poem, who lives in a free or independent nest; the nest, from this perspective, is transformed into Camila's body and her right and duty to make independent decisions for herself, with her mother's blessing and protection.

Race and gender are also fundamental issues present in the novel during the time of narration in the Dominican Republic and, equally importantly, during the time of writing in the United States. Salomé was dark skinned and so were her children—Max, Pedro, Francisco, and Camila—who lived in the United States and interacted with US culture. Pedro delivered the prestigious Charles Eliot Norton Lecture at Harvard University from 1940 to 1941, and Camila held a faculty appointment at Vassar College from 1942 to 1959 and during those same years at the Middlebury College language and literature summer program, an institution also known to Álvarez. While the novel is based on Dominican history and the biographies of the Henríquez Ureña family, the narration also responds to the context of the time and place of writing in the United States. Just as the contexts of both Cuban and US history shaped Villaverde's *Cecilia Valdés*, as I noted earlier, so too the themes discussed in Álvarez's novel have been retrieved from Dominican history, but the narrative focus can be found layered in contemporary US culture—the women's movement, sexual preferences, and race relations—and these are used to uncover their representation in the Dominican past. And just as Villaverde relied on the ideas promoted by the women's suffrage movement, whose leaders saw a relationship between the condition of blacks and women, Álvarez also coalesces these two ideas in her novel. Current Dominican culture does not consider its citizens to be black but rather *indios*; black is a pejorative term more appropriately used with Haitians. Álvarez, drawing on notions of race in the United States, reappropriates the use of race in Dominican culture and restores it to its rightful place in history, to Salomé and her children. The situation of women is evident in the way Dominican men have been accustomed to following the sexual patterns promoted by Salomé's father and husband, and by the former dictator Rafael Leonidas Trujillo, who enjoyed sexual favors with many women and had a voracious appetite for virgins.[16] Race relations in the United States become a fundamental vehicle for exploring matters of race in the Dominican Republic.

Even though the United States desired a presence in the Caribbean during the nineteenth century, it could not accept Pedro Santana's invitation to annex the Dominican Republic at a time it was experiencing its own civil war. The emerging empire was beginning to consolidate its strength and surface as a world power. Some eighteen years after the Spanish-American War, the United States expanded its dominion and occupied the

Dominican Republic, from 1916 to 1924, and placed in power Trujillo, who became the nation's dictator from 1930 to 1961. To strengthen his control, Trujillo allowed race to become an oppositional space and foster a sense of national identity. Many Dominicans were descendants of enslaved people brought to Hispaniola during the Spanish colonial period and of Haitians during the occupation, but, as I have mentioned, Dominicans reject a black identity. To solidify his power and preserve a sense of Do-minicanness, Trujillo orchestrated the massacre of Haitians living along the Massacre River, also home to many dark-skinned Dominicans. Freddy Prestol Castillo's *El masacre se pasa a pie* (1974) and Edwidge Danticat's *The Farming of Bones* (1998) are two important works that refer to this tragic period that resulted in the deaths of some twenty thousand Haitians. Dominican identity is based on rejecting a sense of blackness, Haitian blackness, though many Dominicans and Haitians share a common Afri-can ancestry. These racial markers highlight an Afro-Dominican identity a large portion of Dominicans on the island still consider a national dis-grace.[17] But Dominicans on the mainland are beginning to work with a different concept of race, as my reading of Álvarez's novel shows.

VIII

The rise of the Spanish empire in the Caribbean was assured by the so-called discovery and colonization of the New World, accompanied by the massive death of the Amerindians, regardless of whether the extinction was due to forced labor, disease, or massacre. This "muerte grande," as Neruda would call it when exploring death in "The Heights of Macchu Picchu," initiated the displacement of large numbers of people from Europe and Africa, and then China toward the middle of the nineteenth century. The same colonial control secured the economic wealth of the empire in precious metals but also in valuable crops such as sugar, coffee, and tobacco. As the wave of in-dependence movements spread throughout the Americas, anticolonial forces coordinated their activities from the growing empire to the north, which many made their adopted homeland. Both empires had a lasting impact on the Spanish-speaking countries of the Caribbean. During the early part of the nineteenth century, writers and politicians from Cuba sought sup-port for their ideas in the political turmoil affecting the colonial center, and these sentiments were reflected in their writings when forging Cuban culture many decades before the island became a republic. As the Spanish empire waned and the US empire waxed, the latter's presence in countries outside of its national borders displaced people from Cuba, Puerto Rico, and the

Dominican Republic and produced a postcolonial condition in which the colonies and colonial powers occupied the same time and space. The empire influenced conditions in the home countries, but in the postcolonial period Caribbean people living in the United States are also fashioning the dominant culture, as Hispanics and Latinos continue to grow in numbers and influence life, culture, politics, and society in the neocolonial empire. The Latino Caribbean population creates a hybrid space in which languages, cultures, literatures, and beliefs are layered with those of the adopted country to produce concepts of identity that will also affect the empire's ever-expanding concept of culture from within.[18]

In the Caribbean, the empire is dead, and the empire lives, and this pattern sets into motion historical cycles with surprising similarities but also differences. The foreseeable end of US empire over Cuba and the rest of the Caribbean suggests the start of another one. Presently, there is an emerging cycle that must not be ignored, one that began with the fall of the Berlin Wall and the breakup of the Soviet empire, and that can be defined more precisely with the rise of the Chinese empire. This other empire, which began toward the close of the twentieth century and is making its presence felt in the twenty-first century, has become Cuba's second-largest commercial partner. But if the Spanish, US, and Soviet empires demanded physical control over the island, the Chinese incursion makes headway through loans and cultural institutions, such as the Confucius Institute, and employs a form of "soft power." With planned airplane flights and economic investments from that new empire to the Caribbean island, Chinese culture will alter life on the island, just as the culture of earlier empires did. And, with the passage of time, we will anxiously await the influence the periphery will have on the center. In the Caribbean, the empire is dead; long live the empire.

Notes

1. See Vico.
2. See Artola.
3. See Thomas for the Soles y Rayos de Bolívar (101–2) and Narciso López's expeditions (213–17).
4. See, for example, Cohn.
5. "There are laws of political as well as physical gravitation; and if an apple severed by its native tree cannot choose but fall to the ground, Cuba, forcibly disjoined from its own unnatural connection with Spain, and incapable of self-support, can gravitate only towards the North American

Union which by the same law of nature, cannot cast her off its bosom"
(cited in Franklin 3).

6. See, for example, Ortiz, *Los negros esclavos*.
7. Zapata Olivella best expresses this idea in his chapter on Colombia. See his
    monumental novel, *Changó, the Biggest Badass*.
8. See, for example, Paquette. However, some twenty years after the event,
    Francisco Calcagno maintained that Plácido was an innocent victim. Also
    see Luis, *Literary Bondage*.
9. For the content of the notebook, see Lewis Galanes.
10. See Kanellos.
11. See *Patria*. Also see "Patria," *Diccionario de la literatura cubana* (2:716–19)
    and Ripoll.
12. Hernández and Rivera-Batiz 2 (table 1). According to the 2010 US Census,
    from 2000 to 2010, Dominicans grew from 764,945 to 1,414,703, almost
    doubling (84.9%) in a ten-year period (Ennis).
13. Luis, *Dance Between Two Cultures*. In particular, see the section on US
    Puerto Rican poetry.
14. Luis, *Dance Between Two Cultures*. See the sections on Cuban Americans.
15. See, for example, Moya Pons.
16. This topic is best discussed in Mario Vargas Llosa's *The Feast of the Goat*.
17. On 23 September 2013, the Dominican Constitutional Tribunal ruling
    168-13 denied Dominican citizenship to Dominicans of Haitian descent
    born as far back as 1929.
18. See my "Latino Identity and the Desiring-Machine."

Works Cited

Álvarez, Julia. *In the Name of Salomé*. Chapel Hill, NC: Algonquin Books, 2000.

Andreu Iglesias, César, ed. *Memoirs of Bernardo Vega: A Contribution to the History of the Puerto Rican Community in New York*. Trans. Juan Flores. New York: Monthly Review, 1984.

Artola, Miguel. *La España de Fernando VII*. Madrid: Espasa-Calpe, 1999.

Bahamonde, Ángel, and Jesús Martínez. *Historia de España, siglo XIX*. Madrid: Cátedra, 2011.

Benítez Rojo, Antonio. *La isla que se repite*. Hanover: Ediciones del Norte, 1989.

Calcagno, Francisco. *Poetas de color*. Havana: Imprenta Mercantil, 1887.

Carpentier, Alejo. *The Kingdom of This World*. Trans. Harriet de Onis. New York: Collier Books, 1970.

Carr, Raymond. *Spain, 1808–1939*. Oxford: Clarendon, 1966.

Cohn, Deborah. *History and Memory in the Two Souths: Recent Southern and Spanish American Fiction*. Nashville: Vanderbilt UP, 1999.

Colón, Jesús. *A Puerto Rican in New York, and Other Sketches*. New York: International, 1982.

Crenshaw, Ollinger. "The Knights of the Golden Circle: The Career of George Bickley." *American Historical Review* 47.1 (1941): 23–50.

Danticat, Edwidge. *The Farming of Bones*. New York: Soho Press, 1998.

Ennis, Sharon R., Merarys Ríos-Vargas, and Nora G. Albert. "The Hispanic Population: 2010." *2010 Census Briefs*. United States Census Bureau. May 2011. Web. 5 Feb. 2015.

Diccionario de la literatura cubana. Havana: Editorial Letras Cubanas, 1984, vol. 2.

Franklin, Jane. *Cuba and the United States: A Chronological History*. New York: Ocean Press, 1997.

Friol, Roberto. *Suite para Juan Francisco Manzano*. Havana: Arte y Literatura, 1977.

García, Cristina. *Dreaming in Cuban*. New York: Ballantine Books, 1992.

Griswold del Castillo, Richard. *The Treaty of Guadalupe Hidalgo: A Legacy of Conflict*. Norman: U of Oklahoma P, 1990.

Harter, Hugh A. *Gertrudis Gómez de Avellaneda*. Boston: Twayne, 1981.

Heredia, José María. "Oda al Niágara." *Poesías completes*. Mexico City: Editorial Porrúa, 1974.

Hernández, Ramona, and Francisco L. Rivera-Batiz, "Dominicans in the United States: A Socioeconomic Profile, 2000." Dominican Research Monographs, CUNY Dominican Studies Institute. 6 Oct. 2003. Web. 5 Feb. 2015.

Kanellos, Nicolás, and Helvetia Martell. *Hispanic Periodicals in the United States, Origins to 1960: A Brief History*. Houston: Arte Público Press, 2000.

Laviera, Jesús Tato. *La Carreta Made a U-Turn*. Houston: Arte Público Press, 1992.

Lewis Galanes, Adriana. "El álbum de Domingo del Monte." *Cuadernos Hispanoamericanos*, nos. 451–52 (1988): 255–56.

Luis, William. *Dance Between Two Cultures: Latino Caribbean Literature Written in the United States*. Nashville: Vanderbilt UP, 1997.

———. "Latino Identity and the Desiring-Machine." *The Other Latin@: Writing Against a Singular Identity*. Ed. Blas Falconer and Lorraine M. López. Tucson: U of Arizona P, 2011.

———. *Literary Bondage: Slavery in Cuban Narrative*. Austin: U of Texas P, 1990.

———, ed. *Autobiografía del esclavo poeta y otros escritos*. By Juan Francisco Manzano. Madrid: Iberoamericana, 2007.

Lutz, Alma. *Susan B. Anthony: Rebel, Crusader, Humanitarian*. New York: Beacon, 1959.

Marqués, René. *La carreta*. Río Piedras, PR: Editorial Cultural, 1969.

———, ed. *Cuentos puertorriqueños de hoy*. Río Piedras, PR: Editorial Cultural, 1981.

Martí, José. *Nuestra América*. Buenos Aires: Losada, 1980.

Mata-Kolster, Elba. "Gertrudis Gómez de Avellaneda." *Latin American Writers*. Ed. Carlos A. Solé. New York: Charles Scribner's Sons, 1989. 1: 175–80.

May, Robert E. *The Southern Dream of a Caribbean Empire, 1854–1861*. Baton Rouge: Louisiana State UP, 1973.

Moya Pons, Frank. *The Dominican Republic: A National History*. New York: Markus Wiener, 1998.

Ortiz, Fernando. *Contrapunteo cubano del tabaco y el azúcar*. Ed. Enrico Mario Santí. Madrid: Cátedra, 2002.

———. *Los negros esclavos*. Havana: Editorial de Ciencias Sociales, 1975.

Paquette, Robert L. *Sugar Is Made with Blood: The Conspiracy of La Escalera and the Conflict between Empires over Slavery in Cuba*. Middletown, CT: Wesleyan UP, 1990.

Patria. New York. 14 March 1892 to 3 August 1895.

Pérez, Louis. *Cuba: Between Reform and Revolution*. New York: Oxford UP, 2011.

Pérez Firmat, Gustavo. *Next Year in Cuba*. New York: Anchor Books, 1995.

Prestol Castillo, Freddy. *El masacre se pasa a pie*. Santo Domingo: Taller, 1998.

Ripoll, Carlos. *Patria: El periódico de José Martí; registro general (1892–1895)*. New York: Eliseo Torres and Sons, 1971.

Rodríguez, José Ignacio. *Vida del Presbítero Don Félix Varela*. Miami: Editorial Cubana, 2002.

Sampson, Robert D. *John L. O'Sullivan and His Times*. Kent, OH: Kent State UP, 2003.

Sinnette, Elinor Des Verney. *Arthur Alfonso Schomburg, Black Bibliophile and Collector*. Detroit: Wayne State UP, 1989.

Soto, Pedro Juan. *Spiks*. Mexico: Los Presentes, 1956.

Thomas, Hugh. *Cuba: The Pursuit of Freedom*. New York: Harper and Row, 1971.

Tinajero, Araceli. *El Lector: A History of the Cigar Factory Reader*. Trans. Judith E. Grasberg. Austin: U of Texas P, 2010.

Vargas Llosa, Mario. *The Feast of the Goat*. Trans. Edith Grossman. New York: Farrar, Straus, and Giroux, 2001.

Vico, Giambattista. *The New Science*. 3rd ed. Trans. Thomas Goddard Bergin and Max Harold Fisch. Ithaca, NY: Cornell UP, 1984.

Villaverde, Cirilo. *Cecilia Valdés*. Havana: Letras Cubanas, 2001.

Wagenheim, Olga Jiménez de. *Puerto Rico's Revolt for Independence: El Grito De Lares*. Princeton: Markus Wiener, 1993.

West Side Story. Farmington Hills, MI: CBS/Fox Video, 1984. Videorecording.

Zapata Olivella, Manuel. *Changó, the Biggest Badass*. Trans. Jonathan Tittler. Lubbock: Texas Tech UP, 2010.

PART IV

Cultural Legacies of Empire

8
_____

The Spanish Empire on the Wane
Africa, Galdós, and the Moroccan Wars

Michael Ugarte
University of Missouri-Columbia

Before the world was no longer young and before
History became elderly, it was possible to detect and
confirm the ruin and decadence of all things human
and their slow decomposition from the sublime to the
small, from beauty to vulgarity, as today's greatness
falls giving way to the greatness of those to come, and
the purest of ideals disappear into vile reality. Empires
decay, races fall apart, the strong become weaker and
beauty succumbs to wrinkles and white streaks of hair.
(Galdós, *Aita Tettauen* 97)[1]

Aita Tettauen (in transcribed Arabic, the "Tetouan War" of 1859–1860)
is a novel in a series of *Episodios nacionales* (National Episodes) by canonical Spanish author Benito Pérez Galdós (1843–1920), a man whose
life traverses what many consider the Spanish empire's definitive end circa
1898. In these opening sentences, Galdós's typically sardonic third-person
narrator declares what we as readers all know, no matter where we are from
or in what age we are living: empires, no matter how strong, will eventually
fall as new ones emerge. Yet, given that the Tetouan War was by today's
standards as much a pathetic skirmish as an all-out war, the reader wonders just how "great" Spain's greatness was. Wars beg for narration, and

this particular one was no exception: several well-known Spanish writers were eager to tell its story. Yet unlike *War and Peace* and other epic war novels, *Aita Tettauen* (1905) and its sequel, *Carlos VI en La Rápita* (1905), relate the conflict with an ironic-picaresque tone that prefigures modern and, to some extent, postmodern sensibilities. Moreover, as I argue, they interrogate the orientalist discourse of war novels written from the subject position of an empire.[2]

The publication of these two novels does not mark the first time Galdós manifested his preoccupation with the end of Spain's empire. Two years earlier, Madrid saw the debut of an earnest lamentation responding indirectly to the loss of the colonies: *Alma y vida* (1902). While the dramatic work's subject matter pointed to the oppressive social relations of late eighteenth-century Spain, which was consistent with several of the *Episodios nacionales*, Galdós made clear in his prologue that he intended to express his concern for the end of Spain's past glory:

> I was moved by an unmeasured ambition, not exempt from uneasiness, to set to work on a notoriously difficult enterprise: to pour into a dramatic form, an abstraction, more a vague sentiment than a precise idea, a malaise looming over the Spanish soul for the last few years, like an opaque grief. . . . I saw it as a sign for me to express this sentiment at the end of a heraldic Spain carrying forth its glorious legend and historic splendor toward the fading of its lights. (933)

Adding to these grandiloquent, albeit melancholy, words, Galdós compares his "enterprise" to a Beethoven symphony (933), most likely the Eighth (the *Pathetique*). In the play's protagonist, Laura, the sickly duchess of Ruydíaz (a suggestive allusion to Spain's shining star of the eleventh century), the dramatist suggests a reference to the pathos of the end of empire. Laura engages in a pathetically heroic struggle to rid herself of the tyranny of an opportunistic administrator of her estate. Her ultimate death notwithstanding, Galdós left his audience with a sense of hope in the figure of Cienfuegos, an "hidalgo" (of the lower nobility) who organizes a rebellion against the administrator. We see in his name an indirect allusion to the famous Battle of Cienfuegos in 1898; Spain won the battle but eventually lost the war. In the lengthy prologue to this play, uncharacteristic of most of Galdós's works, the dramatist declares that he wanted his readers to reflect on the end of Spain's legendary days of glory. The prologue is reminiscent of Machado's famous poem, "El mañana efímero" (The Ephemeral

Tomorrow), as the creator of *Alma y vida* refers to the "solid" values of the "people" (*el pueblo*): "Veía también el pueblo vivo aún y con resistencia bastante para perpetuarse, por conservar fuerza y virtudes macizas" (933; I also saw that the people were still alive and resilient enough to conserve its force and solid virtues). Indeed, as in his novels about the Moroccan War (or incursion) of 1859, Galdós wants his readers and spectators to think about Spain's downfall as the younger members of the so-called Generation of 1898 had thought about it.

However, the grandiloquence and earnestness of both the prologue and the text of *Alma y Vida* belie the Canary Island writer's playful irony and mischievous criticism of Spanish society. This is the transgressive Galdós of the two historical North African novels, *Aita Tettauen* and *Carlos VI en La Rápita*. While the critique of the end of the Spanish empire is very much on the novelist's mind in virtually all of the works he wrote in the first years of the twentieth century, these two novels present questions that anticipate modern and postmodern thinking about empire and its aftermath. Unlike anything else Galdós thought or wrote about the end of the Spanish empire, these two novels situate themselves in a land that falls victim to the expansionist policies of that empire.

Spain's role in the colonization of northern Africa in the late nineteenth and early twentieth centuries was ambivalent. An empire (Spain) in clear decline was competing with another one (France) beginning to assert its colonial power, particularly in Africa. France, by the end of the nineteenth century, had gotten the upper hand in the grab for Africa's bountiful resources, and it had done so through diplomatic maneuvers highly detrimental to Spain. With Edward Said's critique of the West's orientalist discourse and its appropriation of culture and the history of colonization in the background, one can see that Spain had already been orientalized by France in the famous dictum (attributed to Alexandre Dumas) that "Africa begins at the Pyrenees." This statement was put forth not coincidentally with the Napoleonic invasion of Spain at the commencement of the nineteenth century, indicating a rivalry between the two empires: one on the wane, the other on the path to glory. Indeed, in Said's history of orientalism, the emperor Napoleon figures among the most foundational perpetrators of orientalist discourse (79–88).[3]

How does this ambivalence unfold in terms of cultural production and the orientalist episteme that dictates how the world apprehends those areas of the globe dominated by the Occident? Put another way, if orientalism is a "discourse" (Said, *Orientalism* 3), how does that discourse manifest itself, and how does it become an object of interrogation? I believe two of

Galdós's *Episodios nacionales—Aita Tettauen* and *Carlos VI en La Rápita—* shed light not only on the nature of orientalism as a colonizing discourse but also on its ambiguities in light of Spain's diminishing (if not defunct) empire around 1905, the year of Galdós's two narratives. Thus, I argue that the waning empire may in fact contribute to that ambivalent status of an orientalizing and orientalized culture.[4]

Galdós's narrator refers in the first lines of *Aita Tettauen* to a time "antes de que el mundo dejara de ser joven" (97; before the world was no longer young). As we later see, this supposed loss of grandiose innocence has to do with the prehistory of the Moroccan War of 1859. But considering that when he was writing these words Spain had recently lost what many considered its last vestige of empire in the Americas, the *mundo* (world) was even older—that is, the decay had nearly reached its culmination around 1898. Considering this pivotal circumstance not only in Spanish history but also in Spanish letters, Galdós seems to suggest in his two Moroccan novels that 1898 was an instance of history repeating itself. One recalls Karl Marx's famous (sardonic) opening statement of *The 18th Brumaire of Louis Bonaparte*: "Hegel says somewhere that all great historic facts and personages recur twice. He forgot to add: Once as tragedy, and again as farce" (5). But Spain's humiliation at the hands of North African forces not willing to concede to Spanish domination did not occur twice but many times, and this is precisely what Galdós suggests. In fact, given the continuation throughout the first half of the twentieth century of the conflict he describes in these novels, we might see Galdós as something of a visionary.

While the Spanish are victorious in *Aita Tettauen*, the reader senses we have not seen the end of the conflict.[5] Indeed we have not. The narrator of *Carlos VI en La Rápita* bids Africa farewell only to find himself later in a skirmish comparably pathetic: an aborted Carlist coup. The pithy, ironic, and multireferential opening passage of *Aita Tettauen*, typical of Galdós's beginning sentences,[6] is an indication not only of what Galdós thought of the end of the Spanish empire but also of what some latter-day postcolonial theorists might think of the Spanish empire: "It was possible to detect and confirm the ruin and decadence of all things human and their slow decomposition from the sublime to the small, from beauty to vulgarity, as today's greatness falls giving way to the greatness of those to come, and the purest of ideals disappear into vile reality" (*Aita Tettauen* 97). As the narrator asserts in a tone clearly irreverent and mock-heroic, so-called reality engulfs the grandiosity of the empire and turns it into something pathetic.

But we need some literary and narrative specificity. Galdós's reference to the Tetouan War is at once allegorical and multireferential. From the title, readers suspect that these words refer to something historical, but at the end of the paragraph they become aware of the crux of the matter—that is, the specific circumstances of the story they are about to read. While the narrator's subject is empire's decay, it is also the diminishing beauty of a woman, Lucila, "hija de Ansúrez" (Ansúrez's daughter), after she had turned thirty.[7] She has a sickly son, Vicentito, whom she coddles by asking her husband to move the family to Madrid from a small town so that her little boy, who is enamored of things military, can watch the Spanish soldiers parade in all their imperial pomp and circumstance along the Calle Mayor in full view of the Ansúrez-Halconero family. They could not have moved at a better time, for Madrid is filled these days with military parades as Spain prepares for the Moroccan crusade with an excitement similar to that at the outset of the Spanish-American War. And to make matters bizarre, we learn that Lucila's brother, Gonzalo, is living in Morocco as a renegade Spaniard, a convert to Islam. His new name and identity is "Sidi El Hach Mohammed Ben Sur El Nasiry" (111).

So begins this curious dramatic history in which all or most of the historical participants in the Moroccan War of 1859 appear: Generals O'Donnell and Prim, as well as Pedro Antonio de Alarcón, whom Galdós parodies in his references to the war chronicles in *Diario de un testigo de la guerra de África* (Diary of a Witness of the African War).[8] The historical/literary figure of Alarcón appears in the form of a Perico, a journalist who, like Alarcón, is commissioned to report on the war and to extol the grandeurs of Spain. Alarcón wanted to restore imperial pride by showing the Moroccans who were questioning Spanish sovereignty that they could not attack Spanish military bases outside of Ceuta with impunity. The Spanish sent military troops to reinforce Spanish hegemony in Ceuta and, ultimately, to continue the campaign by moving southward to Tetouan. This action was designed to give the Moroccan rebels a lesson on the civilizing nature of the empire, as well as to remind them of the superiority of the Spanish military. Alarcón says as much in his chronicles, which become the object of Galdós's parody as Perico sings the war's praises.

Yet Galdós is by no means content to allow his rendering of Spanish imperialism to stand as clear social criticism unencumbered by ambiguity or ambivalence. These two novels are filled with paradoxes, serendipitous happenings, and rarities that reveal how Spanish culture and history are at once a producer of orientalist discourse and an object of it. The author contrasts Perico Alarcón, in all his nationalism, to Santiuste, a writer who witnesses the Moroccan War not to sing the glories of Spain but to observe; as he does so, he changes his perspective. Santiuste, who ends up as the real protagonist of this multilayered novel, is transformed by the experience, and in *Carlos VI* he becomes the narrator. At some points his renditions of the battles read like a modern-day pacifist denunciation in which the war has little by which to redeem itself. Interestingly, Alarcón's *Diario* shared the pathetic view of the horrors of war and the acknowledgment that, after all, the Moroccans are human too, but Alarcón concludes that in the long run there will be a greater good as a result of the war, a position more patriotic than humanistic, as Martin-Márquez points out (*Disorientations* 112–13). The contrast between Santiuste and Alarcón, which takes the form of a parody of the latter, is "dialogical" in a Bakhtinian sense (Bakhtin 75–76).[9] The comparison between the two characters allows the reader to reflect on this period of Spanish history indicating the decline of a once-heroic past. These events have much to tell us about the early twentieth century in which Galdós is writing, a time that for many marks the definitive end to Spain's old "greatness." Thus, by considering the historical dialogue between the conflicts of 1859 and 1898, Galdós plants the seeds of skepticism in the minds of his readers. Some liberal politicians of his day affirmed that the triumph of Spain in this war cost more than four thousand Spanish lives among a conquering army of some forty thousand (Márquez Villanueva 19). In this novel Galdós reminds us that Moroccan lives were lost as well.

On the other hand, to characterize *Aita Tettauen* and *Carlos VI en La Rápita* as historical war novels would be inaccurate. They fall into several categories: picaresque, romance, adventure, and perhaps even intrigue, as characters constantly seem to change identities. With all this implicit political and historical dialogue, there is another crucial factor related to Said's concept of orientalism. Particularly in *Aita Tettauen*, Galdós takes great pains to describe issues of cultural and religious identity. He includes in his cast of characters not only Christian Spaniards but also Jews and Muslims, along with the most curious of all, El Nasiry (Gonzalo Ansúrez), the would-be Spanish Muslim who plays a crucial role in the narrative project of both works.

As he creates El Nasiry and has him narrate the third part of *Aita Tettauen*, Galdós is an unwitting precursor of today's debates about postcolonialism: the result is a dialogue on the notion of reality according to one's subject position. Our Canarian author interrogates the very reality he is describing by rendering it through the eyes of a self-proclaimed Muslim—something of a Lawrence of Arabia figure, a man who, in addition to donning all the accoutrements of being a male Arab, also espouses Islam (unlike T. E. Lawrence). While the first and second parts of the novel have to do with the war itself as filtered through the eyes of Santiuste, the narrative voice in the third part undergoes a major change in register. In this third part a man from the other side narrates the history of the Moroccan War.

Thus, Galdós inserts his own brand of cultural authenticity with references to Allah, descriptions of battles won by valorous Arabs, and exultations of the Moroccan combatants, along with mentions of Christians as infidels (249, 252, 253). While it is tempting to imagine a privileged subject position on the part of this convert to Islam, a careful reading of the text within Galdós's cultural and historical framework suggests that positing El Nasiry as a vehicle for historical or cultural truth is reductive. Galdós is by no means a Spanish version of the Mexican Miguel León Portilla (*Visión de los vencidos*) who pretends to offer the "real" history of the Moroccan War from the point of view of the conquered Moroccans. He never loses sight of the fact that his Muslim narrator is originally Spanish; indeed, he is a renegade, something of a crackpot who decided to cross to the other side. His narration is not always reliable, even though his defamiliarizing assessments of things both Spanish and Moroccan are worth the reader's pondering. In Cadalso's *Cartas marruecas* and Montesquieu's *Lettres persanes*, the Western authors force their presumably Western readers to look at their own culture through the eyes of the Moroccan other—in Said's terms, through the eyes of an oriental subject. Said himself intuited the effect of this kind of discourse when he remarks in *Orientalism* that, in the late eighteenth century, the Orient becomes "an integral part of European material civilization and culture" (3). Indeed, this ambivalent cultural dialogue emerges in part from Spain's loss of imperial world status.

One might say that the way Galdós renders his reality is as orientalist as Alarcón's: it is a poor imitation of how a Muslim might speak. He resorts to mock clichés such as "Allah's blessings," "trusting the protection of Heaven," and "the infidels spend their time in ridiculous practices" (*Aita Tettauen* 249). There seems to be no free will (as an orientalist description of Islamic beliefs might assume); truth is written in the Qur'an; Allah's wish will win no matter what. Indeed, Galdós's own rendition of how an Arab, or a self-assumed Arab, might speak is orientalist.[10] On the other hand, Galdós's orientalism is self-conscious: in part 4 El Nasiry takes back much of what he said in part 3 since he was writing at the behest of his protector, El Zebdy, "according to Islamic sensibilities" (356). Galdós knew what he was doing; there is no pretense of offering the "real" picture of the Arab perspective on the Moroccan War. Márquez Villanueva's discussion of Galdós's determination to present the other side of the conflict is too celebratory. He designates the change in narrative voice in the third part of the novel as Galdós's most accurate achievement (34), but, more importantly, it is the way our canonical nineteenth-century realist problematizes reality itself by juxtaposing several subject positions: that of Alarcón (and his nationalist and orientalist ilk), that of Santiuste, and that of this curious renegade Muslim convert. Galdós's orientalist discourse becomes itself the object of interrogation as Spain continues to lose world power.

Perhaps the clearest criticism of Spanish imperialist culture in these novels is the way they show how some in Spain construct North African identity in a way that resembles Castilian sensibilities. The most significant example of this is the discourse of old Halconero, Lucila's father, who is convinced there is a racial connection between Spaniards and North Africans. "Moors and Spaniards are more akin than it seems; if you don't count a bit of religion or language, the resemblances in kinship and style are surprising. . . . What's a Moor, other than a Spanish Muslim? . . . Their harems are different from ours only in that theirs are open" (105). Halconero goes on like this for over a page before his daughter interrupts him. With his typical wit and perception of human foibles, Galdós has rendered a Spanish archetype, an ultrapatriot who constructs a bond between what he conceives as essentially Arab or Moorish and the Spanish national character. In essence, Spaniards and Moors are kindred spirits despite the difference in religions; they are cultures coming from the same roots.

If we trace this archetype, we see permutations throughout Spanish history, including in the 1920s and 1930s among the so-called Africanista generals, those waging the imperialist wars in Morocco and also plotting the insurrection against the Second Republic. Among them was none other than Francisco Franco,[11] notorious for his insurrection, an event that Galdós seems to predict in a variety of ways. Halconero is himself an "Africanista"; he is an unapologetic Spanish orientalist absorbed by the construction of Arab culture, a man who knows what he knows not through experience but through the assimilation of conventional knowledge. But along with Halconero, we also become intimately familiar with his son-in-law Gonzalo, who is living the life of an Arab and goes by El Nasiry. The unlikely contrast and the playfulness with which our author structures it further indicate the fall and ultimate disappearance of Spain's imperial prestige on the world stage.

Much of the same exploration of the Spanish-Arab connection manifests itself in *Carlos VI en La Rápita*.[12] Galdós transitions seamlessly from one war or skirmish to another: the next one is an aborted coup, perhaps even more pathetic and risible than the war in Morocco. When Santiuste, now the first-person narrator, hears rumors of a pending attempt to force

Queen Isabella II to abdicate and bring Carlos Luis de Borbón (Carlos VI) to the throne, he breaks out into hysterical laughter. Not long after arriving back in Madrid from Africa, the wife of his benefactor, the marqués de Baramendi, informs him there is a conspiracy afloat:

> "Who is conspiring? The absolutists. . . . They assure me
> that two illustrious related families control the thread of this
> intrigue, . . . and that's what I'm calling the [royal] *Palace*,
> because *Palace* is synonymous with Nation for its ancestral and
> noble side. Doesn't it make you tremble? . . . I'll tell you in all
> honesty that I laughed at the story of this conspiracy as I've
> laughed at one of those comedies, like those masterpieces on the
> art of the ridiculous. . . ."
>   I could not keep myself from letting out an unfettered laugh,
> like a child, as infected as I was by this illustrious woman, the
> two of us laughing in unison without being able to utter a single
> word. (*Carlos VI* 136–38)[13]

A farce indeed, and in this case, as Galdós seems to be saying unwittingly, the farce has occurred before, the first time as history and the second time in *Aita Tettauen*.

The parallel he designs between the Tetouan War and this failed coup highlights Galdós's critique of Spanish imperialism. At one point in the novel, the so-called Arcipreste, the Carlist in whose custody Santiuste finds himself as he reports on the coup at the behest of Baramendi, suggests that the timing of the insurrection is linked to the signing of the peace resolution in Morocco, an event that General Ortega thought mistakenly, as Santiuste explains, would have rallied all Spain to his side (*Carlos VI* 196–97). The ironic and playful debunking of the "greatness" of the Spanish empire manifests itself further in the narration of the curious events and strategic details of these skirmishes; all are anything but grandiose.

Moreover, both novels highlight the development of the main characters, Santiuste and El Nasiry, who are on a quest to find an identity unencumbered by things Spanish, particularly the Spanish empire. Almost geometrically, Galdós juxtaposes these two very different characters estranged from their own culture, and, as he does so, he explores what it is to be Spanish. Suggesting that our author does not fall into the traps of orientalism or that he remains impervious to stereotypes, as does Márquez Villanueva (26), is not in my view accurate. Rather, he uses the orientalism of his two characters to question their own constructions of reality.

Questions about identity abound in this novel, as we see in the development and creation of the main character, Santiuste, also known as Confusio. The narrator is just that, confused, and his confusion becomes the
reader's. As he says at the opening of *Carlos VI*, he is no longer sure of
his own name: Yahía is what the Arabs call him, Alarcón mockingly calls
him Profetángano, Don Bíblico, and for other Arabs, not confident of his
honorable intentions, he is Djinn (a little devil) (5). In these beginning
sentences he talks about himself and his own writerly enterprise:

> God is witness, I don't know what my name is anymore! . . .
> Don Toro Godo has nicknamed me Confusio (spelled with an
> s). . . . I have come to realize that I am the one named Juan
> who came from Spain with O'Donnell's army, wearing pretty
> much what he had on, with a humble and pure surname, that
> I believe was Santiuste. . . . That's who I am, that's who I was.
> I want to reconstruct my synthetic self and base it on the new
> consciousness I need after so many mishaps in my African life,
> a life so downtrodden and exuberant. (*Carlos VI* 5)

It is precisely Confusio's "new consciousness" that is also the foundation of *Carlos VI en La Rápita*, Galdós's sequel to *Aita Tettauen*. Yet that
consciousness is hardly a steadfast conviction or ideology. On the contrary,
its ideology is confusion—ambivalence in the wake of empire.

As a complement to Confusio, the man who does not seem to know what
he believes or whom he loves, we have his foil, El Nasiry, who also has an alias.
He is, by contrast, the Muslim convert who seems confident in his own beliefs, no matter how out of touch they would appear to virtually all of Galdós's
readers at the time the text was written, as well as to those of us whose twenty-
first-century sensibilities are more akin to Santiuste's than to El Nasiry's. At the
same time, El Nasiry represents a curious African Other because he himself,
like Juan Sin Tierra and T. E. Lawrence who will follow him, has read and assimilated the construction of Moorish identity and presents it to the members
of his former tribe. However, perhaps unlike the cultural figures I have mentioned, El Nasiry demonstrates a level-headedness that defies (perhaps even
subverts) the orientalist designs of his former identity group as they create
knowledge through discourse. A clear example is the assessment he provides to
Santiuste of the causes and effects of the Tetouan War:

> Well, just so you know, in this land [Morocco] Don Quixotes
> and Cids don't have much to do. And since you have brought

them with you, let them go back with you to Spain. . . . You
know, my son, that honor and chivalry here are replaced
by just living as one can, abiding by religious customs and
obligations. . . . In the Spain on this side of the sea, honor does
not yield anything to eat, and money is not frowned upon, no
matter where it comes from. (*Carlos VI* 40)

The end of empire has given Santiuste, Gonzalo, and Galdós the opportunity to reflect on Spanish culture. Moreover, particularly in this passage, it allows us a glimpse of Spain through the eyes of a Spaniard who
has jumped ship.

In the last analysis, both novels and both characters, Juan Santiuste
(aka Confusio) and Gonzalo Ansúrez (aka El Nasiry), represent Galdós's
critical, dialogical, skeptical, and mischievous deconstruction of the
Spanish empire at the turn of the century. Recalling Galdós's earnestness
in the prologue to *Alma y vida*—"Veía . . . el pueblo vivo aún y con resistencia bastante para perpetuarse" (933; I saw . . . that the people were
still alive and resilient enough to perpetuate itself)—he seems to take a
different path in these two subsequent war novels as he distances Spain
from itself. The recreation of the Moroccan War has made Galdós move
from the tone of Machado's "pasado macizo de la raza" (solid past of the
race, as he says in the prologue to *Alma y vida*) toward radical skepticism.
Santiuste says as much in the final words of *Carlos VI*: "Farewell, past
happenings that I am putting down on paper. . . . Future happenings,
where shall I go to find you?" (303). Perhaps the answer to his question
is the next Moroccan War.

Notes

1. All translations are mine unless noted otherwise.
2. Francisco Márquez Villanueva's "Estudio Preliminar" to the most recent
   edition of *Aita Tettauen* and *Carlos VI en La Rápita* (2004) is perhaps
   the most exhaustive analysis of the work to date and makes specific
   (albeit passing) reference to the pertinence of this novel to the concept of
   "orientalism" (26). Márquez Villanueva's notes, in addition to his preliminary
   analysis, are remarkably informative. I also rely on Susan Martin-Márquez's
   pioneering book, *Disorientations*, as well as her articles on the cultural
   presence of Africa in Spain, and vice versa. See also Tofiño-Quesada's
   pertinent exploration of "Spanish Orientalism" for an explanation of the
   persistence of orientalism in Spanish cultural practices in the twentieth-

century colonization of African territories. Another indirectly related study is Kirsty Hooper's "Reading Spain's African Vocation," which explores the "Moorish Priest" as a prominent figure in three late nineteenth-century Spanish novels. Interestingly, *Aita Tettauen* fits into Hooper's analysis. See also Carl Jubran's dissertation, *Spanish Internal Orientalism*. Many Hispanists await the publication of this work as a book.

3. Susan Martin-Márquez, in her penetrating analysis of the fraught relations between Spain and Africa in the modern era, makes this point compellingly (*Disorientations*). See also her essay, "Here's Spain Looking at You." Similarly, Fernández Cifuentes describes the orientalist ways in which Andalusia (or the Orient within the Spanish Orient) has been represented in Spain's own twentieth-century writing (Ortega, Lorca, Alberti), as well as in travel literature of European cultures outside of Spain. See also Santiáñez; Hooper; and Jubran. Regarding the pertinence or application of Spain within the debates on orientalism, see Linhard. In the prologue to the Spanish translation of *Orientalism*, Said addresses his omission of Spain.

4. The conventional wisdom on Galdós's "National Episodes" is that they are popular works that Galdós wrote both to entertain and to fatten his pocketbook (Berkowitz 101). However, many Hispanists have questioned this wisdom with excellent literary analyses of the "Episodes" (Tsuchiya; Urey).

5. See Márquez Villanueva (17–21), as well as Álavarez Chillida (122–29), on the African war.

6. We see this, for example, in *Misericordia*: "The parish of San Sebastián has two facades, like some people" (11).

7. Lucila, as the embodiment of Galdós's comments on the decadence of empire, suggests the feminine nature of the empire in decay: while robust, masculine, and shrewd in the days of Hernán Cortés, the loss of the final colonies points to the figure of an aging woman.

8. See Nil Santiáñez's article on Alarcón's orientalist discourse in his *Diario*. It is interesting that Galdós intuitively perceived the nationalist and paternalistic tendencies in the way his "Perico" Alarcón reports on the war. Galdós's take on the war not only questions Alarcón but, in his own way, echoes Said's critique. See also Joseph Schraibman's article comparing Alarcón's assessment of the Tetouan War with that of Galdós, as well as Martin-Márquez's *Disorientations* (124–26).

9. In *The Dialogical Imagination* Bakhtin asserts that the use of parody is an indication that a word, style, or way of thinking has become or is becoming outdated.

10. See Martin-Márquez's interesting take on Galdós's linguistic appropriation (*Disorientations* 44–45).

11. See Madariaga.
12. La Rápita is a town on the Ebro Delta from which Don Carlos launched his Carlist coup.
13. For those unfamiliar with the particularities of nineteenth-century Spanish history, the Carlists and Carlism are something of a sui generis Spanish phenomenon originating in 1833 with the death of Ferdinand VII, who died without a male heir, and whose brother, don Carlos Luis de Borbón, contested the coronation of Ferdinand's daughter Isabel. Beyond that, Carlism as an ideology is linked to absolutism, as well as to local (that is, regional) control of land. It is also seen as ultra-Catholic and traditionalist, as it reacted against land reforms and the extension of suffrage. Spain suffered three Carlist (civil) wars, all of which had ended when Galdós wrote this novel but one of which had not been fought at the time setting of *Aita Tettauen* and *Carlos VI en La Rápita*.

Works Cited

Alarcón. Pedro. *Diario de un testigo de la guerra de África*. Ed. Alberto Navarro González. Madrid: Ediciones del Centro, 1974.

Álvarez Chillida, Gonzalo. *El antisemitismo en España: La imagen del judío*. Madrid: Marcial Pons, Historia, 2002.

Bakhtin, M. M. *The Dialogical Imagination*. Ed. Michael Holquist. Trans. Caryl Emerson and Michael Holquist. Austin: U of Texas P, 1981.

Berkowitz, Hyman Chonon. *Pérez Galdós, Spanish Liberal Crusader*. Madison: U of Wisconsin P, 1948.

Fernández Cifuentes, Luis. "Southern Exposure: Early Tourism and Spanish National Identity." *Journal of Iberian and Latin American Studies* 13 (2007): 133–48.

Hooper, Kirsty. "Reading Spain's 'African Vocation': The Figure of the Moorish Priest in Three *fin de siglo* Novels (1890–1907)." *Revista de Estudios Hispánicos* 40 (2006): 171–95.

Jubran, Carl. *Spanish Internal Orientalism, Cultural Hybridity, and the Production of National Identity: 1877–1940*. Diss. University of California, San Diego, 2002.

León Portilla, Miguel. *Visión de los vencidos*. Mexico City: Universidad Nacional Autónoma de México, 2008.

Linhard, Tabea. "In the Precarious Exilic Realm: Edward Said's Andalusian Journeys." *Edward Said and Jaques Derrida: Reconstellating Humanism and the Global Hybrid*. Ed. Mina Karvanta and Nina Morgan. Cambridge: Cambridge Scholars, 2008. 140–57.

Madariaga, María Rosa de. *Los moros que trajo Franco*. Barcelona: Martínez Roca, 2002.

Márquez Villanueva, Francisco. "Estudio preliminar." Pérez Galdós, *Aita Tettauen* 7–94.

Martin-Márquez, Susan. *Disorientations: Spanish Colonialism in Africa and the Performance of Identity*. New Haven: Yale UP, 2008.

———. "Here's Spain Looking at You: Shifting Perspectives on North African Otherness in Galdós and Fortuny." *Arizona Journal of Hispanic Cultural Studies* 5 (2001): 7–25.

Marx, Karl. *The 18th Brumaire of Louis Bonaparte*. Trans. Daniel De Leon. Chicago: Charles H. Kerr, 1907.

Mignolo, Walter. *The Idea of Latin America*. Malden, MA: Blackwell, 2005.

Pérez Galdós, Benito. *Aita Tettauen*. Ed. Francisco Márquez Villanueva. Madrid: Akal, 2004.

———. *Carlos VI en La Rápita*. Madrid: Casa Editorial Hernando, 1925.

———. *Misericordia*. Madrid: Austral, 1984.

Said, Edward. "Andalusia's Journey." *Travel and Leisure* May 2009. Web. Jan. 2011.

———. *Orientalism*. New York: Vintage, 1979.

———. *Out of Place: A Memoir*. New York: Vintage, 1999.

———. "Travelling Theory." *The World, the Text, and the Critic*. Cambridge, MA: Harvard UP, 1983. 226–47.

Santiáñez, Nil. "De la tropa al tropo: Colonialismo, escritura de guerra y enunciación metafórica en *Diario de un testigo de la guerra de África*." *Hispanic Review* 76.1 (2008): 71–93.

Schraibman, Joseph. "Pedro Antonio de Alarcón y Galdós: dos visiones de la guerra de África (1859–1860)." *La Torre (Homenaje a Albert A. Sicroff)* 1 (1987): 539–47.

Tofiño-Quesada, Ignacio. "Spanish Orientalism: Uses of the Past in Spain's Colonization of America." *Comparative Studies of South Asia, Africa and the Middle East* 23.1–2 (2003): 141–48.

Tsuchiya, Akiko. "History as Language in the First Series of the *Episodios Nacionales*: The Literary Creation of Gabriel de Araceli." *Anales Galdosianos* 23 (1988): 11–25.

Urey, Diane. *The Novel Histories of Galdós*. Princeton: Princeton UP, 1989.

9

Inscribing Indianos into Modern Imperial Histories

Lisa Surwillo
Stanford University

The Spanish empire in America may have officially ended with the Spanish-American War, but the flow of human and economic capital continued and an imperial mindset survived the victories of the United States. In this essay I take the theme of this volume in two directions. First, I question the finality of this end of the Atlantic empire. While the Spanish government did not maintain legal control of Puerto Rico or Cuba after 1898 (although it did retain colonies on the African Atlantic), an imperial storyline survived among northern Spanish emigrants who continued to move to the Americas in an attempt to strike it rich, known as *hacer las Américas*, well into the twentieth century. My focus also diverges from Hispanism or Regenerationism as political and ideological questions on a national scale. My questions are grounded instead in the local stories that framed empire as it was lived in daily life in Spain. Second, I consider the ends of the tales of empire, taking into account both their denouement and their present social function. In other words, to what ends has the story of nineteenth-century empire (and the continuation of some of its practices into the twentieth century) been recast in recent years? The emigrants who returned, known as *indianos*, remain vital figures for local, regional, and global identities. This chapter examines the ways in which the *indiano* arc, as a narrative, is rewritten in literature, popular culture, and the architectural legacy of indiano houses.

From the beginning of the colonization of the Americas, the Spanish monarchy carefully monitored emigration. Carlos Martínez Shaw describes its regulations: "It hardly forced anyone to move to the new lands; however, it did not permit free access to a continent that it considered its exclusive patrimony existing for the benefit of its subjects" (27). The exact nature of emigration policies varied considerably over the first three hundred years of Spanish colonialism in its American territories, but the Spanish monarchy always attempted to control the movement of persons and goods across the Atlantic. After 1824, the Spanish government lightened restrictions on emigration to the Antilles in order to facilitate the influx of Spaniards from the Iberian Peninsula; the policy reflected Spain's concerns about maintaining the loyalty of Puerto Rico and Cuba after the wars of independence in Central and South America. However, as Birgit Sonesson has discussed, the government also attempted to keep these emigrants in Spanish territories and to prevent them from departing the islands for Venezuela. In 1848, the Spanish government outlawed emigration to South America outright, but lifted the ban in 1853 (15). The military and demographic impact of emigration was too high for Spain to allow population and economic growth in lands now out of its sphere of influence. Spaniards aspiring to escape a stifling economic situation—or, sometimes, military service—maintained a vision of the Americas as a land of economic opportunity. Such a belief was both a literary hyperbole, of which Galician peasant Ildara's fantasy of stooping to collect gold coins rolling down the street in Emilia Pardo Bazán's short story "Las medias rojas" is characteristic, and an incentive for emigration. The American dream survived the political upheavals of political independence during both the first third and final years of the nineteenth century. Official emigration policies continued to evolve, but even after 1898, the official end of the empire in the Americas, the former colonies continued to serve as a place for emigrants to enrich themselves. Moreover, during and after the political empire, emigration perpetuated an imperialist discourse that supposed the right of Spaniards to *hacer las Américas*.

According to the Asturian government, between 1835 and 1930 a full 41 percent of the population was directly impacted by emigration, through their own or their family member's departure to the Americas (Asturias Paraíso 18). In just one year, 1860, nearly twenty-five hundred departure papers were granted in Asturias (Martínez Cachero 251). Many were seasonal laborers in other parts of Spain, others emigrated abroad for a limited term and returned with sufficient earnings to live comfortably, and a few managed to climb the social ladder. The discussion of remittances documented the sustained goal to *hacer las Américas* and confirmed long-standing financial dependencies. Underscoring Spain's undiminished financial linkages with the Americas, the newspaper *ABC* reported that during 1923 Asturians abroad remitted staggering amounts back to Spain. In this one year, Asturians in Argentina and Uruguay sent 441 million pesetas; those in Cuba, 31 million pesetas; in Mexico, 11 million pesetas; in Brazil and Chile, 10 million pesetas each; in Bolivia, Puerto Rico, and Ecuador, 1 million pesetas from each country (Penzol 86). The focus on American money in Spain pointed to established historical trends. Although scale, geography, government, and nearly every other structural aspect of Spanish-American relations had changed, money had not ceased to flow eastward. (As a very general comparison, remittances from the Americas constituted 23 percent of the official budget in 1560 under King Philip II [Tortolla and Comín 141].) Emigration to the Americas, as well as to Europe, continues today, but explicit imperial language of conquest and triumph faded by the first third of the twentieth century.

Emigrants not only followed the money, they also followed their families: consistent with established patterns, itineraries were often based on community ties. When chain migrants met success abroad, friends and relatives from their hometowns joined them. Thus, for example, the *indianos* in the towns of Malleza (concejo de Salas), Somao, and Labarces went to Cuba, whereas those from Luarca, Llanes, and Colombres went to various cities in Cuba, Mexico, and, in lesser numbers, Guatemala. Local dynamics of space and relations transcended national or imperial limits, as villages and families were partially reconstituted abroad.

The degree of success among migrants varied immensely, and not all emigrants returned to Spain. Among those who did return, generally known as indianos because of their experience in the "Indies," only a much smaller subset wielded significant political and economic power, yet their trajectories have tended to shape the narrative of nineteenth- and early twentieth-century emigrations. The most spectacular rags-to-riches stories of the nineteenth century were those of poor emigrants who rapidly ascended through direct or indirect participation in the slave trade as financiers. For example, Domingo Aldama emigrated from the Basque Country to Havana in the first years of the nineteenth century. He initially worked as a clerk in a textile warehouse, invested his savings in slave trafficking during its transition from a licit to illicit trade, and quickly became one of the richest men in Cuba.[1] Julián Zulueta, the *príncipe de los negreros*, followed a similar path from the Basque Country to Cuba. He arrived in Havana poor in the 1830s and labored for several years until he inherited enough money to start his own businesses. After his marriage to Francisca de los Dolores Samà, Zulueta became perhaps the most powerful force in the transatlantic slave trade, an influential landowner, businessman, and politician. He ultimately returned to Madrid and assumed a position in the Senate. His wife's uncle Salvador Samà i Martí was himself a major slave trader who had emigrated to Cuba when young and entered the trade with his uncle Pau Samà, later investing in the sugar and wine trades. Zulueta formed part of the third generation of Samà slaving interests. In his meteoric rise, Salvador Samà founded the Primer Banco Español de la Isla de Cuba, served as mayor of Havana, and profoundly influenced Antillean politics (Rodrigo, "Con un pie"). Ultimately, Salvador Samà was granted the title of Marqués de Marianao by Isabel II and became a lifelong member of the Senate. While he did not return permanently to Spain, his heir, Salvador Samà i Torrents (twice mayor of Barcelona), used his great-uncle's *negrero* money to hire the talents of Antonio Gaudí and José Fontsere y Mestres (who also created Barcelona's Ciutadella) and built the lush Parc Samà in Cambrils (near Tarragona). Today, the Parc Samà offers couples the opportunity to purchase the imperial experience in a unique way: the romantic, colonial garden is available as a wedding location that explicitly evokes the lost paradise of not Eden but the Antilles.

The frames for interpreting migrations, and the activities of the *indianos* in the Americas, differ across Spain. For example, in twentieth-century Galicia, the master narrative of that region's migration casts the mass exodus as "a contribution to the higher cause of 're-Hispanizing America'" (Núñez 240). Clearly part of a neo-imperial regenerationist discourse, Galicians in America and, to a lesser extent, in Spain more generally presented their migrants as the front line in keeping the Spanish-speaking Americas "Hispanic" in the twentieth century (Núñez 240). Today in Galicia there are competing interpretations of what twentieth-century migration has meant to the *patria*, and ethnonationalism has been engaged by political groups of all ideologies. Various parties cultivate a positive memory of migration in an attempt to garner the votes of the offshore Galician community. Yet no one doubts the right of Spaniards to live and work, as Spaniards, in the Americas.

In the case of Asturias and Cantabria, the standard narrative of emigration, economic conquest, and triumphal return during the century bracketing the official end of empire (1830–1930) was punctuated by the construction of American-style mansions with vibrant colors and unique structure in the *indianos'* hometowns. The mansions, which currently attract tourists, offer a space from which to narrate the nineteenth-century empire, a period beyond the grand narrative of the age of discovery or the age of conquest (depending on who is remembering). These showpieces are the most visible monument to nineteenth- and twentieth-century emigration to the Americas. But while each unusual building symbolically represents the individual owner's displacement to a foreign land and display of success, more systemically, *indiano* architecture demonstrates a community's American roots. As Morales Saro has written, the typical Asturian (and to a lesser extent Cantabrian) *indiano* house also can be attributed to an "affective impulse, somewhere between nostalgic and presumptuous" (16). A town anchored by one or more of these mansions proclaimed its American ties in its new character.

Indiano architecture refers both to a particular sociology of architecture and, especially, "to a given environment that this architectural presence confers distinct characteristics. It is the summary consequences of a construction boom and of urbanistic growth in small population centers whose economies had only one visible transformation: the arrival of money from America and with it, highways and byways, reservoirs, wells, parks, statues from a grateful citizenry [etc.]" (Morales Saro 16). Indeed, in addition to his mansion, the indiano often built up the urban core of his village, distributing his spoils according to both family expectations and also moral and civic concerns. Through the construction of schools, buildings for religious communities, and community centers, indiano wealth acquired a moral legitimacy.[2] (One oft-visited example is the *conjunto cívico* in Somao, discussed below.) Their interventions materially improved lives in innumerable small towns and sometimes weakened the influence of the clergy on the local population. In *La Regenta*, Clarín satirizes this display of devotion and moral anxiety by the American wealthy in the character of Francisco Páez. However, while it is impossible to gauge the actual ethical code of the returned emigrants, high-minded concerns for the "people" should be considered with some caution: one nominal requirement for the granting of a noble title (in addition to cold hard cash) was the demonstration of public works and actions dedicated to the good of Spain. Some indianos constructed both their private mansions and civic structures, and tourists may visit an array of constructions that display their American triumphs. Of course, my aim is not to judge the intentions of specific indianos but rather to consider how they are remembered today in imperial terms.

Many of the indiano mansions that draw tourists are integrated into a route or have been profiled in the media. Principal among the mansion sites are the Cantabrian village of Comillas and the Asturian hamlet of Somao. The latter was rebuilt in the early twentieth century by progressive indianos who returned from Cuba, postempire, with a project to civilize their homeland in Spain. The current historical discourse about these indiano mansions places the majestic and the domestic in dialogue. In the town square of Somao, a plaque announces that this village "is the center possessing the most and best examples of indiano architecture. The church, the cinema and the schools were constructed with capital imported by emigrants in Cuba." The sign also notes the modernist style, the imagination, and the quality of the structures. Tourists visiting Somao can read a placard outside each mansion, detailing its architectural splendors: staircases, wrought ironwork, arts and crafts style, and, in the case of *La Casona*, a modernist mausoleum. Somao is noteworthy for its collective identity: not only are the private homes balanced by the construction of civic buildings (and a playground for the local children), but the hamlet as a whole is characterized as an indiano enterprise rather than as a village saved by the support of a single triumphant indiano.

The small Cantabrian town of Comillas was originally a set to stage the importance of its most successful indiano, Antonio López, for royal eyes. López succeeded in demonstrating his expansive influence and fortune to King Alfonso XII in order to maintain a foothold in the Bourbon regime. López ultimately gained preferential treatment in banking and shipping, acquired the tobacco monopoly, and was granted the title of Marquis by Alfonso XII. The same staging is now used to tell a similar story but to a different audience of Spanish tourists. Similar to Zulueta, Aldama, and Samà, López arrived in Cuba while still a minor, "to all appearances, fleeing from the justice system" (Rodrigo, "La casa de comercio" 255). He married the daughter of his landlord, Andrés Bru, and moved with her family to Barcelona. With his father-in-law's money, he made his initial fortune by participating intermittently in the illegal slave trade and through real estate (in the late 1840s early 1850s). In his study of López's life and finances, Martín Rodrigo establishes that the slave trade grew López's capital quickly (Rodrigo, "La casa de comercio" 256). It allowed him to diversify and expand his holdings, both in Cuba with coffee and sugar plantations, as well as shipping lines, and in Barcelona, where he invested significantly in projects such as the large bank Crédito Mercantil, transatlantic shipping companies, and the Philippine tobacco monopoly. The epitome of the self-made man, his influence in Spain seemed limitless. A visit to Comillas today brings this version of Antonio López's biography to life. His son Claudio López may be in the process of beatification, but the town venerates Antonio López, the first marqués de Comillas, as its savior. Staff members at the tourist office recount his rise from poverty and his return and gift of beneficence to the town of his birth as a near miracle.

Tourists continue to see the American presence, as Morales Saro notes; it is most evident in the villages that visibly break with autochthonous architecture. Most visits to indiano mansions today present an uncomplicated view of conquest and triumphal return, of overseas gains transformed into public works and domestic self-promoting monuments that announce their inhabitants' American provenance. But other emigrants who opted for the social and aesthetic agenda of integration upon their return from the Americas bought or built traditional mountain-style houses that imitated the aristocracy to which they aspired. While the grand palaces tell a story of triumph and glamour, not all indianos returned and built sumptuous modernist palaces painted in vibrant tropical colors. Their American history also is embedded in small Cantabrian towns where stories are personal and recalled individually, neither figuring on any government-sponsored route nor rounding out a unified narrative.

Maria Luisa González Torre, the great-granddaughter of a would-be indiano who never returned from Cuba, walks interested outsiders through her village of Labarces, near San Vicente de la Barquera, past large stone mansions whose austere exteriors give a different face to the story of conquest (foreign and domestic) by the families within. Here the indianos did not proclaim the American origins of their wealth in aesthetically eccentric terms but, instead, immersed themselves in a traditional architectural idiom. González Torre estimates that 10 percent of the homes in this tiny village were built with American money. The houses may not be flamboyant, but the indiano families of this town were major players in the transatlantic economy, including a vice president of the Banco Hispano-Americano (recently merged with the powerhouse Banco de Santander, which is as involved in overseas politics today as it was in the nineteenth and early twentieth centuries). In Labarces, one witnesses the full integration of Cantabrian indianos as heroes and conquerors. When not showcased in modernist architecture, the story is neither as obvious nor as celebratory. The fortunes of conquest were used to the same ends of public display and private alliances as in other towns: construction and acquisition of large homes, consolidation of political influence, and intermarriage with aristocracy. For example, the Gil de Reboleño family has a pantheon within the parish chapel, while another indiano family with Cuban money obtained a coat of arms from a down-and-out aristocratic family during the Spanish Civil War, supposedly in exchange for a sack of flour. It now is displayed as their own on an exterior wall near the street. Such opportune acquisitions were strategically used as aesthetic and cultural markers of the solid influence of these families, who were granted the title of don from villagers and treated as heroes and *triunfadores*. The rhetoric of the self-made man, the discourse of conquest, and the policy conserving riches remained tightly braided even as they adapted to the reigning political ideology. These families tilted politically to the right during the Civil War and throughout the twentieth century. In 2010, the flag of fascist Spain (featuring the black eagle) was still visible in the village: the adoration of Spanish imperial grandeur appeared alive and well.

Even when integration was not the indiano's primary goal, the story of indiano triumph overshadows precise knowledge of what the emigrants who left Spain to *hacer las Américas* actually did. Over time, these historical figures became larger-than-life myths, and, then, the secrets of the empire were slowly lost. The accomplished epidemiologist Julián Zulueta, socialist mayor of Ronda, nephew of Julián Besteiro, and student of Francisco Giner de los Ríos recounted to Spanish radio listeners in 2011 that he only discovered that his ancestor Julián Zulueta was a slave trader from a novel by Pío Baroja. His father dismissed the fact as "foolishness by Baroja" ("Julián"). The moderator of the radio show *Siluetas* helpfully suggested that Zulueta was a "good slave trader," and although Dr. Zulueta retorted, "I wouldn't say he was good," he praised his ancestor as the savior of Cuba who organized the island's defense during the Ten Years' War (1868–1878) without help from the central government in Madrid. In sum, according to Dr. Zulueta, the "prince of the slave traders . . . kept Cuba functioning" ("Julián"). Although the family knew little of Zulueta's American story, today in Vitoria the Zulueta Palace, built in the early twentieth century with money brought from Cuba by Julián Zulueta, is openly acknowledged as a slave palace. It was the headquarters of the Sancho el Sabio Foundation from 1991 to 2009 and a symbol of Euskadi culture, even as it was a material witness to Basque participation in imperialism and Spanish nationalist projects during the nineteenth century. Today, the uncertain fate of the palace has sparked frank discussion of its genesis and the place of buildings created with slave money (Góngora).

Contemporary media, too, has explored the question of how to reinscribe indianos and their various legacies from the Americas. Their money, their ideas, and their role in both plantation economies and Asturian industry awaken conflicting attitudes toward the past. The most attractive story to tourists who wish to relive a historical moment of imperial grandeur and social mobility presents an uncomplicated narrative grounded in the indiano mansion and shrines to the Compañia Transatlántica, such as the Casa del Indiano, a theme restaurant in the Mercado del Este in Santander. This narrative celebrates indiano contributions to Spain and the Americas without considering the actual economic realities of transatlantic travel and what was extracted by and from emigrants while abroad.

The story of the end of empire in Asturias has been staged on television, where the exotic elegance of the indiano mansions sets the scene for the discovery of Antillean secrets in the roots of the new modern Spain that emerged in the 1920s. *La Señora*, a three-season dramatic series directed by Jordi Frades that aired on RTVE between 2008 and 2010, was a hit by any measure: its final episode broke all records in Spain, with over five million viewers. The domestic settings and characterization revolve around the rich indiano and tobacco trader Ricardo Márquez and his daughter Victoria (the titular "señora"). His principal adversary, the false nobleman Gonzalo, is revealed in the final episodes to be both a commoner and a confidence man. Gonzalo acquired his title through marriage whereas Ricardo Márquez made his way in the Americas before marrying into money (although he is a widower at the beginning of the series). After Ricardo's death, divisions between the families collapse and Gonzalo ultimately marries Victoria by means of underhanded dealings and collusion with the clergy. Various other characters (such as Márquez's ally and shipyard baron, Álvaro de Viana), as well as filming on location in Colombres and Garaña de Pría, provide a veritable set of highlights of the Asturian indiano and his story. However, although the memory of indiano transgressions and the shadows of nineteenth-century colonialism abound, particularly during the first season, they are profoundly transformed. In an active manipulation of the historical past, the show modifies elements of the indiano story in order to align all aspects of colonial transgression within one or two characters.

The place of Cuba in Asturias is narrated in the first season through these same two principal male characters. Ricardo Márquez is a heroic liberal indiano who brought new energy to Asturias. His progressive ideology is demonstrated through friendship with Benito Pérez Galdós, the contents of his library, his business practices, and a refusal to collaborate with the church and the aristocracy. He uses his money to stimulate the economy, support locals, and educate his children. His well-ordered house, the famous Casa Roja of Colombres, symbolizes his triumphant return and reintegration into Spain. Although Ricardo Márquez lived in Cuba (seas. 1, ep. 5, 35:00), he returned morally intact. The sins associated with slavery in Cuba are instead placed in the antagonist's family, composed of Gonzalo de Castro; Irene, the marquise de Castro; and Catalina, Irene's half-sister. Catalina is the illegitimate daughter of the old marqués de Castro and is Gonzalo's confidante. Mystery envelops Gonzalo's sister-in-law, and over the course of the first season we discover that "the blood of a black slave runs through her veins" (seas. 1, ep. 5, 29:00). Catalina, played by Spanish actress Laura Domínguez, is phenotypically white but bears the shame of miscegenation. Her secret is not just racial impurity but also imperial impurity that has returned to Spain with Antillean money. Catalina not only embodies many stereotypes of Afro-Hispanic slaves and their knowledge of the world but also represents Spain's inability to articulate the human implications of empire.

Catalina is in love with her sister Irene's husband Gonzalo, and there is more than a whiff of incest. Through the character of Catalina, *La Señora* effectively imports the Antillean narrative of the tragic *mulata* from novels such as Cirilo Villaverde's *Cecilia Valdés* (Catalina even wears whiteface in an attempt to win Gonzalo's affection in seas. 1, ep. 10, 47:00). A subversive force, indomitable except through love, Catalina ultimately poisons a pregnant Irene and thus destroys the ancient Castro family line: Irene and her fetus die. In other words, Catalina embodies the danger of the invisible, unspoken foundations of modern empire unleashed in the metropolis. Most explicitly, she practices a form of Santería and is shown wielding dolls and herbs in her attempts to harm both Victoria and Irene (seas. 1, ep. 5, 70:00; ep. 10, 26:00, 57:00, 70:00). However, Gonzalo controls Catalina through racial blackmail, and his characterization as a villain is intensified by both his knowledge and articulation of Catalina's heritage. In scenes of melodramatic intensity Gonzalo makes visible the logic of slavery, physically forcing Catalina to look at the portrait of the marqués, the silent witness to the family's (and Spain's) transatlantic secrets. Gonzalo points to a series of half-buried transgressions: "This is your father, take a good look at him: this same man was Irene's father, yet you don't look anything alike at all, for the blood of a black woman runs through your veins" (seas. 1, ep. 12, 71:00). He soon repeats his denunciation of her bloodlines and threatens to reveal her secret to the entire city: "It would be better for you if you kept your mouth shut, Catalina, because I swear to you that if you don't, the whole city is going to know who you really are" (seas. 1, ep. 12, 71:00–73:00). Through fear, intimidation, and force, Catalina's identity and eventually her existence are eliminated from the indiano town.

Catalina is envious of both Victoria and her own half-sister, but, significantly, she never appears in the famous Casa Roja (Ricardo Márquez's house in the series). By separating the Márquez family from Catalina and allying her with the evil Gonzalo, the series illustrates the neat division in contemporary narratives about Spaniards in former Spanish colonies—

before and after actual political independence. It would be plausible for Ricardo Márquez to have brought an Afro-Cuban woman with him to Spain, but because he is a melodramatically good character, the imperial crime of slavery behind such relations is transposed onto the Castro family. That is, the means (slavery) and the ends (return of capital) of empire are divided. Viewers condemn Gonzalo's machinations, question his friendship with Miguel Primo de Rivera (another figure tied to Cuba), and frown at the Castro family's association with African slavery as well as Gonzalo's repudiation of it. Yet, Ricardo remains idealized, as do the ends to which his money it employed. In spite of the illogical connections, the networks of slavery, family secrets, indianos, aristocracy, and Asturian economy in *La Señora* are reunited. The series' exploration of the economic ends of empire, however, extends to Victoria's generation and her response to inherited ownership of mines and tobacco factories, much as Antonio López's son Claudio López intervened with striking miners in the creation of Bustiello in order to neutralize social unrest. But the suggested parallels in the series point to unresolved issues in society at large. The historical question of how the culture of colonialism intersected with the lived experience of the general populace in Asturias after the end of empire has yet to be satisfactorily addressed. Generous indianos certainly donated their wealth to hospitals and schools, thus linking the Spanish poor with Antillean economics. But beyond the works of charity funded by Cuban sources, how did the sugar refineries, tobacco factories, and mines founded and developed by indianos import the realities of the Americas into the lives of Spaniards employed by these same indianos?

In conclusion, the relationship between the economic gains from a Spanish presence in the Americas before and after the empire's legal end in 1898 and the lived experience of an enduring culture of colonialism in the Iberian Peninsula is far more complex than the triumphant narrative of the wealthy indiano and his unique mansion might suggest. The year 1898 did not mark an entirely decisive break, and many migratory and economic practices remained in place after the Treaty of Paris. Their implications for Spanish economic development were decisive. For example, Rafael Anes has documented the relationship between American money and the growth of the Spanish banking system; José Ramón García López's findings suggest that all ships registered in the port of Avilés in the 1860s (as well as many in Gijón) were funded with indiano capital. Moreover, the roles of various prominent indianos in promoting the Asturian economy are well-known. However, the culture of colonialism transcended economics. The financial investment in Spanish industry aside, how was daily life

Americanized by those who determined to *hacer las Américas?* How were the financial ends of empire lived by Spaniards in Spain, not only in the fictionalized 1920s of *La Señora*, but also much earlier? In contrast to the celebratory discourse of tourism at the indiano *casonas*, several museums offer a more critical view of their legacy. The Centro de Interpretación del Poblado Minero de Bustiello celebrates the paternalism of the second marqués de Comillas, son of Antonio López, even as it demonstrates the living conditions of workers in his mines. Similarly, the Museo de La Ciudadela de Capua (opened in 2003) recreates the living conditions of the working class of Gijón starting in the last third of the nineteenth century. Celestino Solar, an indiano who had made his fortune in Cuba, built the housing units. His blocks of twenty-four units with a common latrine set the living conditions of numerous families until well after the Civil War. Such ends of empire endured long after 1898 but remain beyond the narrative of triumphant return and financial investment.

Notes

1. Moreno Fraginals ranks the Aldama clan as the twelfth-largest fortune in Cuba (265, 266).
2. The indianos' demonstrated concern for "the people," a version of aristocratic largesse, is given original treatment by Unamuno in his "San Manuel Bueno, mártir" where the wealthy indiano Lázaro Carballino stages his conversion to Catholicism at the hands of the parish priest, for the good of the village. He gives the moral gift of his soul in lieu of an architectural gift. For an example of the very real benefits indianos did bring to their villages, see Castrillo Sagredo.

Works Cited

Anes, Rafael. "Comerciantes-banqueros y banqueros en los orígenes de la banca regional asturiana." Diss. U de Oviedo, 1985.
"Ángel descubre el secreto de Gonzalo." *La Señora*. Diagonal TV. 3 Apr. 2008. Television.
Asturias Paraíso Natural. "Indianos y emigrantes." *Bajo Nalón*. Ayuntamiento de Pravia, Ayuntamiento de Soto del Barco, and Ayuntamiento de Muros, n.d.
Castrillo Sagredo, Benito. *El aporte de los "indianos" a la instrucción pública, a la beneficencia y al progreso en general de España*. Buenos Aires: n.p., 1926.
"El voluntario." *La Señora*. Diagonal TV. 3 Apr. 2008. Television.

García López, José Ramón. "La marina mercante asturiana, 1840–1900." *Transportes, Servicios y Telecomunicaciones* 13 (2007): 147–73.

Góngora, Francisco. "Zulueta, el negrero y un palacio de Vitoria." *Elcorreo.com.* El Correo, 11 July 2009. Web. 11 Oct. 2010.

"Julián de Zulueta." *Siluetas.* Corporación de Radio y Televisión Española, 29 May 2011. Web. 15 July 2011.

"Mantener las riendas." *La Señora.* Diagonal TV. 3 Apr. 2008. Television.

Martínez Cachero, Luis Alfonso. "Bibliografía de la emigración asturiana." *Bidea* 46 (1962): 250–56.

Martínez Shaw, Carlos. *La emigración española a América (1492–1824).* Colombres: Archivo de Indianos, 1994.

Moreno Fraginals, Manuel. *El ingenio: Complejo económico social cubano del azúcar.* Ed. Luis M. Traviesas. Vol. 2. Havana: Editorial de Ciencias Sociales, 1978.

Morales Saro, María Cruz. *Arquitectura de indianos en Asturias: Exposición organizada con motivo de inauguración del Archivo de Indianos de Colombres.* Colombres: Servicio de Publicaciones del Principado de Asturias, 1987.

Núñez Seixas, Xosé Manoel. "History and Collective Memories of Migration in a Land of Migrants: The Case of Iberian Galicia." *History and Memory* 14.1/2 (2002): 189–228.

Penzol, Pedro. "Mosaico de Asturias." *Bulletin of Spanish Studies* 2.6 (1925): 81–86 .

Rodrigo y Alharilla, Martín. "La casa de comercio de los marqueses de Comillas (1844–1920): continuidad y cambio en el capitalismo español." *Fortuna y Negocios: Formación y Gestión de Los Grandes Patrimonios (Siglos XVI–XX).* Ed. Hilario Casado Alonso and Ricardo Robledo Hernández. Valladolid, Spain: Ude Valladolid Secretariado de Publicaciones e Intercambio Editorial, 2002. 251–74.

———. "Con un pie en Cataluña y otro en Cuba: la familia Samà de Vilanova." *Estudis Històrics i Documents dels Arxius de Protocols* 16 (1998): 359–97.

Senado de España. "Expediente personal del Senador Vitalicio Marqués de Marianao, D. Salvador Samá y Martí." ES.28079.HIS-0267-01. Web.

Sonesson, Birgit. *Catalanes en Cuba: Un estudio de casos.* Colombres: Archivo de Indianos, 1995.

Tortolla, Gabriel, and Francisco Comín. "Fiscal and Monetary Institutions in Spain." *Transferring Wealth and Power from the Old to the New World: Monetary and Fiscal Institutions in the 17th through 19th Centuries.* Ed. Michael D. Bordo and Roberto Cortés-Conde. Cambridge: Cambridge UP, 2006.

Unamuno, Miguel de. *San Manuel Bueno, mártir; y tres historias más.* 5th ed. Madrid: Espasa-Calpe, 1963.

10

Hispanic Studies and the Legacy of Empire

Alejandro Mejías-López
Indiana University

The title of the symposium that was the seed of the present volume was accompanied by a framing chronology: "Empire's End: Transnational Connections in the Hispanic World, 1808–1898." Ostensibly aiming to focus the scope of the discussion on the nineteenth century, the chronology also carried within itself a paradox that I find symptomatic of the way in which both empire and transatlantic relations have been addressed by and large in Hispanic studies. The year 1808 points to the Napoleonic Empire and, particularly, to the French invasion of Spain and the resulting Spanish uprising against the occupying troops. The year 1898 refers to the so-called Spanish-American War and the emergence of the US Empire, rather than to the Cuban wars of independence. Thus, the chronology made visible what I find is a recurrent problem in our discipline: empire's end seems to be only comprehended, paradoxically, through empire itself. Both dates place the end of the Spanish empire in the hands of other empires and not in those of Latin American (or Philippine) revolutionaries.[1] They are only guessed at, invoked as it were, through the lens of empires, an object but not a subject. The phrase "transnational connections," however, seems to work in the opposite direction, evoking networks and flows seemingly void of power relations. The title, then, was an accurate reflection of dominant views of postcoloniality within Latin American and peninsular studies: on the one hand, a mere change of the imperial guard from Spanish to French and Anglo-American; on the other, a network of fraternal relations between

Spanish and Latin American writers, more often than not marginal to the writing of Hispanic literary histories at large.

In what follows I offer a brief reflection on the way these dynamics have shaped and still continue to shape our field and its possibilities for new directions; on the way that literary scholarship has found it so difficult to critically address empire in the postcolonial Hispanic context and to do so without simultaneously resurrecting empire in the process; on how the legacy of empire seems to continually threaten the prospect of reaching empire's end; and, finally, on the possibility that, rather than resurrecting empire or hailing its end, a meaningful and productive way to address the ghost of empire in Hispanic studies may be found by exploring the instances when imperial dynamics were unexpectedly reversed, turned on their head, and new dynamics and structures of power imagined and realized, forcing empire to come to terms with its own end.

The End of Empire: National Literary Histories, Hispanism, and the Construction of a Discipline

During the wars of independence, the subsequent formation of the new republics, and the rise of liberalism as the dominant ideology of the nineteenth century, liberal Spanish American creoles repeatedly declared their open rejection of all things Spanish and, seeing themselves at the avantgarde of modernity in the Hispanic world, relegated Spain to the realm of backwardness. This narrative of futurity, identified by Carlos Alonso as a central engine behind both the formation of an American identity and political independence, would soon turn into a source of tension that would define Spanish American cultural modernity. Although that tension would come about in relation to Europe's own claim to the modern, the geography of modern Europe never included Spain. However, as Spanish Americans undertook the arduous task of constructing modern nations and as literature became one of their central tools, the need arose for writing national literary histories that, tracing the so-called national spirit, helped legitimate the very existence of the nation. In this case, Spain posed a much more difficult challenge, as the notion of a national literature necessarily entailed dealing with the existence of a national language and the construction of a national past. As Beatriz González-Stephan states:

> All *Spanish American* literatures were written in the same
> language and seen, additionally, as the legacy of a metropolis

that was fought at all levels. In this sense, there was a block, not quite resolved, in the well-known debates between Bello and Sarmiento, which illuminate how difficult it was to assume that any of the national literatures had to be established in the Spanish language and, hence, had to also establish ties with the colonial past. (32)[2]

Even though the anti-Spanish fervor of postindependence gave way to a less polarizing attitude toward Spain and even though the very existence of historiography as a discipline demanded "a minimum of positivist objectivity" (32), both national literary histories as well as those of Spanish America as a whole would be eventually written and rewritten keeping Spanish literature at a safe distance—when not simply out of the picture—in the postindependence period. Regardless of the many changes in the relationship between Spanish America and Spain in the following two centuries, Spanish American literary history has been written by and large with its back to Spain, read instead in relation to other European and North American centers. This dominant vision allows Nicholas Shumway to state, "After Independence, Spanish American literature becomes increasingly disconnected from Spain. There are, of course, moments of rapprochement, for example during *modernismo* or among some of the vanguardist poets. But students of twentieth century Spanish American fiction would do better reading Tolstoy, Dostoyevsky, Joyce, Faulkner, and Proust, than Galdós, Miró, Cela, or Goytisolo" (297). Indeed, critics in the twentieth century have framed Spanish American literature in neocolonial terms by, paradoxically, doing away with its actual metropolitan center and shifting it instead to regions with which Latin America never had a colonial relationship to begin with.[3]

Spanish literary historiography has followed a similar path even if for the opposite reasons. By the time the modern concept of literary history and its strong ties to a given concept of nation developed in the nineteenth century, Spain had lost most of its empire, and power had irrevocably shifted to northern Europe. Thus, nineteenth-century Spanish nationalism was founded in a manner not unlike that of Spanish America—that is, through a war that was soon understood, and has since remained in the Spanish national imaginary, as a "war of independence." While Spain did not have to deal with the problems posed by a colonial past and indeed the heyday of imperial Spain was soon considered the golden age of Spanish letters, its literary production thereafter was inevitably mediated by Spain's newfound marginal position within the new European geopolitical order, particularly by its always complex relationship to France (Torrecilla). Hence, if Spanish Americans established a new relationship with northern Europe in part out of spite for Spanish cultural heritage, Spaniards established a similar relationship with their neighbors to the north out of what was perceived as the loss of its cultural glory. The literature produced in the former colonies could no longer be considered Spanish, and Spanish historiography, fixated as it has been on the place of Spanish literature within Europe, all but ignored Spanish American letters. Thus, through the opposite view of the past but a similar reaction to the political shifts of the nineteenth century, Spanish peninsular and Spanish American literary histories were written with their backs to each other and their eyes set on France and other northern European powers.

And yet, while the end of empire was behind the constitution of national literary histories, which for political and ideological reasons kept Spanish American and Spanish peninsular literatures apart, the end of empire was simultaneously responsible for generating a countercurrent that aimed to prevent that very separation and to understand the literatures written in Spanish on both sides of the Atlantic as parts of a larger entity, whose center remained in Spain. This new ideology that valued transnationalism over national insularity, transatlantic commonalities over and above other European referents would eventually be known as *hispanismo*, grounded on the commonality of language and the legacy of Spain in the Americas.[4] Thus, as the Spanish empire came to an end, hispanismo attempted to fill that void by positing the existence of a transnational Hispanic community that, nevertheless, assumed the "natural" leadership of Spain, both as historical agent and as birthplace of the language over which it claimed ownership. Embraced first by conservatives from both sides of the Atlantic but soon enough by Spanish liberals as well, hispanismo would become consolidated in the second half of the nineteenth century, emerge as a central discourse during the long years of the Franco regime in Spain (permeating also, as Sebastiaan Faber has shown, much of Spanish intellectual discourse in exile), and then be incorporated seamlessly with some updates into the official discourse of post-Franco Spain (Escudero; Pérez de Mendiola). Spanish literary history showed no interest in exploring its connections to the literatures produced in Spanish America, which remained largely absent from it. Yet, at the same time, Spanish American literature became an important and necessary component of hispanismo, a reminder and remainder of empire, so long as Spanish American letters maintained a subordinate position to the authority of the parental figure of Spain.

Today, the field of Hispanic literary studies is still marked by the opposite forces of separation and unification described above. On the one hand, the sharp division between Spanish peninsular and Spanish American literatures as virtually "disconnected" entities, to use Shumway's expression, remains central to the organizing principle of the discipline. Spanish peninsular and Spanish American post-Enlightenment literary studies, in particular, have remained mostly oblivious to each other and focused, each in its own particular way, on a northern European center. On the other hand, the discipline as a whole still finds its main justification in a tacit understanding of a commonality of language and literary traditions that grants Spain a prominent place, which justifies the dominant perception that, rather than representing one of more than twenty nations with literatures in Spanish, Spanish peninsular literature somehow represents, in the imaginary of the field, about 50 percent, one of two ostensibly equal halves—Spain and Spanish America.[5]

So the end of empire and its symbolic continuation have been fundamental elements in both the constitution of literary histories and their study. But the consequences of this inherited trajectory have been rather different for the study of literature on both sides of the Atlantic. In the case of Spanish American literary criticism, empire, rather than its end, changed hands and continued existing as a relevant category: as a source of literary and cultural influence in earlier traditional and philological approaches, and in the form of new metropolitan centers of the neocolonial period that independence inaugurated. In the case of Spanish literary criticism, on the other hand, the very same center against which Spanish literature has also been perennially measured was never articulated in metropolitan terms but rather in those of exclusion and inclusion, of being European or not European enough.

Neither the historical forces that propelled the study of Spanish American and Spanish literatures apart nor the way these forces became naturalized in the field can be overstated. As a result, over two centuries of literary relationships, conflict, exchange, encounters, and confrontation have remained mostly unexplored in any systematic way that might have opened up a more sophisticated understanding of the trajectories of the literatures written in Spanish, expanding their often too unidirectional relationship with the North Atlantic, decentering and perhaps dismantling Hispanism as a concept and as a field, and stimulating new, more complex paradigms from which to think through the ever problematic division between monolithic centers and peripheries.

Despite their marginal place in literary histories, these connections existed. The nineteenth century was marked by transoceanic voyages of peoples and texts in both directions. Even if France and England had emerged as the new centers of cultural prestige, Spanish authors, from Larra and Espronceda to Galdós and Pardo Bazán, continued to be read and published in the new American republics. Likewise, from Zorrilla's "México y los mexicanos" (1857), an essay on Mexican literature written while in Mexico in the form of a letter to the duque de Rivas, to the better-known *Cartas americanas* and *Nuevas cartas americanas* by Juan Valera in the 1880s and the *Antología de los poetas hispanoamericanos* from the 1890s, peninsular writers were aware of what was being produced across the Atlantic. Besides, Spanish newspapers both reported on American news from early on and began publishing literary texts by American authors. This trend grew steadily in the middle of the century with publications such as *La América, El correo de España, Revista del Nuevo Mundo, Revista Hispano-Americana, La ilustración española y Americana,* and *Revista de la Unión Iberoamericana,* among others, venues that disseminated Spanish American literary production in the peninsula. In addition to texts, writers were also moving in both directions, including Zorrilla, Emilia Serrano, Valle-Inclán, Sarmiento, Gómez de Avellaneda, Blest-Gana, Martí, Darío, and most of the *modernistas,* to name but some of the best known. Nineteenth-century literary production in Spanish was far from compartmentalized and separated by the Atlantic—quite the contrary. Yet few of these exchanges have left any significant mark in the telling of Hispanic literary histories.

If at times these exchanges could be qualified as "moments of rapprochement," to use Shumway's phrase (297), at times they were certainly mired in conflict and, in most instances, haunted one way or another by ghosts of the colonial past.[6] As the nineteenth century gave way to the twentieth, transatlantic relations in the Hispanic world, brewing for decades, reached a turning point with the advent of modernismo in the peninsula and, as I have argued elsewhere, the subsequent reversal of literary authority. If for over a century Spanish American creoles and their narrative of futurity had been relegating Spain to the premodern, Spanish American *modernistas* took it upon themselves to modernize the literature of the former metropolis, thus turning the ideologies of Hispanism and Spanish colonialist discourse on their heads. From Juan Ramón Jiménez, Gerardo Diego, and Federico García Lorca early in the century to Antonio Muñoz Molina, Rosa Montero, Javier Marías, and Enrique Vila-Matas at century's end, Spanish writers have time and again acknowledged the modernizing influence that Spanish American letters have had in Spain.[7] Yet, to an extent, each generation has discovered Spanish American literature anew, due in no small part to the way Spanish literary history has resisted incorporating that modernizing impulse into its telling, much preferring to propose a direct, unmediated, French and European influence. Only when the towering presence of a writer like Rubén Darío was impossible to hide did Spanish literary history acknowledge it, but only by naturalizing him—that is, by incorporating him into Spanish literature and turning his Spanish Americanness into a mere footnote, a birthplace, and by completely isolating him from his peers, as if modernismo were a one-man enterprise and he a mere "catalyst."[8]

Yet, because of modernismo, the nineteenth-century maternal metaphor, so prevalent in writers like Valera and Unamuno,[9] was no longer sustainable and slowly transformed into a discourse of fraternity, a metaphor consolidated by the break of the Spanish Civil War and the prolific collaboration between writers, artists, and institutions. Allegedly egalitarian, the discourse of fraternity has also been used, however, to hide, rather than highlight, changes in relationships and structures of power in the development of literatures in Spanish. Neither fully Spanish nor foreign, Spanish American writers parade through twentieth-century Spanish literary history both present and absent at once, foreigners in the homeland, to use Mario Santana's fortunate expression about the Boom writers. The transforming presence of their literary texts in Spanish letters remains largely hidden under vague metaphors of kinship that ultimately only help avoid contemplating the possibility that the modernization of Spanish letters did not come from Europe after all, but rather from America.

Transatlantic Studies and the Ghost of Empire

Certainly, there have been changes in peninsular literary studies in the past few decades. As Spain became a full member of the European Union and its "Europeanness" has finally been secured, the field of peninsular studies has experienced a progressive transition from reading Spain as the exception, in an always conflicted relationship with Europe, to understanding it as an integral part of and in tune with the rest of Europe.[10] The "Europeanness" of its object secured, peninsular literary criticism seems to be doing a 180-degree turn in relation to empire in the twenty-first century. Largely ignored until now as a category of inquiry (or rather sublimated in

Hispanism), empire has recently begun to take center stage in peninsular literary studies.

In his 2003 article "Historical Memory, Neoliberal Spain, and the Latin American Postcolonial Ghost," Joseba Gabilondo reads Latin American post-coloniality as a ghost of Spanish historiography: "Latin American processes of independence (1810–1825) are absent from most Spanish historiography but, at the same time, they haunt the very fundamentalist refashioning of a contemporary Spain to the point of constituting it" (252). From the field of historiography itself, Christopher Schmidt-Nowara in his "La España Ultra-marina: Colonialism and Nation-Building in Nineteenth-Century Spain" also shows how contemporary Spanish historians dismiss the colonies as he examines the close relationship between national and colonial histories in the nineteenth and early twentieth centuries. Peninsular literary history and criticism have traditionally not fared much better in addressing the many ties between Spain's literary production and its postimperial history with the exception of perfunctory references to *el desastre* when studying what used to be known as the Generación del 98.

In recent years, however, there seems to be a trend in the opposite direction—that is, a critical effort to bring empire back to the forefront of our understanding of Spanish literature. This welcome effort has taken different forms: first, a renewed interest in exploring how the imaginary of empire shaped the manifestation of a given aesthetics, like romanticism and nationalist discourses in Spain;[11] second, a new reading of nineteenth-century Spain as still fully imperial that aims to show how empire articulates nineteenth-century Spanish literature;[12] and, finally, new attention to Spain's imperial ventures beyond Latin America and the Philippines—that is, a focus on North Africa and Equatorial Guinea.[13] Judging by these new approaches, however, empire has indeed returned with a vengeance. The significant and provocative body of scholarship studying empire and its multiple manifestations is beginning to address the ghost of empire that Gabilondo identified a decade ago as haunting contemporary Spain. This necessary and welcome task is bound to alter our understanding both of Spanish literary and cultural production and of transatlantic histories. Nonetheless, the unquestionable importance of recent scholarship on empire notwithstanding, the question remains about the extent to which this recent critical surge, if unaccompanied by an equally thorough critical inquiry into the shift in power relations across the Atlantic, will ultimately and unwittingly perpetuate the very imperial impulse under critique. In other words, by only focusing on Spain as empire (and thus reinstating its former colonies in the realm of the colonial), recent scholarship runs the risk of reimperializing, as it were, both the field and its object of study. Rather than engaging the ghost of empire, these recent approaches might end up, instead, resurrecting Spain's imperial body.

This is, in part, the fear expressed by some critics regarding what in the last decade has become known as "transatlantic studies" or "transatlantic approaches" within Hispanic studies, rubrics under which much of the scholarship mentioned above has been inserted. Criticism has come from both the peninsular and the Spanish American camps, the two sides of the great divide that has marked the history of the field and that transatlantic studies allegedly aims to bridge. No small part of the criticism has to do with the geopolitical, economic, and academic environment in which transatlanticism has emerged in Hispanic studies. Early on, Joseba Gabilondo, one of the earliest proponents of the critical possibilities of what he labeled as the "Hispanic Atlantic," made a connection between transatlanticism as a field of inquiry and Spain's neoliberal and neo-imperialist policies toward, mainly, Latin America.[14] In fact, Gabilondo saw those practices as the reason behind the Latin American ghost in Spanish historiography: "At this point, Spain is the second largest investor in Latin America and the latter has become the main scenario for Spanish neoimperialist, capitalist fantasies—hence the need to approach Latin America in a ghostly manner" ("Historical Memory" 252).

Concomitant to these political and economic developments, Gabilondo ("One Way") and other critics such as Brad Epps and Luis Fernández Cifuentes, Sebastiaan Faber ("Economies"), Mabel Moraña, Joan Ramon Resina, and Abril Trigo have also identified a specifically academic component behind the recent shift in scholarship: peninsular studies have been losing ground vis-à-vis Latin American studies, mainly although by no means exclusively in Anglo-American academia.[15] For these critics, transatlantic approaches have developed as a compensatory measure, a type of colonization of the field of Latin American studies by Peninsularists in order to stay relevant.[16] Thus, as the term "transatlantic" keeps gaining currency in our field, critics have raised voices of concern if not outright rejection, seeing it as the reincarnation of neo-Hispanism, an old wolf in new sheep's clothing. Coming from the field of Latin American studies, Trigo, in his thorough critique of transatlantic studies, explains:

> As an outcome of [this] global realignment, the intellectual crisis of U.S. Hispanism and Spain's freshly acquired international status, Hispanic Transatlantic Studies adopts this dual shift and

adapts it to a renovated Pan-Hispanism. This complicates things further, insofar as it involves the overlapping interests of Spanish capitalism and transnational corporations, so that the first is put to work at the service of the latter under the pretense of a shared cultural tradition, and Hispanic imperial nostalgia becomes an alibi for global geopolitics.

Trigo wonders what transatlantic studies can offer that Latin American studies does not and concludes that there is nothing. Along this line, though Trigo does not make this argument, it can certainly be said that transatlanticism itself is not quite so new.

Indeed, as Eyda Merediz and Nina Gerassi-Navarro have recently reminded us, transatlantic studies have had a long tradition in Latin American studies. This is true not only of the colonial period but also of postindependence: it is hard to find, just to give one example, a more transatlantic text than Mary Louise Pratt's *Imperial Eyes*. As a matter of fact, from the very moment that Latin American studies understood itself in relation to an imperial center located across the Atlantic, transatlanticism has always been part and parcel of the field to a lesser or larger degree. There must be, then, another reason Latin Americanists have generally been more skeptical of transatlantic studies than their peninsular colleagues, and I suspect that the reason is that the eastern end of this new Atlantic is now located in Spain and not northern Europe. In other words, it is *not* transatlanticism itself that bothers critics like Abril Trigo; rather, the "Hispanic" element attached to it suddenly brings Spain back into a picture from which it had long been vanished. This has been understood, perhaps not without some reason, as yet another imperialistic move.

Criticism has also come from peninsular studies. Joan Ramon Resina, for instance, placing even stronger emphasis on Latin Americanism's increased symbolic capital as a crucial element in certain approaches to the Atlantic that operate to the detriment of peninsular studies, also dismisses the whole enterprise as a mere adjustment of the latter with nothing new to offer:

> Through the growing hegemony of Latin American literature, the field has added regions even as it has lost periods. In the US the trend has reached the point where it is nearly impossible to publish scholarly work on Spanish subjects. As a result of these strictures, a "new field" in "trans-atlantic studies" has arisen, permitting "Peninsularists" to reposition

themselves nearer the dominant Americanism. There is nothing particularly "interdisciplinary" or "border-crossing" in most of these moves, which in fact reinforce the discipline's traditional reliance on the legacy of empire. Merely inverting the signs of the discourse turning the apology of colonialism into a post-colonial critique changes nothing, as detractors turn objectively into accepters. (96)

A problem with Resina's assessment, to an even larger extent than Trigo's, is the degree to which it refuses to reflect on and critically engage with the implications of the increased symbolic capital of both Latin American literature and studies. There are many factors behind these processes, to be sure, but certainly one of them resides in the renewal and innovation brought about by both Spanish American literature and Latin American studies as a discipline. As Epps and Fernández Cifuentes have put it: "The vigor of peninsular studies . . . is surpassed . . . by that of an expanded Latin Americanism" (19). Resina's rejection effectively avoids having to deal with the agency of Latin American literature and studies in bringing about these changes, instead reverting back to a monolithic view of Spanish imperial discourse reinventing itself. In this sense, the debate on transatlantic studies may seem at times like a reenactment of the debates surrounding the advent of modernismo or the narrative boom in Spain, a refusal to accept that change and innovation in Spanish literature, as in Spanish studies, have come from across the Atlantic.

Ultimately, both Trigo and Resina end up throwing the baby out with the bathwater. They rightly identify some of the possible problems surrounding the emergence of transatlantic studies, as part of the associated scholarship may, if left to stand alone, unwittingly bring empire back. Yet both tend, in different ways and degrees, to see transatlantic studies as an unmediated result of political and economic agendas, and thus they unnecessarily reduce its complexity, dismiss its achievements, and, more importantly, ignore its potential. Critics of transatlanticism have failed to acknowledge the central role played by Latin American literary and intellectual output in pushing the field in this direction. More importantly, they have not meaningfully engaged its potential to find new ways to understand Spanish American and Spanish peninsular histories and production and to rearticulate a field still weighed down by two centuries of troublesome rejections and nostalgic unity. In this sense, critics of transatlantic studies have reproduced the very same gesture they set out to criticize in the emerging field: the perpetuation of imperial dynamics by which Latin America can only be the object and Europe only the subject and by which ideas can flow only from east to west. But the story of transatlantic literary relations between Spanish America and Spain, emerging in the nineteenth century and becoming consolidated in the twentieth, is more often than not an altogether different one, one that does not fit well within inherited patterns of Hispanism, center/periphery, and neocolonialism/postcolonialism.

In their introduction to a special issue of *Revista Iberoamericana* on transatlantic and Latin American studies, Eyda Merediz and Nina Gerassi-Navarro state: "The challenge resides in how to transcend a field of transatlantic studies that always imagines itself trapped between Spanish global expansionism, North American dominant academia, and Latin American indifference" (614). I find the *modernista* concept of inverted conquest (Díaz Rodríguez 61) a fruitful point of departure to imagine transatlantic studies otherwise. It engages with the ghost of empire, yet it does so without resurrecting the imperial body. On the contrary, it encourages us to explore the way in which Spanish American literature has been for over a century: not only the object of imperial forces but also the subject of creative and intellectual impulses that have successfully and profoundly transformed the production of the former empire and beyond in systematic and sustained ways. In doing so, it asks us to challenge the inertia with which we all too often think of monolithic notions of center, periphery, and modernity.

Turning the rise of transatlantic studies into an opportunity for re-imagining new critical possibilities not only entails addressing Spain's imperialism past and present, however important that may be; taking advantage of this opportunity also requires addressing the subordinate position of twentieth-century Spanish literature in relation to that of Spanish America, acknowledging that the former would not be what it is without the constant renewing and modernizing presence of the latter. Likewise, Spanish American literary criticism would do well to explore the many instances in which Latin American agency has profoundly shaped the way others—including Spaniards—think and write.

This is by no means a call to adopt a celebratory or uncritical stance toward Latin American cultural production, nor is it an attempt to convert Spanish literature into a passive receptacle or to consider it irrelevant and derivative. It is rather an opportunity to open new spaces of critical thinking and inquiry and new theoretical paradigms; it is an opportunity to explore the unique space that colonial and postcolonial relations have formed in the Atlantic, a space of collaboration, surely, but also and often of power struggles for symbolic capital and authority, of resistance to imperial ideologies, and of the creation of new and unexpected power dynamics. Neither transatlantic studies nor its critics should content themselves with reproducing, yet again, paradigms of postcoloniality thought out elsewhere for specific contexts that are subsequently universalized. Rather, practitioners in the field would do well to engage in new theorizations that can help us reimagine the circulation of culture and power across the Atlantic.

Notes

1. This was further reinforced by the images that framed the program: Francisco de Goya's powerful *The Third of May 1808* and a period postcard showing a US soldier waving an American flag under the phrase "On to Havana."
2. All translations are mine unless otherwise noted.
3. As Silvia Molloy puts it: "If Latin America is 'writing back' anywhere . . . one could argue that it is writing back to the 'wrong' address" (191).
4. See the seminal studies by Van Aken and Pike, and more recently the collection edited by Mabel Moraña. See also Francisco Morales Padrón, Carlos Rama's classic study on nineteenth-century relations, and Marina Pérez de Mendiola's pioneering transatlantic volume. For a reading of the use of Hispanism and *Hispanidad* by Spanish American *modernistas*, see Mejías-López.
5. This is as true in Anglo-American academia as it is in universities across Latin America, Spain, the rest of Europe, and beyond. In the case of Latin America, Spanish literature sometimes represents, at worst, a third of the field, on equal footing with Latin America as a whole and each respective national literature. Other literatures in Spanish (including those from the Philippines and Equatorial Guinea) have remained completely marginal within this major division of the field. Fortunately this is beginning to change, as I will discuss in the next section.
6. See, for instance, the anecdote mentioned by John Dowling about Zorrilla's ambiguous welcome in Mexico. For the debates and their colonialist undertones surrounding the advent of Modernismo to Spain, see Mejías-López; see also Mario Santana; and Joaquim Marco and Jordi Gracia on the reception of the Boom.
7. Although he would later temper his enthusiasm, Juan Ramón Jiménez's admiration for Rubén Darío is well known. Perhaps less known is that he was also a fervent reader of José Enrique Rodó's *Ariel*, referring to him in letters, as he referred also to Darío, as his "master" (Mejías-López 125–26); Jiménez wrote of José Asunción Silva that "he influenced me and every one, as he truly was one of the main precursors of *modernismo* in Spain"

(qtd. in García Morales 106). Gerardo Diego dates Vicente Huidobro's visit to Madrid in 1918 as "decisive" for Spanish writers (Videla 48), and, according to César González Ruano, young Spanish writers welcomed the Chilean poet to Madrid as "a sort of Messiah of a new literary age" (Videla 38). In Federico García Lorca and Pablo Neruda's well-known "discurso al alimón" on Rubén Darío, Lorca states: "He taught in Spain both old masters and children, with a sense of universality and of generosity that we need in the poets of today" (229). At the other end of the century, Muñoz Molina has often expressed his debt to the Boom writers. See his "Una orgía perpétua" in which he recalls the impact that Spanish American fiction had on his generation. For Javier Marías, the Latin American Boom "was a current of fresh air and the demonstration that it was possible to write in Spanish in a less academicist form than it was common in Spain," while Rosa Montero states, "I believe that the Spaniards of my age educated ourselves in the literature of our own language through the 'boom'" ("El boom"). Enrique Vila-Matas, for his part, has said, "Perhaps the majority of the writers that interest me, because of their narrative freedom and literary family, are Spanish American" (Azancot).

8. Arturo Pérez Reverte, reporting from the Feria del Libro in Bogotá, expressed well this ongoing trend as he chastised the attitude of many of his fellow Spaniards toward Spanish American writers: "And I insist on their Colombian nationality because here, in order to accept greatness, we usually take them out of context, as if they were stateless or Spaniards wrongly censured, without a fixed home address, as if they had been born there by mere accident."

9. Writers like Valera and Unamuno, among the most open to Spanish American letters, could generally not think about the relationship between Spain and Spanish America beyond the idea of *madre patria*, the spiritual and cultural parent/leader of the former colonies. For Valera, for instance, American national literatures made no sense without Spain to give them unity (see Mejías-López 86–90, 178).

10. As Sebastiaan Faber has rightly noted in the context of US Hispanism: "Recognizing that the exceptionalist claim no longer serves, the new legitimizing strategy is to claim commonality. Spain is just like the rest of the West; therefore, Hispanic Studies is just as important and interesting as French, English, or American Studies" ("Economies" 27).

11. In addition to Gabilondo's studies, see, for instance, the studies by Christopher Britt-Arredondo, James Fernández, Robin Fiddian, Michael Iarocci, and Ángel Loureiro, among others.

12. Alda Blanco persuasively makes that case in "Spain at the Cross-Roads"; see also the recent work by Lisa Surwillo, Joyce Tolliver, and Mary Coffey, among others.

13. See, for instance, the recent work by Michael Ugarte and Benita Sampedro, as well as the several special issues that have recently come out on these subjects, coedited by Ugarte and M'baré N'gom; Ugarte and Teresa Vilarós; Sampedro and Baltasar Fra-Molinero; and Barbara Fuchs and Yuen-Gen Liang.

14. Julio Ortega, another early proponent of transatlantic studies and one of the most visible representatives of the field, in contrast, related its emergence to the alleged exhaustion of theory and the rise of a post-theoretical moment. See Trigo for a critique of Ortega's vision of transatlantic studies, particularly the way in which it seems to free the field from a consideration of issues of power (33–35).

15. See the edited volumes by Moraña and by Epps and Fernández Cifuentes.

16. Relevance does not only apply to the object of study but is also connected to the economics of university life and thus to funding for peninsular studies, from courses to faculty positions to publishing.

Works Cited

Alonso, Carlos. *The Burden of Modernity: The Rhetoric of Cultural Discourse in Spanish America*. Oxford: Oxford UP, 1998.

Azancot, Nuria. "Enrique Vila-Matas: 'Dejaré de escribir el día que no tenga enemigos.'" *El cultural* 21 Nov. 2002. Web. 13 Oct. 2014.

Blanco, Alda. "Spain at the Cross-Roads: Imperial Nostalgia or Modern Imperialism?" *A Contracorriente: A Journal on Social History and Literature in Latin America* 5.1 (2007): 1–11. Web. 13 Oct. 2014.

Britt-Arredondo, Christopher. *Quixotism: The Imaginative Denial of Spain's Loss of Empire*. Albany: State U of New York P, 2005.

Coffey, Mary. "Galdós's 'locas aventuras' and the Madness of Spanish Colonialism." *Studies in Honor of Vernon Chamberlin*. Ed. Mark A. Harpring. Newark, DE: Juan de la Cuesta, 2011. 37–48.

Díaz Rodríguez, Manuel. *Camino de perfección*. Caracas-Madrid: Edime, 1968.

Dowling, John. "José Zorrilla en el Parnaso Mexicano." *Actas del IX Congreso de la Asociación Internacional de Hispanistas*. Ed. Sebastián Neumeister. Frankfurt: Vervuert, 1989. 527–34.

"El Boom, influencia y aire fresco para los autores españoles." *El Diario Vasco* 3 Nov. 2012. Web. 13 Oct. 2014.

Epps, Brad, and Luis Fernández Cifuentes, eds. *Spain beyond Spain: Modernity, Literary History, and National Identity*. Lewisburg, PA: Bucknell UP, 2005.

Escudero, María A. "Hispanist Democratic Thought versus Hispanist Thought of the Franco Era: A Comparative Analysis." Pérez de Mendiola, *Bridging the Atlantic* 169–85.

Faber, Sebastiaan. "Economies of Prestige: The Place of Iberian Studies in the American University." *Hispanic Research Journal* 9.1 (2008): 7–32.

———. "'La hora ha llegado': Hispanism, Pan-Americanism, and the Hope of Spanish/American Glory (1938–1948)." Moraña 62–104.

Fernández, James. "America Is in Spain: A Reading of Clarín's 'Boroña.'" Pérez de Mendiola, *Bridging the Atlantic* 31–43.

Fiddian, Robin. "Under Spanish Eyes: Late Nineteenth-Century Postcolonial Views of Spanish American Literature." *Modern Language Review* 97.1 (2002): 83–93.

Fuchs, Barbara, and Yuen-Gen Liang, eds. *A Forgotten Empire: The Spanish-North African Borderlands*. Special issue of *Journal of Spanish Cultural Studies* 12.3 (2011).

Gabilondo, Joseba. "Historical Memory, Neoliberal Spain, and the Latin American Postcolonial Ghost: On the Politics of Recognition, Apology, and Reparation in Contemporary Spanish Historiography." *Arizona Journal of Hispanic Cultural Studies* 7 (2003): 247–66.

———. Introduction to *The Hispanic Atlantic*, special issue of *Arizona Journal of Hispanic Cultural Studies* 5 (2001): 91–113.

———. "One Way Theory: On the Hispanic-Atlantic Intersection of Postcoloniality and Postnationalism and Its Globalizing Effects." *Journal of Iberian and Latin American Literary and Cultural Studies* 1.1 (2001). Web. 13 Oct. 2014.

García Lorca, Federico. *Obras completas*. Vol. 3. Ed. Miguel García Posada. Barcelona: Galaxia Gutemberg, 1997.

García Morales, Alfonso. "Juan Ramón Jiménez, critico de José Asunción Silva: sus anotaciones manuscritas." *Thesaurus: Boletín del Instituto Caro y Cuervo* 46.1 (1991): 88–110.

González-Stephan, Beatriz. "La historiografía literaria hispanoamericana: agenda de problemas para una historia de la literatura nacional." *Revista de Estudios Colombianos* 4 (1987): 29–33.

Iarocci, Michael. *Properties of Modernity: Romantic Spain, Modern Europe, and the Legacies of Empire*. Nashville, TN: Vanderbilt UP, 2006.

Loureiro, Ángel. "Spanish Nationalism and the Ghost of Empire." *Journal of Spanish Cultural Studies* 4.1 (2003): 65–76.

Marco, Joaquim, and Jordi Gracia, eds. *La llegada de los bárbaros: La recepción de la literatura hispanoamericana en España, 1960–1981*. Barcelona: Edhasa, 2004.

Mejías-López, Alejandro. *The Inverted Conquest: The Myth of Modernity and the Transatlantic Onset of Modernism*. Nashville, TN: Vanderbilt UP, 2010.

Merediz, Eyda, and Nina Gerassi-Navarro. "Introducción: confluencia de lo transatlántico y lo latinoamericano." *Revista Iberoamericana* 75.228 (2009): 605–36.

Molloy, Silvia. "Latin America in the US Imaginary: Postcolonialism, Translation, and the Magic Realist Imperative." Moraña 189–99.

Morales Padrón, Francisco. "La imagen de Hispanoamérica en la España de los siglos XIX y XX." *Estudios Latinoamericanos* 6.1 (1980): 199–236.

Moraña, Mabel, ed. *The Ideologies of Hispanism*. Nashville, TN: Vanderbilt UP, 2005.

Muñoz Molina, Antonio. "Una orgía perpetua." *El País* 28 Nov. 2009. Web. 13 Oct. 2014.

Ortega, Julio. "Post-teoría y estudios transatlánticos." *Iberoamericana* 3.9 (2003): 109–17.

Pérez de Mendiola, Marina, ed. *Bridging the Atlantic: Towards a Reassessment of Iberian and Latin American Cultural Ties*. Albany: State U of New York P, 1996.

———. "The Universal Exposition Seville 1992: Presence and Absence, Remembrance and Forgetting." Pérez de Mendiola, *Bridging the Atlantic* 187–203.

Pérez Reverte, Arturo. "Los pobres indiecitos." *El país semanal* 5 May 1994. Web. 13 Oct. 2014.

Pike, Fredrick. *Hispanism, 1898–1936: Spanish Conservatives and Liberals and Their Relations with Spanish America*. South Bend, IN: U of Notre Dame P, 1971.

Pratt, Mary Louise. *Imperial Eyes: Travel Writing and Transculturation*. London: Routledge, 1992.

Rama, Carlos M. *Historia de las relaciones culturales entre España y la América Latina, siglo XIX*. Mexico City: Fondo de Cultura Económica, 1982.

Resina, Joan Ramon. "Cold War Hispanism and the New Deal of Cultural Studies." Epps and Fernández Cifuentes 70–108.

Sampedro, Benita. "Engaging the Atlantic: New Routes, New Responsibilities." *Bulletin of Hispanic Studies* 89.8 (2012): 905–22.

Sampedro, Benita, and Simon Doubleday, eds. *Border Interrogations: Questioning Spanish Frontiers*. Oxford: Berghahn Books, 2008.

Sampedro, Benita, and Baltasar Fra-Molinero, eds. *Equatorial Guinea*, special issue of *Afro-Hispanic Review* 28.2 (2009).

Santana, Mario. *Foreigners in the Homeland: The Spanish American New Novel in Spain, 1962–1974*. Lewisburg, PA: Bucknell UP, 2000.

Schmidt-Nowara, Christopher. "'La España Ultramarina': Colonialism and Nation-Building in Nineteenth-Century Spain." *History Quarterly* 34.2 (2004): 191–214.

Shumway, Nicholas. "Hispanism in an Imperfect Past and an Uncertain Future." Moraña 284–99.

Surwillo, Lisa. *Monsters by Trade: Slave Traffickers in Modern Spanish Literature and Culture*. Palo Alto, CA: Stanford UP, 2014.

————. "Representing the Slave Trader: Haley and the Slave Ship; or, Spain's Uncle Tom's Cabin." *PMLA* 120.3 (2005): 768–82.

Tolliver, Joyce. "Framing Colonial Manliness, Domesticity, and Empire in 'Página suelta' and 'Oscuramente.'" *Revista de Estudios Hispánicos* 46.1 (2012): 3–24.

————. "Over Her Bloodless Body: Gender, Race, and the Spanish Colonial Fetish in Pardo Bazán." *Revista Canadiense de Estudios Hispánicos* 34.2 (2010): 285–301.

Torrecilla, Jesús. *La imitación colectiva: Modernidad vs. autenticidad en la literatura española*. Madrid: Gredos, 1996.

Trigo, Abril. "Global Realignments and the Geopolitics of Transatlantic Studies: An Inquiry." Paper presented at the Title VI 50th Anniversary Conference, Washington, DC, 19–21 Mar. 2009. Web. 13 Oct. 2014.

Ugarte, Michael. *Africans in Europe: The Culture of Exile and Emigration from Equatorial Guinea to Spain*. Urbana: U of Illinois P, 2010.

————, and M'baré N'gom, eds. *Equatorial Guinea in Spanish Letters*. Special issue of *Arizona Journal of Hispanic Cultural Studies* 8 (2004).

————, and Teresa M. Vilarós, eds. *African Spain*. Special issue of *Journal of Spanish Cultural Studies* 7.3 (2006).

Van Aken, Mark. *Pan-Hispanism: Its Origin and Development to 1866*. Berkeley: U of California P, 1959.

Videla de Rivero, Gloria. "Huidobro en España." *Revista Iberoamericana* 45.106–7 (1979): 37–48.

Index

www.ingramcontent.com/pod-product-compliance
Lightning Source LLC
Chambersburg PA
CBHW030648270326
41929CB00007B/256